Visit us at

www.syngress.com

Syngress is committed to publishing high-quality books for IT Professionals and delivering those books in media and formats that fit the demands of our customers. We are also committed to extending the utility of the book you purchase via additional materials available from our Web site.

SOLUTIONS WEB SITE
To register your book, please visit **www.syngress.com**. Once registered, you can access your e-book with print, copy, and comment features enabled.

ULTIMATE CDs
Our Ultimate CD product line offers our readers budget-conscious compilations of some of our best-selling backlist titles in Adobe PDF form. These CDs are the perfect way to extend your reference library on key topics pertaining to your area of expertise, including Cisco Engineering, Microsoft Windows System Administration, CyberCrime Investigation, Open Source Security, and Firewall Configuration, to name a few.

DOWNLOADABLE E-BOOKS
For readers who can't wait for hard copy, we offer most of our titles in downloadable e-book format. These are available at **www.syngress.com**.

SITE LICENSING
Syngress has a well-established program for site licensing our e-books onto servers in corporations, educational institutions, and large organizations. Please contact our corporate sales department at corporatesales@elsevier.com for more information.

CUSTOM PUBLISHING
Many organizations welcome the ability to combine parts of multiple Syngress books, as well as their own content, into a single volume for their own internal use. Please contact our corporate sales department at corporatesales@elsevier.com for more information.

T0363870

Building a Digital Forensic Laboratory

Building a Digital Forensic Laboratory

Establishing and Managing a Successful Facility

Dr. Andy Jones
Dr. Craig Valli

Foreword by Dr. Gerald Kovacich

Unique Passcode

20749562

PUBLISHED BY
Butterworth Heinemann and Syngress Publishing, Inc.
Elsevier, Inc.
30 Corporate Drive
Burlington, MA 01803

Building a Digital Forensic Laboratory

Printed and bound in the United Kingdom

Transferred to Digital Print 2011

ISBN 13: 978-1-85617-510-4

Publisher: Laura Colantoni
Acquisitions Editor: Pamela Chester
Developmental Editor: Matthew Cater
Project Manager: Andre Cuello

Page Layout and Art: SPI
Copy Editors: Audrey Doyle, Michael McGee, Adrienne M. Rebello
Indexer: SPI

Library of Congress Cataloging-in-Publication Data
Application Submitted

We dedicate this book to all of those security, law enforcement, and private investigative professionals around the world who dedicate their lives to protecting their organization, the public, and their nation from the miscreants who use digital technology to violate the laws and morals of society and who leave traces of their crimes in the digital realm.

Lead Authors

Dr. Andy Jones, MBE, directed both intelligence and security operations during a full military career and briefed the results at the highest levels and was awarded the MBE for his service in Northern Ireland. After 25 years of service with the British Army's Intelligence Corps he became a business manager and a researcher and analyst in the area of information warfare and computer crime at a defense research establishment. In Sept 2002, upon completion of a paper on a method for the metrication of the threats to information systems, he left the defense environment to take up posts as a principal lecturer at the University of Glamorgan in the subjects of network security and computer crime and as a researcher on the threats to information systems and computer forensics. At the university he developed and managed a well equipped computer forensics laboratory and took the lead on a large number of computer investigations and data recovery tasks. He holds a Ph.D. in the area of threats to information systems. In January 2005 he joined the Security Research Centre at British Telecommunications where he is currently the Head of Security Technology Research. His current research includes work on risk management and computer forensics.

Andy wrote Chapter 1, *"An Introduction to Digital Forensics,"* Chapter 2, *"Types of Digital Forensic Investigation,"* Chapter 3, *"Establishing and Managing a Digital Forensics Laboratory,"* Chapter 5, *"Developing the Business Plan,"* Chapter 10, *"Responding to Crimes Requiring Digital Forensic Investigation,"* Chapter 14, *"High Technology Crimes: Case Summaries,"* Chapter 16, *"The Digital Forensics Laboratory: Strategic, Tactical, and Annual Plans,"* Chapter 17, *"Networking, Liaison, and Sources of Information,"* Chapter 19, *"Workload Management and the Outsourcing Option,"* Chapter 20, *"Developing a Career in Digital Forensic Management,"* Chapter 21, *"A Summary of Thoughts, Issues, and Problems,"* Chapter 23, *"The Future of Digital Forensics in the Criminal Justice System,"* Chapter 24, *"Conclusions and Final Thought's" Appendix A: Digital Forensic Resources,"* and *"Appendix B: Risk Assessment Template"*

Dr. Craig Valli is currently the Head of School and an Associate Professor (Network and Computer Security) within the School of Computer and Information Science at Edith Cowan University (ECU) in Perth, Western Australia. He has over 20 years of experience in the IT industry. In addition to his teaching and research at ECU, Craig regularly serves as a consultant to industry and law enforcement on digital forensics, and computer and network security issues. He has been the architect of successful postgraduate and undergraduate courses in computer and network security and digital forensics at ECU. He is the Chair and Founder of the Australian Digital Forensics Conference and Co-Chair of the Australian Information Security Management Conference. Craig is also the Editor of the Journal of Network Forensics and Co-Editor of the Journal of Information Warfare. Craig also serves on numerous security-related conference committees.

Craig wrote Chapter 4, "Scoping the Requirement for the Laboratory," Chapter 6, "Laboratory Location," Chapter 7, "Selecting the Staff," Chapter 8, "Education and Training," Chapter 11, "Management of the Collection of Evidence," Chapter 12, "Management of Evidence Storage," Chapter 13, "Quality Assurance," Chapter 15, "Understanding the Role of the Digital Forensic Laboratory Manager," and Chapter 22, "The Future of Digital Forensics and Its Role in Criminal Investigations"

Contributing Author

Mr. Phil Swinburne has enjoyed a long career in the U.K. Metropolitan police force, during which he gained experience in criminal investigations and then specialized in the area of fraud investigations. In 1996, he became the head of the Metropolitan Police Computer Crime Unit, one of the first of its kind in the world. As part of the role he worked on developing the international relationships that are so essential to this type of investigation. He was the U.K. representative to INTERPOL and EUROPOL and was responsible for the training of police officers from a large number of European and former Soviet countries. In 2000, he retired from the Metropolitan Police and became Head of Hi-Tech Crime for the National Crime Squad of England and Wales and led a multi-agency team, which devised the first Policing Strategy for Hi-Tech Crime in the U.K. and created the U.K. National High Tech Crime Unit (NHTCU) in 2001. He then took up a role as the Specialist Policy Advisor for the NHTCU. Since his retirement from the NHTCU he has become an independent contractor, has been appointed as a director for a QCC Information Security Ltd. and has been contracted by the U.K. Home Office as part of a team writing the U.K. manual of advice and best practice for Managers of Hi-Tech/Computer Crime Units. He has also been contracted by Skills for Justice in the U.K. to write a framework detailing the skills required by network investigators and forensic computing practitioners. He regularly lectures at the National School for Government and at a number of universities on computer crime.

Phil wrote Chapter 9, "Legislation, Regulation, and Standards," and Chapter 18, "Computer Forensics Investigation Unit Metrics Management System"

Foreword Contributor

Dr. Gerald Kovacich has over 40 years of experience in the fields of counterintelligence/counterespionage, security, criminal and civil investigations, anti-fraud, information warfare, and information systems security. He has served in the U.S. government as a special agent. He has also worked for numerous technology-based international corporations as an information systems security manager, information warfare technologist, investigations manager, and security audit manager. Dr. Kovacich is also an international lecturer, writer, and consultant on these topics in the United States, Europe and Asia.

Contents

Foreword

Once upon a time, there came along some bright folks who invented a machine we now call the *computer*.

Initially, computers were massive, test-tube-loaded, hot-running monsters that were kept in air conditioned rooms which were so cold they could double as meat storage lockers if the computers didn't give off so much heat. Well, that was true in the twentieth century, and since then computers have become cooler, cheaper, more powerful, and smaller as the microprocessors—the heart of these machines—also became cheaper, more powerful, and smaller. As a result, computers were able to move from those air conditioned labs to businesses and even homes around the world.

Then, some other smart folks decided to connect computers into networks, and subsequently into that mother of all networks, the Internet. Later, other smart folks decided to connect computers through wireless networks, and still others decided to enhance them with GPS capability, cameras, telephones, e-mail capability, search engines, storage devices, and even the ability to play your favorite music while instantaneously sending Grandma a digital photo of yourself after winning your latest downloaded game against other gamers halfway around the world whom you have never met.

Today the computer is our business, social, government, and personal environment where we work, play, and basically hang out. However, along with these developments, or *progress*, as some call it, came "computer enthusiasts," also known as *hackers*, who were eager to learn as much as they could about these new toys, and in the process committed vandalistic acts which led to general criminal activities such as fraud and theft.

On their trail were law enforcement professionals. But whereas the cybercriminals had incentives fueled by greed and were willing to work whatever hours were necessary to claim their treasures, the law enforcement professionals had to work with funding, training, and support that were severely lacking. As a result, they were always trailing but seldom able to catch the cybercriminals. Because the priorities of law enforcement are to fight violent crimes as demanded by the public, law enforcement officials had—and many still have—little time for "white collar crimes" such as computer crimes, unless the crimes are so massive as to gain the interest of the public and, subsequently, the politicians who demand action.

But that is now changing.

The first computer crime investigations were conducted by IT professionals within businesses and government agencies; if law enforcement became involved they had to ask for IT support in collecting evidence, as they did not have a clue (pardon the pun) how to work in this new crime scene environment. Gradually, some smart IT people saw a business opportunity and developed software to assist in conducting high-tech investigations such as finding hidden files on computer storage devices and finding evidence of a computer crime on a victim's system.

That worked fine for awhile, but when computers became networked and went national and then global in their connections, the new crime scene covered the world. Trade secrets, pornographic material, and every other bit of information, photos, and digital things of value could be stolen and sent to the other side of the world in a nanosecond!

At first, finding cybercriminals and bringing them to justice was nearly impossible because each national boundary these miscreants crossed brought with it political issues, treaties, sovereignty issues, and nations where no law had yet been written to cover their acts; therefore, their acts may not have even been considered illegal. This is gradually changing, but the obstacles are still immense.

Most law enforcement agencies around the world have developed and improved their forensic crime labs so that blood, hair, ballistics, and other evidence collected during a criminal investigation can be analyzed by experts; that evidence and the experts' testimony can then be used in a court of law to help prosecute the criminals. Only in the past few years was the idea of dedicated digital forensic laboratories and digital forensic experts specialized in conducting inquiries and investigations into high-tech crimes even considered.

As with law enforcement in general, the tools these professionals use are not always the best in the world compared to those used by the criminals, but these dedicated crime fighters are making progress; slowly they are beginning to bridge the gap, and sometimes even close the gap, between themselves and the cybercriminals they are after.

Yes, we are still in the days of the "Wild West" of high technology, where the sheriffs still carry a badge and a gun, but they also now tote a laptop as they pursue criminals. In addition, they are being joined by antiterrorist specialists who are after global terrorists who use high-tech tools to commit such crimes as identify theft, to gain funds and access other targets. This may help drive the increased need for digital forensic labs and units staffed with high-tech experts.

This book will be of immense benefit to these law enforcement and antiterrorist support professionals. It provides readers with the basic information they need to understand this new high-tech crime environment, to conduct high-tech investigations, and to establish and manage a digital forensic laboratory and unit.

To those readers who will take on this challenge, good luck, and good hunting!

—*Dr. Gerald L. Kovacich, CFE, CPP, CISSP (Ret.)*
Whidbey Island, Washington
United States of America

Preface

Because of society's continuing reliance on digital technology, the use of high-tech devices and systems to conduct illegal activity in the worldwide information environment continues to grow at an ever-increasing rate. And because of the rapid integration and globally expanded use of these devices and systems in all aspects of our professional and personal lives, we are increasingly becoming the targets of high-tech, or cyber, criminals. These criminals are also, in some ways, becoming more likely to leave traces of their activity in the digital environment.

Toward that end, in the past five years or so we have seen a huge increase in the number of universities, colleges, and specialist companies offering courses in digital forensics, and in the number of companies delivering tools and services to address the increasingly complex area of digital forensic investigations. Although we are making progress, unfortunately this expansion in the availability of training and tools is not keeping pace with developments in technology and crime and the problems they cause.

Many law enforcement and civilian training agencies provide basic and advanced instruction in modern digital forensic methods and technologies, but few have the resources to offer the necessary range of in-depth, technical training in digital forensic investigations and none currently offer training on establishing and managing a digital forensic laboratory or unit.

Our goals for the readers of this book are as follows:

- To gain an understanding of digital forensic investigations and related issues

- To be able to develop a plan for establishing and managing a digital forensic laboratory and high-tech crime investigation unit

- To be able to manage digital forensic investigations

- To prepare for what the future may hold in terms of high-tech crime and digital forensic investigations

This book consists of four sections comprising a total of 24 chapters. It is not intended to be a "how to" book, although how-to aspects are presented. Instead, it is intended to provide an overview of establishing and managing digital forensic investigations and laboratories, both now and into the future. The art and science of managing a digital forensic investigation require a very different set of skills, experience, and knowledge from those required to carry out a typical criminal investigation. The manager of a digital forensic investigation must understand all aspects of the investigation and his or her role in helping to bring the cybercriminal to justice.

With that said, regardless of whether you have an investigative or a technical background, or whether you're from a business, law enforcement, or government agency environment, if you want to become a manager in this area this book is for you. In addition, this book will offer a few insights and perhaps will act as an *aide memoire* for seasoned veterans. At the very least, we hope this book provides some enjoyable reading.

Although only a small number of people officially carry the title of "digital forensic investigator" or something similar, there is a growing need for highly trained, technically competent digital forensic investigators within the private and public sectors of every information-dependent, Information Age nation and corporation in the world.

It is clear that in the high-tech environment of today and in the one we anticipate for the future, digital forensics is becoming increasingly important in investigating all types of incidents. It is also clear that, as in any forensic discipline, effective management and good governance of the processes involved will be essential to the credibility and success of these investigations.

To those who rise up to take on the challenge, we wish you good luck and continued success!

Dr. Andy Jones
Ipswich, England
United Kingdom

Dr. Craig Valli
Perth, Western Australia
Australia

Acknowledgments

We wrote this book to fill a gap in publications that guide readers on managing digital forensic investigations in the global information environment, and on establishing and managing a digital forensic investigative unit.

Toward that end, we would like to thank the following individuals who helped us in achieving our goal:

- Phil Swinburne, president of Swinburne Associates, for the guidance and support he provided and for the guest chapters he wrote

- Dr. Jerry Kovacich and Bill Hutchinson, for the friendship, guidance, and mentoring they have given us over the years

- Bill Millar, security technical director at Capgemini UK, a true security professional and a good friend who told us when we were wrong

We would also like to thank our project team and the publishing professionals of Butterworth-Heinemann—Pam Chester, Matthew Cater, and Andre Cuello—for their continued support and the professionalism they've shown in this and all our previous projects.

In addition, we would like to acknowledge our wives, Kath Jones and Robyn Valli, for their ongoing support, patience, and tolerance of the book-writing process. Without their wholehearted support, we know we would not have been able to complete this project.

Finally, we thank all of you who are reading this book. We hope the information we've provided contributes to your professional success! Please send your comments to us through our publisher, Butterworth-Heinemann.

Creating a Digital Forensics Laboratory

This section will provide a background explanation of digital forensics and address management issues related to the creation of a laboratory and a computer forensic investigations unit. The section will include an introduction to computer forensics and the types of investigation that may be encountered, and will give advice on things that need to be considered when establishing a laboratory. The section will give advice on how to develop a workable business plan and an insight into where to locate the lab and how big it should be. Finally the section looks at staff selection, training, and support; and the regulations, standards, and legislation with which the lab will need to comply in order to be credible and successful.

Chapter 1. An Introduction to Digital Forensics. This chapter provides an overview of the important concepts associated with digital forensics. It describes the potential sources of evidence available in the typical microcomputer device, how to conduct a search for evidence, and a method of conducting a search in a systematic and effective manner.

Chapter 2. Types of Forensic Investigation. This chapter includes the reasons for carrying out the investigation and the type of investigation that is being undertaken; for example single computer, network, or mobile devices.

Chapter 3. Establishing and Managing a Digital Forensics Unit. The chapter discusses the basic "how-to's" for establishing and managing a digital forensics unit based on real-world experience, and is not a theoretical discussion by authors who have never had such an experience.

Chapter 4. Scoping the Requirement for the Laboratory. This chapter draws upon the experience of the authors to provide guidance on how to scope out the requirement for the laboratory. This includes guidance on the potential throughput and the number of staff, and the quantity and type of equipment that will be required to satisfy the anticipated workload.

Chapter 5. Developing the Business Plan. This chapter covers the development of the business plan for the creation and running of the digital forensics laboratory and the unit.

Chapter 6. The location and size of the Laboratory. This chapter addresses a range of issues that must be considered when deciding on the location of the laboratory. This includes the location of the laboratory in terms of the geographic location, the location with regard to the owning organization, and the location of the laboratory within a building.

Chapter 7. Selecting the staff. This chapter discusses a range of the issues that are related to the selection of the right staff for the laboratory. The chapter includes assessment of the suitability of staff, their qualifications and experience, their references, and if required, their background checks and security vetting. The chapter also deals with the requirement for the provision of support for staff including counseling and psychiatric assessment.

Chapter 8. Training. This chapter addresses the requirement for staff training and achieving the balance between enough training to create and maintain an effective unit and excessive training, which is likely to cause unnecessary costs and to leave the organization vulnerable to poaching of staff by rival companies or organizations. It will also address a strategy for the development of specialist areas within the teams.

Chapter 9. Legislation, Regulation, and Standards. This chapter looks at a range of the international, national, and local legislation and regulations that must be addressed if the unit is to be credible and efficient. The chapter also looks at issues such as data protection and human rights laws and the impact that this may have on the resources and methods used to carry out investigations.

This section is the foundation for the remainder of the book, and it introduces the topic of digital forensics and introduces the issues that will need to be considered not by an investigator, but by the person who will have to manage the laboratory. There are already a range of excellent books available that assist and instruct the digital forensic investigator; however, the areas of knowledge and experience that the manager requires, though complimentary, are very different.

In this way, the security professional, consultant, or private investigator who is going to be the manager of a unit can have an understanding of the issues that need to be considered when creating a digital forensic laboratory for an agency or corporation, whether this is as a fee-earning business or as an additional capability for the organization.

This section is focused on the individual manager or aspirant who is to build such a digital forensic laboratory for an agency or a corporation. The issues that have been addressed have been approached from a management perspective to support the individual who will be responsible for such a unit using the basic philosophies of management and business.

Chapter 1

An Introduction to Digital Forensics

For gauging the scientific validity of evidence, it should be seen whether the technique in question can be or has been tested; whether the technique has been subjected to peer review and publication; its known or potential error rate; the existence of standards controlling its operation and whether the methodology in question has attracted widespread acceptance within the relevant scientific community.

—U.S. Supreme Court in Daubert *v.* Merrell Dow Pharmaceuticals, Inc., 509 U.S. 579, 113 S.C.T. 2786 (1993); popularly referred to as the "Daubert Standard"

Introduction

As computers and microprocessor-controlled devices become more capable and have a greater number of services available, they have become more ubiquitous and are increasingly integrated into our everyday lives. They are used in an growing number of ways, and as a result of this, more and more information is stored on computers of all types, from the ubiquitous desktop computer to the laptop, the personal digital assistant (PDA), and an ever-increasing range of other devices. As a result of this, the term "digital forensics" is used throughout this book wherever possible since it more accurately reflects our environment than "computer forensics."

The increasing ubiquity of digital devices, and our reliance on them, will result in digital forensics playing an ever-greater role in both civil and criminal litigation. It has been estimated[1] that over 85 percent of all crimes committed today leave a trail of digital evidence.

Digital forensics is in a state of transition from "art" to "science" and is moving from the domain of a small number of highly skilled experts to an integral component of the information security enterprise. This change has been driven by factors that range from the increasing maturity of the area to the growing reliance in all areas on computers. As organizations have steadily adopted new technologies and services, more and more volumes of information have been stored electronically. Partly as a result of this, legislation has been introduced to ensure this information is processed and stored in a suitable manner so privacy, corporate governance, and a range of other concerns can be appropriately satisfied. The transition of digital forensics from art to science has been assisted by the introduction and acceptance of procedures, as well as improved and more widely accepted digital forensic software. The growing maturity of the subject area has meant an increasing number of practitioners with experience, and academic institutes that are providing suitable courses and qualifications.

Some History

Digital Forensics emerged as a scientific discipline initially developed in the U.S. by federal law enforcement agents in the mid- to late 1980s. The development started shortly after the introduction of personal computers (PCs) into businesses at the start of the 1980s when U.S. federal law enforcement organizations noticed the rise of white-collar crimes that were aided by these new personal computers. In the period since then, the processing power, storage capacity and speed of PCs has increased enormously.[2] The field of digital forensics has had to keep pace with these developments and been forced to diversify so that today it has expanded to encompass a range of disciplines involving computers, networks, telecommunications, security, law enforcement, and the criminal justice system.

From the outset, it is important to understand that the examination of computers and their associated peripheral devices is not only related to criminal offenses, but also addresses the general business environment for civil litigation issues. A failure to follow the correct procedures in either criminal or civil cases may render the evidence that has been gained, often at considerable effort and expense, worthless and unusable.

A number of important concepts have been developed as the art and science of digital forensics has evolved. Computing and information technology is relatively young in scientific terms, and is still in its infancy in legal terms. Digital forensics is a new discipline that has been born of this highly volatile and uncertain environment.

It is worth starting this book with a definition of digital forensics, but as with anything related to information technology, the term has a range of interpretations. The first definition given here is from one of the earliest and most respected of organizations, the Scientific Working Group for Digital Evidence. It defines digital forensics as:

> Any information of probative value that is either stored or transmitted in binary form.

This definition is very concise, but at the same time generic and all encompassing, but for the practitioner it is not, in many ways, particularly helpful. A more useable definition is that:

> Computer forensics is the collection, preservation, analysis, and court presentation of digital-related evidence.[3]

Another useful definition that has been attributed to Mark Pollit,[4] a retired FBI special agent is:

> Digital forensics is the application of science and engineering to the legal problem of digital evidence. It is a synthesis of science and law.

The US-CERT defines digital forensics as:

> …the discipline that combines elements of law and digital science to collect and analyze data from digital systems, networks, wireless communications, and storage devices in a way that is admissible as evidence in a court of law.

The point that all these definitions make is that digital forensics is not just about science, but also about the law. A failure to satisfy either aspect will mean that any investigation has failed.

Digital evidence is obtained from digital devices and associated peripheral devices through the application of digital investigation and analysis techniques, the data from which is preserved in a scientifically sound manner in an electronic form. The evidence can then be analyzed using acceptable and repeatable processes without fear of the evidence being contaminated by the analysis process. Once the analysis is completed, the necessary reports can be produced in a suitable form.

Principles of Digital Forensics

As the art and science of digital forensics has developed, four underlining principles have evolved and are now widely accepted. As defined in the UK Association of Chief Police Officers (ACPO) Good Practice Guide for Computer-Based Electronic Evidence, the principles are:

- Principle 1: No action taken by law enforcement agencies or their agents should change data held on a digital device or storage media which may subsequently be relied upon in court.

- Principle 2: In circumstances where a person finds it necessary to access original data held on a digital device or on storage media, that person must be competent to do so and be able to give evidence explaining the relevance and the implications of their actions.

- Principle 3: An audit trail or other record of all processes applied to digital device-based electronic evidence should be created and preserved. An independent third party should be able to examine those processes and achieve the same result.

- Principle 4: The person in charge of the investigation (the case officer) has overall responsibility for ensuring that the law and these principles are adhered to.

These principles have been developed within the law enforcement environment, which should not be surprising since it was law enforcement that was the first adopter in order to gather evidence for criminal cases. In the commercial environment, these principles hold equally true, and it should never be forgotten that an investigation started for civil litigation may become a criminal investigation.

Forensic evidence of all types must be collected by following rigorous and well-tested procedures in order to protect any such evidence from contamination or destruction, or from becoming subject to claims of tampering and improper handling, and to establish and preserve the chain of custody. Digital forensic evidence is no different. By following good scientific principles, the fragile and easily altered evidence collected will be provably sound and authentic. Any failure to follow the strict procedures developed and agreed upon may result in some digital evidence being excluded or limited by the courts.

The typical computer- or microprocessor-controlled device contains a range of potential sources of evidence to the skilled investigator. In modern computing devices, the places where information can be stored include the hard disk, the random access memory (RAM), CDs, DVDs, thumb drives, flash memory devices, and other external storage or processing devices that may be connected by wires, Bluetooth, WiFi, or infrared. To deal with this range of places where information that may be of evidential value can be stored, employing the specific knowledge and tools in order to safely access the information requires an increasing range of skills and experience.

Procedures

In order to satisfy the four principles, it is essential that the digital forensic investigation be undertaken using a set of procedures that have developed as the science, technology, and law have evolved. The procedures detailed next generate part of the evidence that demonstrates that the principles have not been breached. Some of the procedures in the digital forensic process are:

- **Log all Actions:** All actions taken in the investigation should be logged. This provides a record of all of actions taken at all stages of the investigation and serves a number of purposes. In addition to providing a record that all of the required actions were taken and carried out in the proper manner, this can also be used as a checklist for the investigators to make sure they have not missed anything.

- **Record the Scene:** Before any of the equipment at the scene is disturbed, either photographs or a video should be taken of the scene, including all of the connections related to the equipment. Once the initial photos of the scene have been made, it may be necessary to move the equipment slightly to give access to the rear of the equipment and the connections. If photographic or video equipment is not available, a diagram should be made to record the information; however, these days, this should be the exception. This will again form part of the evidence, but will also provide vital information if it becomes necessary to reconstruct the equipment in the laboratory. There is nothing worse than removing a large number of cables and devices, storing them and transporting them, following the appropriate procedures, only to find you cannot put it back together the way it was originally configured because you do not have the necessary information.

- **Screen Information Recording:** If the system is turned on, it is important to record the information visible. If any files are open, they should be saved, preferably to an external device (such as a floppy disk of a pen drive) and the action recorded.

- **Cable and Socket Labeling:** Once the connections have been photographed, all cables should be labeled as they are removed to denote which devices they were connected to and which socket they were removed from. This helps with the reconstruction of the system if it is required.

- **Checking for Passwords:** During the initial examination of the scene and the subsequent activity to record and dismantle the system for transport, the investigator should always remember that it is not unusual for people to record passwords and store them in the vicinity of the digital device. If any passwords are found, they should be recorded for use later in the process.

Phases of a Digital Forensic Investigation

The Digital forensic process is made up of a number of phases. The first phase is the collection of the evidence, the next is the preservation of the evidence, then the analysis of the information, and finally the presentation of the results. These phases are described in the following:

- **Evidence Collection:** The collection phase of the digital forensic process is when any items that could be considered to be of evidential value are identified and collected. Normally, these are items that may contain digital data in the form of computers, or devices that will contain random access memory (RAM), disk drives, flash memory drives, or other forms of digital media.

- **Evidence Preservation:** The preservation phase of the digital forensic process is the preservation of the items in a manner that is reliable, complete, accurate, and verifiable. This process may include the documentation of all of the items and the use of cryptographic hashing and checksums to ensure that items of data have not been altered. The terms reliable, complete, accurate, and verifiable are all significant and are described more fully as:

  - *reliable*, in that it yields consistent results and are dependable

  - *complete*, in that it contains all of the relevant information, not just that which supports one side of the case

- *accurate*, in that it is free from error
- *verifiable*, in that any other investigator could come to the same conclusion if they were to examine the same information
- **Evidence Analysis:** The analysis phase of the digital forensic process addresses the extraction of the individual elements of information that may be of significant to the case. For evidence to be of any use, it must have a number of characteristics. These include it being:
  - **admissible:** It must be acceptable for use by the courts or other bodies.
  - **authentic:** It must be possible to show that the evidence is relevant and relates to the incident.
  - **complete:** It must be complete and not just material that provides evidence of the guilt of the suspect and should also include evidence that may prove their innocence.
  - **reliable:** It must be reliable and the procedures adopted for the analysis must not cast doubt on the authenticity and/or veracity of the evidence.
  - **believable:** It must be clearly understandable and believable to a judge, jury, or tribunal.
- **Evidence Presentation:** The fourth phase of the digital forensic process is when the evidence that has been gained as a result of the previous three phases is presented in what may be a variety of forms. The aim of this phase is to present the evidence obtained in a form that is an accurate representation of the facts and that is understandable to the intended audience. The presentation, in whichever form is selected, will normally be supported by documentation, which may include declarations and depositions.

The specific knowledge and skills needed to investigate crimes involving digital devices will change from case to case; however, investigators must understand how a computer operates and how each of its components interacts with the others. Major components include the following:

- The central processing unit (CPU) and its interaction with the RAM
- How the various operating systems utilize the RAM, and how paging and swap files are used
- How individual devices and components interact with each other
- The ways in which these components store and retrieve data to and from physical storage media, such as hard disks

In addition to knowing how the basic components of the computer interact, an understanding of the specific operating systems, applications, and file systems involved in the investigation will be required.

Common Mistakes

A number of common mistakes can occur during investigations. The first and most frequent of these is the failure to maintain the proper documentation. The creation and maintenance of the documentation is both tedious and demanding, which is why this is one of the most common mistakes. Another is the inadvertent modification of data by opening files on the original evidence.

Just opening a file to look at the contents results in the time stamps of the file being changed. This may hinder the subsequent investigation or result in the evidence being rendered unusable. Another is the destruction of potential evidence as a result of the installation of software on the evidence media. The writing of software to the memory of the digital device or to a disk may result in evidence that was stored there, but not protected, being overwritten.

While all of these mistakes may appear to be avoidable, there are times in some investigations where it is necessary to open a file on the original evidence before it has been copied, or to install software in order to recover evidence. This is particularly true of investigations into large networked systems that cannot easily be isolated or turned off. When it is necessary to carry out such actions, it is essential they be recorded, together with the reason such actions were taken.

Another common mistake made is failing to adequately control access to the digital evidence and maintain the chain of custody. When this occurs, it is almost impossible to prove the evidence has not been compromised.

Yet another instance is a failure by the investigator to know when they have reached the limits of their knowledge and to ask for assistance. We all like to think we are experts in our field, but in the area of digital forensics, the subject is now so vast and complex it is not possible for one person to have the necessary level of knowledge in all its relevant areas. Once the investigator exceeds their area of expertise, any evidence they recover will be of questionable value and may be challenged in the courts. These are just a few examples; more will be addressed later in the book.

Chain of Custody

Chain of custody is a legal term that refers to the ability to guarantee the identity and integrity of the article from the time it is collected through the time the results of the analysis are reported and subsequently disposed of. The chain of custody assures continuous accountability, which is important because, if it is not properly maintained, an item may not be admissible in court.

The chain of custody consists of a chronological record of those individuals who have had custody of the evidence from its collection until its final disposition.

Each person in the chain of custody is responsible for all aspects of the care of the article of evidence while it is under their control. Because of the sensitive nature of evidence, it is normal practice to nominate one person as an evidence custodian, to assume responsibility for the evidence when not in use by the investigator of one of the other authorized people involved in the investigation.

In the past, documentary evidence was limited to paper documents, and where the best evidence rule applied, the original document was produced. However, with the rapid transition to the information age, documents are now rarely handwritten or produced on a typewriter and are created using word processing software on personal computers. Increasingly, these documents are no longer printed and are regularly e-mailed or faxed to the recipient directly from the computer.

These changes in the way people communicate and information is distributed has meant that the rules of evidence have had to change as well. Copies of digital files are now considered to be as good as the original electronic document (as long as it is possible to produce evidence such as hash files).

Potential Sources of Evidence

In the past, in the early days of computing, the only viable sources of evidence on a digital device were considered to be the hard disk (or tape cassette) and floppy disks. The volatile memory was limited in size and there was no concept of potential evidence being recovered from it. On the modern digital device, a huge range of potential sources of electronic evidence exist. The sources that the investigator of today needs to consider include:

- Hard Disk (Internal or External)

- Floppy Disks

- CDs/DVDs

- Pen Drives (Dongles)

- Flash Drives

- Modems

- Routers

- Mobile Phones

- Tapes

- Jaz/Zip Cartridges

- Cameras

- MP3 Players

- Network Devices

- Bluetooth-connected devices

- InfraRed Devices

- WiFi Devices

This list is intended to indicate the scope the investigator needs to consider and is not intended to be an exhaustive one (it would undoubtedly be out-of-date before this book appeared on shelves). What must also be borne in mind is that standard forensic procedures must be followed at the same time digital forensic evidence is being collected and preserved. It may well be that the convincing element of evidence is the fingerprint on the keyboard rather than the material on the digital device, or it could be the password written on a piece of paper that is stuck to the inside of the drawer that allows the investigator access to the evidence. Digital forensics is one of the tools and techniques that can be applied to any investigation, and the way it is managed must ensure it is integrated into the other parts of the investigation and be in line with the appropriate standards, as well as the organization's policies and procedures. For example, if fingerprints must be taken from a floppy disk, at what point should they be taken and what should be used to take them? A floppy disk drive is highly sensitive to dust and foreign objects—particularly when the dust in question is a metal oxide, so it is possible that if the recovery of data from the floppy disk and the testing for latent fingerprints is not coordinated, some or all of the potential evidence could be lost.

The Digital Forensic Examiner

The role of the digital forensic examiner is to discover data that exists on a computer system and associated devices. This may require them to recover deleted or erased, damaged, or encrypted information, or to recover passwords in order to gain access to the contents of files. The investigator must be aware that any information discovered during the analysis may be used by either side during litigation, whether civil or criminal. This raises two separate issues: the role of the forensic investigator and the amount of time spent on an investigation.

The task of the digital forensic investigator is to discover the facts. While the investigation will have been initiated as the result of a suspicion that something has occurred, they must always remember that their function is to determine the facts relevant to the incident.

It is normal that when sufficient information has been obtained to prove the case, any data that has not been used remains untouched. This is a simple expedient of the use of resources. If sufficient evidence has been gathered to prove the case, it would not be sensible or economical to investigate further. The problem with this approach is that it may leave evidence behind, or further crimes may remain undiscovered, or even information that may prove the suspect innocent may not be found.

Unfortunately, this is a reality that must be faced. With the volumes of storage now in common use, the time that would be required to examine all of the information potentially available on a digital device means that judgements must be made with regard to when the investigation should end. It should be borne in mind that it is not uncommon for an investigation into one type of crime to uncover evidence of another totally different type of crime.

The other situation that is not uncommon is for the person in charge of an investigation to ask for all of the information that can be recovered from the disk, without any concept of the volume of information, most of which will be irrelevant to the investigation. It is one of the roles of the digital forensic lab manager to intercept such generic requests and ensure that the accepted requests are targeted and will produce the required information (if it exists).

Increasingly, laws are being passed that require organizations to safeguard the privacy of personal data. It is becoming more and more necessary to prove that your organization is complying with computer security best practices. If there is an incident that affects critical data, for instance, the organization that has added a digital forensics capability to its arsenal will be able to show it followed a sound security policy and thus potentially avoid lawsuits or regulatory audits. Anyone who is responsible for the management or administration of information systems and networks needs to have an awareness and understanding of digital forensics and the legal implications of digital forensics.

The wider topic of forensics deals primarily with the recovery and analysis of latent evidence. Latent evidence is evidence that potentially exists, but which cannot be immediately seen. Latent evidence can take many forms, as most people now understand from TV shows such as *CSI*, and this may include things like fingerprints recovered from a weapon, to gunshot residue found on skin or clothing, to DNA evidence recovered from skin or body fluids to, in the case of digital forensics, the files on a digital device or its associated devices. Taking the example of a "latent fingerprint," there may be a fingerprint on an object, but it cannot be seen until an action is taken to make it visible. The same applies to digital evidence—it potentially exists on the computer systems, but steps must be taken to reveal it. With the fingerprint, it may be necessary to identify the relevant print from a whole range of other fingerprints present on an object. On the digital device, it is necessary to identify the evidence from a vast range of other data present.

Digital forensics is important to the organization because it has the potential to save it money. An increasing part of IT (and particularly IT security) budgets is being spent on measures to protect systems with technologies such as firewalls and antivirus software and to detect malicious activity with measures such as intruder detection systems (IDS) or intruder protection systems (IPS). This investment can only be sensible if the correct information is collected and then stored in a forensically sound manner. Then, if necessary, at some time in the future it can be accessed in the knowledge that it has not been altered or contaminated in any way and that it can be used, if necessary, for any subsequent civil or criminal suit against the perpetrator.

Types of Data

Two basic types of data are encountered and collected during a digital forensics investigation. The first type is persistent data. An example of this is the data stored on a hard disk or a CD/DVD and which persists (is preserved) when the digital device's power is turned off.

The second type is referred to as volatile data. This is any data that exists in memory, or in transmission, that will most probably be lost when the digital device is shut down. The most common locations for volatile data is in the registries of the devices, the cache, and random access memory (RAM).

It is important that the investigator understands both of these data types since decisions may be needed during an investigation as to which is more important to preserve in order to capture the required evidence of activity. As an example, consider an investigation into computer hacking. A decision may be necessary as to whether to capture the volatile memory, where the evidence of the perpetrator's most recent actions may be captured, or just capture the persistent data. The risk is that in attempting to capture the volatile memory, persistent data may be lost because it will be necessary to keep the system running for longer and the attacker may use the opportunity to remove evidence.

System administrators and security personnel must also have a basic understanding of how routine computer and network administrative tasks can affect both the forensic process (the potential admissibility of evidence at court) and the subsequent ability to recover data that may be critical to the identification and analysis of a security incident.

Forensic Readiness

One of the factors any person responsible for the management or administration of computer systems or networks must be aware of is the procedures they need to establish during normal operations that will make the collection of evidence and the recovery from an incident easier. These actions are increasingly being referred to as forensic readiness and according to Rowlingson,[5] there is a ten-step process that can be used by any organization to ensure that, in the event of an incident, they will be capable and prepared for the collecting and storing of the information that will be required for a successful investigation. Rowlingson describes the steps as:

1. **Defining the business scenarios that require digital evidence:** It will never be possible to predict all of the scenarios that may occur, but those that are considered to be the most likely, or those that would cause the organization the most concern, can be identified. Different types of organizations will be sensitive to different scenarios depending on the type of systems used and the way in which they are used. The benefits of defining these scenarios will include:

    ■ *A reduction in the impact of a computer-related crime.* If you have thought about the factors that will affect the likelihood of an incident and the impact of such an incident on the organization, you will have enhanced the awareness of the organization to its vulnerable points and the steps that can be taken to minimize the likelihood and level of impact of an incident.

- *Legal requirements.* By understanding the legal requirements for the collection, storage, handling, and disclosure of information, it will be possible to organize the collection and storage in order to retain only that information that is most likely to be required and store it in such a way that any legal requirements can be met without undue disruption to the workings of the organization.

- *Production of evidence.* It may be necessary to demonstrate compliance with a range of regulatory or legal requirements or to produce evidence for use in either internal disciplinary or external criminal or civil cases. Each of these cases may require that different types of information be stored. If a range of scenarios have been considered, the appropriate data can be identified and stored to meet these requirements.

2. **Identify available sources and different types of potential evidence:** Undertaking this process will, in itself, aid any subsequent investigation since the potential sources of information will have already been identified. The very act of identifying the information sources may help highlight gaps in the information currently being collected and stored and allow for changes in the type of information collected or the positioning of sensors. The procedures created as a part of this activity will ensure that the level and type of information collected will be suitable for any investigation.

   - In this process, some of the issues to be considered include the format of the data, the period of time it is stored for, the storage locations, the control of the data and who has access to it, other sources of information that may be required, how it can be made available to an investigation and in what form, and whether any legal or regulatory constraints surround its release (Data Protection Act, Basel II accord, Sarbanes Oxley, human rights legislation).

3. **Determine the evidence collection requirement:** By considering the issue in advance with the people who will have to carry out an investigation, the system administrators and the legal team, it should be possible to determine the type and range of information that can and should be collected. When the scenarios have been identified and the potential sources of information have been isolated, it will be possible to determine the evidence collection requirements.

   - Issues to be addressed when determining the evidence collection requirements include how the evidence can be collected without undue interference to the organization's working processes, management of the cost of collection and storage of information in proportion to an incident, the legality of collecting the required information and whether there will be sufficient information available to allow for a successful investigation.

   - Once these factors have been considered, it will be possible for the organization to understand the economics of the required data storage and evidence collection and to determine whether any of the identified data is already collected for other reasons. If all of the information that is likely to be required is not already collected, then a business decision must to be made about the economics of collecting and storing the additional information.

4. **Establish a capability for securely gathering and storing evidence in a manner that will make it legally admissible:** This includes the planning to ensure that the tools and facilities are in place to make sure the information is collected and stored in an appropriate manner and that the staff are suitably trained, aware of the requirements, and have practical experience in such procedures, so any evidence collected and stored will be admissible in any legal or internal disciplinary proceedings.

   ■ The issues that need to be considered here include whether the information has been collected in a manner that is legally sound and has been stored in a manner that make it admissible in court. Consideration must be given to the way in which the data is collected. For instance, does the organization have the right to monitor and collect e-mail (have the organization's Internet and e-mail usage policies been written to allow this)? Consideration should also be given to the storage procedures and to which members of the staff will have access to the stored records.

5. **Establish a policy for the secure storage and handling of potential evidence and ensure it is properly and regularly tested:** It is only by planning in advance for the correct storage and handling of the information that it can be ensured it is useable as evidence.

   ■ Ensure that audit and other logs and any other relevant information be stored in such a manner that they cannot be tampered with or modified and that such records are stored in a physically secure and safe manner.

6. **Ensure the monitoring of systems and networks is targeted to both detect and deter major incidents:** This step should be a part of the normal security processes and procedures implemented to protect the systems, but input from an investigator may provide a different viewpoint and improve the defenses and the monitoring systems put in place.

   ■ Monitoring will be guided by a range of factors indicative of different types of activity. For example, fraud activity may be indicated patterns or variations in patterns in financial data. The leakage of IPR from the organization might be revealed by checking information contained in e-mail messages and attachments or records of the copying of files to removable media or of the printing of documents. The abuse of privileges on a system may be indicated by changes in an individual's authorities and access rights or their access to files and areas of the system they would not normally have authority to access. It is only by gaining an understanding of what the investigator will need to look for that the appropriate monitoring can be instigated. To try and monitor everything is pointless and wasteful, as the recovery of any significant information from huge volumes of stored data will be difficult and expensive.

7. **Specify the circumstances in which an incident should be escalated to a full formal investigation:** By considering this in advance, it is possible to think about the scenarios rationally and to get the necessary input from all parties that will be affected or involved. This is a much better time to consider the issues rather than having to make on-the-spot decisions in the heat of the moment during an incident.

   ■ Ensure that the policies for incident management contain sufficient detail for the conditions in which incidents will be escalated and include details of the individuals that should be informed/involved in the identified scenarios.

8. **Train all relevant staff in incident awareness:** In this way, all members of the staff that are likely to be involved will know their role in the digital evidence process and have an understanding of the legal requirements for the collection and storage of evidence. Remember, it will not be possible to train staff and ensure that they have an awareness of the role they will play in the process once it has started. By then, it is too late.

9. **Document an evidence-based case describing an incident and the impact:** By documenting a case, you will be providing a template for the processing and reporting of a real incident and provide the staff with an aide-memoir for any investigation. It will also give those involved in the management of the organization an opportunity to consider the range of impacts and allow them to think about the decisions and actions they will need to take.

10. **Ensure there is a legal review of the procedures developed:** This will facilitate any action taken in response to an incident. By getting a legal review of the policies and procedures that have been put in place to make sure they are legally sound, the organization can have confidence that the steps implemented are effective and correct.

   - Legal advice that should be sought includes the potential liability that may result from an incident, the legal or regulatory constraints that must be taken into account, methods for dealing with members of staff, and any other areas that should be considered that have not been identified until the legal review.

Legal Aspects of Digital Forensics

Anyone responsible for the management of computer or network security must be aware of the legal implications of digital forensic activity. Security professionals must consider the policies they define and implement and the technical actions these necessitate in the context of existing laws. For instance, you must have appropriate authorization before you initiate the monitoring and collection of information related to a computer intrusion. There are also legal ramifications to using a range of security monitoring tools.

As has been stated earlier, digital forensics is a relatively young discipline in the legal community and the issue is further complicated by the rapid change seen in both technologies involved and the ways they are used. As a result, many laws used to prosecute computer-related crimes are out-of-date or are laws that were never intended to be used for digital environment. Not too long ago, phreakers (people who obtained free telephone calls) were prosecuted for the theft of electricity—the only law at the time that could be used. In the UK, the Computer Misuse Act of 1990 was introduced as the first law in the UK to specifically address computer crime, but it was very quickly found that it was difficult to prosecute under this legislation. It has since been updated, most recently in the Police and Justice Act of 2006.

In the U.S., one of the best sources of information with regard to computer crime is the United States Department of Justice's Cyber Crime web site.[6] The site provides an excellent listing of recent court cases that relate to computer crime. The site also provides guides on how to introduce digital evidence into the court and the relevant standards. Laws relevant to digital forensic cases are discussed more fully in a later chapter of this book.

Summary

This chapter offered an introduction to digital forensics and showed why it is necessary. Its definition was covered, as well as its relationship to both science and the law, which has introduced a number of issues that must be considered when managing information systems or conducting or managing digital forensic examinations.

Notes

1. Dr. Ray, I, Presentation on "Digital forensics: Cyber sleuthing solves the case," 1st International Conference on Information Systems Security (ICISS 2005).

2. Moore's Law, coined in 1965 by Intel co-founder Gordon Moore, which states that "the number of transistors on a chip doubles every 24 months."

3. Barbin D. and Patzakis J., article titled "Computer Forensics Emerges as an Integral Component of an Enterprise Information Assurance Program."

4. Special Agent Mark Pollitt, FBI—quoted in *Forensic Computing: A Practitioner's Guide*, (Sammes & Jenkinson).

5. Rowlingson. R, "A Ten-Step Process for Forensic Readiness," International Journal of Digital Evidence, Winter 2004, Volume 2, Issue 3.

6. U.S. Department of Justice's Cyber Crime Web site, http://www.cybercrime.gov.

Chapter 2

Types of Digital Forensic Investigation

Introduction

This chapter will discuss the reasons for carrying out a digital forensic investigation and the type of investigations that might be undertaken—for example, on a single computer, a network, or a mobile device.

Reasons for Conducting a Digital Forensic Investigation

The reasons for undertaking a digital forensic investigation will be wide-ranging and will be dependent, in part, on the type of organization you belong to. The type of investigation that the laboratory will be required to conduct for a federal, state, or local law enforcement organization will normally focus on the whole range of criminal cases. This, in itself, has considerable diversity and as computer devices have increasingly been incorporated into many aspects of our everyday lives, is no longer confined to the older "computer based crimes" category. An example of this is highlighted in a 2002 paper by Carpenter and Perala,[1] which stated that a study of 669 reported cases of computer abuse over the eight preceding years had shown that computers had been increasingly involved in all types of crimes except murder and person-to-person street crimes.

If the laboratory is a part of a corporate entity or a commercial laboratory, the scope may well extend to include data recovery or to support legal service providers for civil discovery where the focus of work will be on the extraction of relevant information to support legal actions. Other areas where a corporate laboratory may be called upon may include support to audit staff and IT security personnel, use as part of an independent incident response and/or disaster recovery, or utilization by human resource staffs for criminal and civil cases or workplace investigations.

The Role of the Computer in a Crime

In any incident, the computer may have played its part in one of three ways. The first is where the computer is the victim of a crime. This is normally where it is the target of hacking, viruses, Trojan horses, or Denial-of-Service type incidents. The second is where the computer has been used as a tool in the commission of a crime—for example, sending blackmail threats. This type of role will cover almost all areas of criminality, including fraud, pedophilia, hacking, industrial espionage, intellectual property crime, and the storage of information relating to any number of other types of crime. The reason for this is due to the role computers and networks play in modern communications and their increasing integration into all aspects of personal and business life. The third way in which a computer may be connected to a crime is in an incidental manner, where it may contain information that relates to crimes such as drug deals that its owner is involved in.

Types of Devices and Systems that May Require Investigation

The range of computerized devices encountered during a normal day that may be potential sources of information and evidence and be considered for forensic investigation is vast. In the home, there is the personal computer and the hub or router that connects it to the outside world, probably a computer games console, a satellite TV box that may have Internet and e-mail capability, the alarm system and control systems for the washing machine and environmental controls, and increasingly other "white goods." In the car, there is the engine management system and the satellite navigation system, which may include a wireless or Bluetooth communications facility. In the office, there will be networked computer systems, access control systems, and alarm systems.

For the individual user, there is the laptop computer and the handheld mobile communications device. The last may seem a strange choice of words to describe what, to date, has been referred to as the "mobile phone," but that term now no longer really describes the devices we all regularly carry with us. Today's device is more and more a mini computer. In addition to making phone calls, it contains an address book and a diary, can download and play music, can browse the Internet, send e-mail, and act as an SMS-capable device.

The types of information that may contain evidence lie in one of three groups; Active, Archival, and Latent Data. Active data is the information that can be seen on the device, such as data files, programs, and the operating system files. This is the easiest type of data to collect. Archival data is data that has been backed up. This may be stored, for example, on DVDs, CDs, floppies, backup tapes, and hard drives. Latent data is the sort of information that may require specialized tools to recover and includes information that has been deleted or may have been partially overwritten.

Issues to Be Considered When Dealing with a Single Computer

For the laptop and the stand-alone personal or work computer, the investigation into a single computer is probably the easiest type undertaken. Even here, the level of difficulty is growing as PCs become more powerful and the size of the storage media increases, and as the ways in which they connect to networks increase and become less obvious (WiFi, WiMax, and Bluetooth). When dealing with a single PC, elements to be considered include:

- The PC
- Peripheral devices
- Storage media
- Associated material

Issues to Be Considered When Dealing with a Networked Computer

Network forensics deals with the capture, recording, and analysis of network events in order to discover evidence and to determine the source of an incident or network-related problem. Network forensics mainly deals with information related to networks on a number of different levels, such as topology, the configuration of the network and the individual elements, network traffic, and the relevant hardware devices that form the network.

According to Garfinkel, the author of a number of books and articles on information security, network forensics can be divided into two main areas:

- The first is where traffic passing through a certain point in the network is captured for subsequent analysis. This normally requires large volumes of storage capacity.

- The second is where each packet passing through the node undergoes a limited level of analysis while it is in the memory of the device. Only information that is considered relevant is then saved for future analysis. This approach requires less storage but is more processor-intensive and may require a faster processor to keep up with the volumes of traffic.

Both of these approaches normally require significant data storage capacity and the first approach may also give rise to potential privacy issues since "end user data" may be inadvertently captured and stored, which may be in contravention with the Electronic Communications Privacy Act (ECPA), since it might be considered eavesdropping or the disclosure of intercepted content if user permission is not obtained.

For the networked computer, all of the preceding elements must be considered, as well as a whole range of other factors. Additional areas to be considered include:

- Routers

- Hubs

- Servers

- Volatile information

Issues to Be Considered When Dealing with Handheld Devices

When dealing with the handheld device, a set of additional considerations must be addressed to ensure that any evidence they contain is captured in a manner that makes it useable in any criminal or civil action. The term "handheld device" is used to describe a range of devices that continues to expand. It includes electronic organizers, personal digital assistants (PDAs), mobile phones (cell phones) and increasingly, as they reduce in size, devices that would previously have been called laptop computers. An increasing convergence in the capabilities of small devices is underway, and the distinction between the whole range of handheld devices is shrinking.

In addition to the types of devices previously detailed, a number of other electronic devices fall into the handheld group that might be encountered during searches, which may contain evidence relevant to the investigation. These include pagers, digital cameras, and MP3 and MP4 players.

Electronic organizers and PDAs range from very small and very cheap devices that may contain anything from a few telephone entries to expensive devices that have as much processing power and storage as the desktop PC of only a few years ago. These devices work on a range of operating systems, such as Linux, Windows CE, the Palm OS, and the Symbian OS. Mobile (cell) phones range from devices capable of making phone calls and storing a small list of phone numbers to modern 3G-capable devices that have the full functionality of a PDA.

Small laptops such as the Nokia N810, the Toshiba Libretto, and the HTC "Shift" are fully functional laptops that have been reduced in size to the point where they are treated very much like other handheld devices.

Despite the range of hardware and operating systems, all handheld devices these days provide a similar level of functionality. They contain a small microcomputer with a miniature or virtual keyboard and a display screen and memory chips or microdisks on which information is stored.

In some of the devices, the memory is volatile and is kept active by the battery. If this fails or is allowed to fully discharge, all information contained in the device may be lost. However, even then, it may be possible to recover data from flash memory.

Other devices have two sets of batteries. The main battery is used to run the device when it is turned on, while a backup battery maintains information in the memory if and when the main battery fails or is fully discharged. When handheld devices are seized, specialist advice should be obtained at an early stage to determine the most appropriate way to handle and store the device. With handheld devices, special consideration must be given to the isolation of the device to prevent data stored on it from being altered or deleted as a result of connection to a network.

The information stored on a handheld device is likely to be held in volatile memory. Consequently, a main concern is to make certain the procedures in place ensure that the evidence stored in the main memory is changed as little as possible. Any changes that occur must take place with the certain knowledge of what is happening internally on the device.

To access most handheld devices, it is typically necessary to switch them on. This means that Principle 1 (shown in Chapter 1) cannot be complied with and, as a result, it is necessary to ensure that Principle 2 is adhered to. In addition, it is not possible to create an image of some handheld devices in a manner that can be repeated to achieve the same hash value, because variables such as the clock time are constantly changing. As a result of this, it is essential that Principle 2 be applied rigorously to ensure any actions taken to obtain the evidence are recorded and verifiable.

Live Forensics

This term describes the collection of possible evidence in real time, while the computers and servers are running. The use of live forensics could provide the opportunity to collect evidence that would otherwise be lost and may give the chance to identify groups of individuals who are communicating and may be working together. The potential to capture this additional information has led to a shift toward live forensics in both government and the private sector. The types of information that can be gathered during live forensics includes running processes, recent e-mail messages, and recently visited Web sites and chat rooms.

Live forensics deals with the extraction and examination of the volatile forensic data that would be lost if the device were to be powered off. It is not a "pure" forensic discipline, in the formal definition, since the use of live forensics will have a minor impact on the underlying operating state of the device. This is one of those exceptions to the basic digital forensics principles, where changes must be made in order to recover the information—the key is that the impact of the actions taken are known and that those actions are fully documented.

Live forensics should be considered for a number of reasons. These range from the capture and recovery of information from systems considered to be business-critical and which cannot be shut down to gaining access to encrypted file systems while they are still accessible. Those systems defined as business-critical will be affected by the type of organization you are working for.

Other reasons for conducting live forensics include the recovery of information from systems where a shut down of the system may create a legal liability for the investigator or an unacceptable commercial cost. These may arise as a result of impeded operations, unintended data loss, or damaged equipment, or when the evidence must be gathered in the least intrusive manner.

Data on a system has different levels of volatility. All data in a main memory is volatile since it is data on a live system. Normally, data from the memory, the swap space, network processes, and running systems processes is the most volatile and will be lost if the system is rebooted. Whenever you collect data, it is sensible to collect the most volatile data first and then proceed on to that which is the least volatile. The order of volatility (as defined in RFC 3227) is:

1. Memory
2. Swap File
3. Network Processes
4. System Processes
5. File System Information

Reasons for Conducting an Investigation

A number of reasons exist for conducting a digital forensics investigation and these will depend, in part, on the type of organization you belong to. The most common types of investigation include:

- Criminal investigations
- Civil litigation investigations
- Data discovery
- Data recovery

Criminal Investigations

Criminal investigations, historically, have been considered the remit of law enforcement and government agencies. While this is understandable, it is incorrect, and this issue is becoming increasingly important. All investigations, whatever the initial motivation for instigating it, should be treated in the same manner. Later in the book, we will deal with the issue of "task creep," where the tasking changes as more information is recovered, but there are occasions where an investigation into a noncriminal incident, such as a virus on a system, will reveal criminal activity. If the correct processes and procedures have not been used from the start, any information collected may be contaminated and rendered unusable. Examples of the types of activity commonly considered criminal include hacking, fraud, distributing viruses, stalking, and blackmail.

Civil Litigation Investigations

The type of activity normally considered to fall into the civil litigation investigation category includes internal disciplinary investigations to gather evidence of system misuse and abuse, or inappropriate behavior that will result in internal disciplinary procedures and potentially the dismissal of a member of staff. Even in this type of investigation, it should always be remembered that if the case is disputed, it may go to an industrial tribunal and, once again, the processes and procedures used should be held up to the same standard applied to any criminal investigation.

Data Discovery

Electronic data discovery (e-discovery) has become increasingly important recently and is now in the mainstream of civil discovery. Recent surveys have indicated that more than 90 percent of all documents produced since 1999 were created in a digital form.

The increased importance of data discovery has been brought about, in part, by recent changes to the Federal Rules of Civil Procedure, which took place in December 2006 and which mandate that discovery is to include electronic discovery. To comply with the new rules and prevent spoilation, e-discovery must commence immediately upon the filing of an action. Elements of the e-discovery process include the preservation of electronic evidence, the creation of a repository of all digital files, and a document retrieval system based on defined search terms. The scope of activity normally covered by e-discovery includes e-mail and documents stored on individual computers and network servers, as well as other devices.

Many attorneys still fail to undertake electronic discovery due to concerns over cost, the time needed, and the complexity of such undertakings, and so fail to appreciate that, compared to the discovery of nondigital information, e-discovery is much more cost-effective. With the digitization of all aspects of business, which has taken place over the last decade or so, there is now an incredible volume of electronic evidence available that can be collected, preserved, documented, and authenticated. The types of cases in which computer-generated evidence is typically relevant include defamation, intellectual property theft, sexual harassment in the workplace, fraud, and breach of contract. It is also increasingly being seen in smaller cases, such as personal injury claims and wage disputes.

Data Recovery

Data is sometimes lost for a variety of reasons. Disk drives sometimes fail, either as a result of mechanical or electronic faults, or due to the corruption of data. Data may also be lost as a result of users being malicious or making mistakes. Data recovery tasks may include the recovery of data that was lost as a result of:

- Logic problems, such as corrupted or destroyed partition tables, boot sectors, or file allocation tables (FATs)

- Mechanical problems, such as hard drives that do not work due to head crashes, where the read/write heads of the disk have become stuck in one position or have made contact with the surface of a disk and failed or a failure to spin up because, for example, the lubricant on the spindle has hardened.

- Malicious activity or errors by the users, such as data deletion, the formatting of disks, or the deletion of partitions

- Malicious software including viruses and Trojan horses

- Lost or forgotten passwords

- Physical damage to the disks as a result of external events like fires and floods

Data recovery tasks involve the recovery of the data that has been identified as required and relevant. This may be all, or just a small portion, of the data available on the media.

Summary

This chapter has discussed the reasons for carrying out the digital forensic investigation and the type of investigations that might be undertaken. The reason for covering these issues was to highlight the range of types of investigation that the laboratory may become involved in and the number of decisions needed. These decisions are particularly important in the very early stages of an investigation to ensure that the right data is captured and collected in the appropriate manner.

If the digital forensic investigation is not managed from the start, effort and resources will be wasted and the objective may not be achieved. It is essential that the manager of the laboratory has put in place the necessary tools, processes, and procedures to support the staff, and that they are appropriately trained and empowered to use them effectively.

Note

1. Carpenter E.M. and Perala D., A Definition of Computer-Related Crime, May, 2002, http://lfa.atu.edu/Brucker/Engl2053/engl2053abstrart1.htm

Chapter 3

Establishing and Managing a Digital Forensics Laboratory

Introduction

This chapter will describe how to establish and manage a digital forensics unit, based on the real-world experience of the authors.

The creation and management of a digital forensics laboratory that is capable of meeting the current and future needs of increasingly high-tech-dependent organizations and environments in government, law enforcement, and the commercial sector is something that should be given considerable thought and planning, since the cost and resource implications are significant. One of the early things to consider in each of these areas is, "Is it a dedicated resource, or is it possible to collaborate and share resources with other groups with a requirement for the same capabilities?"

Resource and capability sharing may be both desirable and even essential for law enforcement and government agencies, where the development and retention of skilled staff is likely to be a significant factor. This can be more problematic in the private sector, but it is possible to create a laboratory that offers value to a number of organizations in the same sector, and which would not be viable for a single organization. Once the rationale for the scope of the laboratory has been established, the development of the business plan can start.

In the United Kingdom, the Association of Chief Police Officers (ACPO), a group that represents all of the local police forces, created the *Advice and Good Practice Guide for Managers of Hi-Tech/Computer Crime Units*. This document was published in 2005 and was developed to give guidance and advice on issues related to the creation of a digital forensics laboratory for a law-enforcement organization. For the non-law-enforcement reader, this may not seem particularly relevant, but the document provides a good basis that is built on years of law-enforcement experience in the creation and management of digital forensics laboratories and has been well tested over a number of years. As a result, it will provide guidance issues that should be addressed in a laboratory in any sector. The amount of thought and consideration that takes place before the laboratory is created will have a huge impact on the likelihood of success and the cost of the investment when the plans are implemented.

It should always be borne in mind that, if the laboratory is not set up correctly in the first place, or is managed poorly following its inception, it is likely that any material processed in the laboratory will not be processed in accordance with relevant regulations and good practice, and may be contaminated or tainted. This will mean it could be liable to being challenged in any criminal or civil proceedings that rely on evidence that the laboratory subsequently produces.

Establishing the Laboratory

The creation of a digital forensics laboratory is not a trivial issue and will be dependent on a number of factors and be constrained by a number of regulations and rules. As alluded to earlier, the initial cost of creating a digital forensics laboratory and the ongoing cost of maintaining it is likely to be relatively high, particularly when it is being introduced as a new function within an organization. The first issue you must overcome (assuming the lab is not being set up as the result of an internal or external regulatory or functional requirement) will be in convincing the organization's management, which has so far managed without forensic capabilities, that the investment is necessary and desirable.

In this, you may be helped by the requirements of changing regulations and the proliferation of technologies that make the creation of such a capability either a requirement or a sensible business decision. Another supporting factor will be the development of a financial model that can demonstrate that the creation of a digital forensics laboratory will provide a return on investment (ROI). This might be achieved by demonstrating that the work being undertaken in the lab will make it cost-neutral in terms of the reduced cost of the organization carrying out its main business. This may be through reduced losses, lower insurance, being able to demonstrate compliance with regulations, or be a result of increasing the value of some other function or service within the organization. Another way in which an ROI can be shown is by demonstrating that the services or facilities of the laboratory can be sold to third parties.

The main message here is that before you start identifying equipment and accommodation needs, you must establish the management support and requirement for the laboratory, and the scope of the task that the laboratory will undertake.

The first step in developing the business case for setting up the laboratory will be to identify the answers to a number of questions. Examples of the types of questions to be answered include:

- What types of activities will the digital forensic laboratory be used for?

- Why is it needed?

- What is the business case for changing from the arrangements you currently have?

- What will the scope of the work to be undertaken by the laboratory include?

- What is the budget required?

- What is the available budget?

Without answers to these questions and others that will be specific to the type of organization the laboratory will serve (and so generate a clear understanding of the rationale for developing it), it will probably fail to come into being, or will fail to achieve its potential.

As an example of the changes that have taken place the last few years, just to answer the first of these questions regarding the type of activity the laboratory will be used for, you must be clear about the requirement. Is the laboratory going to be used for federal, state, or local law enforcement involving criminal cases or will it be used for legal service providers for civil discovery? Alternatively, is it going to be used within an organization for corporate IT security personnel in regards to criminal and civil cases? Will it be used for other corporate human resource investigators for workplace investigations, or will it play an external consultancy role to private investigators or to external computer security consultants in incident response? It may be that the laboratory will be used in more than one of these areas and it is only with clarity of understanding that you will be able to produce a coherent business case for the development of the lab.

The Role of the Laboratory

If the laboratory is to be cost-effective and achieve its potential, a number of steps must be taken before it begins operation. One of the first actions you will need to carry out is to develop the terms of reference for the laboratory. This will, for the most part, be derived from the rationale used for the business case and will outline the customer base that will be supported by the laboratory, as well as the roles of both management and those individuals assigned to the laboratory, and identify (in writing) their job descriptions and individual responsibilities. The terms of reference will also provide guidance about the scope of activities the laboratory will carry out.

Once you have developed the terms of reference for the laboratory, you will be able to identify the roles, duties, and responsibilities of the members of staff. Examples of the types of duties that should be considered for the respective roles are detailed by professional organizations such as the American Society of Crime Laboratory Directors (ASCLD)[1] and, in the UK, the ACPO[2] Good Practice Guide.

The Budget

One element of the budget that will be required in order to establish the laboratory will be what most organizations call capital cost. This is the expenditure that includes the cost of purchasing the equipment and software, and obtaining the accommodation and refurbishing it. These are the "one off" costs required to obtain the infrastructure and equipment and get it into an operational state.

The second element of the cost will be for expenses such as rental costs and maintenance of the accommodation, the cost of staff salaries and training, and ongoing expenses such as the maintenance and upgrading or refurbishment of equipment and software licenses.

The budget you actually obtain will normally depend on the strength of the business case that has been put forward, the priority it receives in the organization and the amount the organization can afford. If the amount allocated by the organization is not as high as that required by the business case, it will be necessary to review the scope of the tasking of the laboratory and modify the level of capability and service you can deliver, to reapply to the organization with a more persuasive case, or to find an alternate source of revenue to support the laboratory.

When you have explored all of these issues and have some answers, then you can start to prepare for setting up the laboratory. A number of considerations, such as the size and type of laboratory, will depend on answers you have obtained to the research you have carried out, but some of the things you will need to address are common throughout.

Detailed in the next chapter is a short business plan for a laboratory. The example shown regards the creation of a laboratory that was being set up to satisfy the requirements of a university. Their requirement was to develop a laboratory that would support the teaching of digital forensics as part of its academic curriculum and also develop a commercial income stream for the university department.

Staff Considerations—Digital Forensics Laboratory Management

It is probable that the person who is doing the business planning will be the first manager of the laboratory or will be heavily involved in the selection of that person. Once the manager has been identified, that person will be fundamental to the development of the roles required to meet the tasking of the laboratory, and the subsequent selection of the staff to meet that tasking.

Depending on the size of the laboratory and the purpose for which it was set up, a number of functions will need to be carried out, and a set of skills will be required to achieve them. The roles will be defined as a result of the identification of the purpose of the laboratory as it was identified in the planning stages. Some of the required skills will be acquired when the staff are selected or recruited, but others will require the training of staff and evolve from hands-on experience.
It is essential that at this early stage of planning the roles and their respective responsibilities be documented from the start, since it will guide the selection of staff and ensure that those people selected will have a clear understanding of their role in the laboratory.

Staff Considerations—Staff Levels and Roles

Depending on the size and purpose of the laboratory being created, some roles that may need to be considered include:

- **Laboratory Manager.** A key role in the laboratory, the laboratory manager will be responsible for all aspects of running the lab. This will include all issues related to the staff, such as recruitment, training, mentoring, counseling, ethical guidance, reward, and retention. They will also be responsible for financial planning and accounting, the equipment and software procurement and management, the allocation of tasks, compliance with standards, and the cost-effectiveness of the lab. A good laboratory manager will have a huge impact on the effectiveness of the lab and should be selected with care.

- **Reception Officer.** The reception officer is effectively the "front man" for the lab and will be recognized as the "point-of-contact" within it, being the person responsible for managing the interface with the "customers." This is the person who will deal, initially, with the investigators and who will decide which tasks are accepted into the laboratory. This person will also normally be responsible for interfacing with any representatives from outside the organization (for example, a defense expert or legal representative), who may require access to the laboratory, the staff, or to specific elements of the evidence. To ensure that a consistent approach is taken when dealing with people from outside the lab, it is essential that whenever possible, only one person carries out this focal role. The person selected for this role will need to have a good knowledge of the investigation process and be able to translate the requests of investigators into realistic tasks for the laboratory. Thus, the employee will need to have good interpersonal skills.

- **Triage Officer.** The triage officer is the person who will be responsible for deciding whether tasks are accepted into the laboratory, and if they are, for allocating the priority in which cases are to be dealt with. As with the reception officer, the role requires a robust character with good interpersonal skills and a good knowledge of both the investigation process and the role of the investigator.

- **Imaging Officer.** This is the role that describes anyone who will be responsible for creating the copy (image) of the seized media and ensuring that the images are created in a forensically sound manner. Depending on the size of the laboratory and the diversity of the tasking, this role may be undertaken by one person or several, each of whom may specialize in a specific platform or software product. The imaging officer will need to be well trained, be experienced in the imaging of media, and must have a good knowledge of the relevant legislation and points of contact, both at home and in other countries where evidence may be located.

- **Analyst.** This is the person who will be responsible for the analysis of the available material and for ensuring that any findings to be presented are in a clear and understandable form that can be reproduced by anyone who needs to do so. During the course of the analysis, they will attempt to find useful information or evidence that relates to the current investigation and may also discover information that relates to other incidents or crimes not known at the time the material was seized. The analyst, with training and experience, should be able to inform management and customers about the progress of the analysis. The analyst will require an in-depth knowledge of the hardware and software, must have good analytical skills, and also good oral and written communication skills.

Depending on the size and scope of the tasking of the laboratory, one or more of these roles may be combined, and it is not uncommon for the laboratory manager to also act as the reception officer or the triage officer, or for the imaging officer to also carry out the role of the analyst.

It is vital you understand that in order to be successful, one of the most important issues to be dealt with will be the selection of staff for the forensics laboratory. You will need to have a clear idea of the purpose and function of the laboratory and the roles that have been identified to be able to select the appropriate staff with the right mix of skills and experience needed. Once the laboratory is established and the staff have been recruited, they will need to have a range of skills that encompasses:

- An understanding of the relevant legal processes
- A diverse range of IT knowledge hardware and software, including mobile phones, PDAs, PCs, networks, and communication systems
- High-tech forensic data acquisition, analysis, and reporting
- Communications, both oral and written
- Administration

Other skills, not listed here, will also be required, but this should give you an idea of the range of skills required.

Getting your recruitment and staff selection right is important, and it is worth investing effort in getting the right mixture of staff. Remember that, in addition to gathering and developing the correct skill sets, the staff must work and function as a team, often in a difficult high-pressure environment. It is also worth considering, from the start, any measures that will be put in place to motivate and retain staff, given you will have invested a significant level of effort and funding in their recruitment, education, and training since the skills they will have and obtain are scarce and there is a general shortage of experienced and skilled personnel available.

Allocation of Duties

In order to ensure the best use of available resources and make certain that staff workloads within the laboratory are spread evenly, it is important that individual levels of expertise be continually developed. This will help ensure that sufficient overlap exists in the skill sets of the staff, which will allow for absences, and for peaks and troughs in the types of tasks being accepted by the laboratory. The digital forensic environment can be stressful and to ensure that the laboratory is running efficiently and that staff are used both effectively and on tasks that they find challenging and satisfying, you must make certain that consideration is given to the fair and appropriate allocation of duties within the laboratory.

Staff Training and Experience

Once the types of tasks that are going to be accepted into the laboratory are decided upon, the software and hardware to be used for the forensic examination of evidence in such cases can be determined. After this decision has been made, it will be essential to ensure that the staff has received appropriate training and has sufficient experience in their use. The staff should never be put in the position of having to defend the results of the work they have carried out, or attest to the "facts" if they have not had suitable training on the use of the software and are not experienced in its use. It would also be sensible to adopt professionally recognized certification or accreditation for any staff working in the laboratory.

When establishing budgets, the fact that training is an ongoing cycle and not a once-only event should be taken into account. For the laboratory to be credible and meet the demands that will be placed on it, staff members will have to operate effectively and continue developing their skills. In order to do this, they must have access to an ongoing program of training that will take account of the changes in technologies and of developments in the tools available. This will be expensive to implement and maintain, but must be supported because any failure to maintain the currency of staff training will lead to disillusioned staff who are not properly skilled to carry out the tasks required of them, and ultimately to the failure of the laboratory to fulfill its role.

Staff and Laboratory Productivity

In the development of the initial business case for the creation of the digital forensics laboratory, assumptions will have been made with regard to the type of investigations that will be undertaken and the anticipated workload. The decision regarding the staffing level for the laboratory will be based on these assumptions and an assessment of the workload that each member of staff will be able to manage. While this is an essential part of the initial planning and justification for the staffing levels, the reality is that, once the laboratory is fully operational, all of these assumptions will need to be revisited in light of the experience gained. The type of investigation will almost certainly change as customers start to better understand the capability of the laboratory, and the workload will almost certainly increase for the same reason. Also remember that consideration should be given to the possibility that the laboratory might be more cost-effective if it is also supporting other types of inquiries or investigations and not just those involving high-tech crimes. The workload that the staff can absorb will also change as the staff gain experience and familiarity with the tools and begin working as a team.

The productivity of both individual members of staff and the laboratory should be continuously monitored to ensure that members of staff are utilized effectively and that the laboratory is operating efficiently. Once the laboratory has been operational for a period of around a year, a review should be carried out and all of the contributory factors should be reviewed to determine whether changes need to be made.

Counseling

Procedures must be put in place for the counseling of staff. The whole area of digital forensics can be extremely stressful, particularly if material being scrutinized relates to serious or gruesome crimes or if pornography or pedophilia are involved. It is essential you have the procedures and arrangements in place for staff not only to have access to counseling services whenever they feel it necessary, but also to have review sessions programmed at predetermined periods. Staff should not be given an option with regard to counseling; there is no place for "macho" acts of bravado, and failure to attend counseling sessions should be investigated and appropriate action taken. A regular well-considered program should be adhered to.

Outsourcing Policies and the Use of External Experts[3]

With the increasing diversification of software and hardware systems and an ever-increasing complexity in the types of systems to be investigated, it is unrealistic to believe that all of the skills and experience required will be available in one laboratory. The policy to be used regarding the outsourcing of tasks (if there is an excess of work to be carried out or if the skills are not available in the laboratory) should be established in advance. In addition, if it is likely you will need to outsource work, potential suppliers should be investigated in advance so their rates are understood, perhaps negotiated, and are acceptable, and that you have checked them out to ensure that their skill sets, integrity, and adoption of standards are up to par. Trying to do all this at the point of need is a guarantee that you will pay the top rate and accept whoever is available at the time, rather than the best.

The policy for which an organization or expert can be called upon, and when, and under what conditions they can be engaged must also be defined in advance so staff are clear on the expectations of the organization. When using external experts, a word of caution on the hiring of "ex-hackers." Hackers, phreakers, or other miscreants are often held up as experts, but if they have been involved in illegal activities, they should not be hired regardless of their expertise. The reality is that, no matter what their skills or expertise, their integrity and trustworthiness will always be questionable and questioned—for example, by a defense attorney.

Accommodation Requirements

The physical size of the laboratory is another issue that should be addressed early in the planning stage. The size of the laboratory you end up with will normally be a balance between what you would like and what you can afford. What is essential is that the laboratory is large enough to meet the role you have identified in terms of reference. Another issue that will affect the accommodation will be the location selected for the laboratory. This will probably be driven by a number of factors: the center of gravity concerning your organization's work (if you have a headquarters in Chicago and satellite offices along the East coast, you probably wont find it suitable or justifiable to put your laboratory in California!), the location of available staff, the relative proximity to other organizations or functions (for example, the disaster recovery team or the audit staff), security, and other issues.

You will need to take into account that the facility will need to have a level of enhanced security. In order to achieve this and improve the survivability of the laboratory from natural disasters and accidental damage, it is normal to avoid locating it in a basement or on the ground floor. On the other hand, you probably want to avoid locating the laboratory on the top floor of a high-rise building since you often have to move equipment that is heavy and bulky.

You must also consider how many staff are likely to be employed in the laboratory and the types of procedures expected to be carried out within it. You should not base this purely on the startup numbers, but should try and project forward for growth, if that will likely be a factor. You will need enough space for each member of staff and for work areas to allow for the dismantling of systems and for the storage of equipment and evidence, for rest facilities, and for meetings. If the laboratory is likely to deal with cases of a particularly sensitive nature, you may need a room that is separate from the main area of the laboratory in order to minimize the number of people who have access to the information revealed as a result of these investigations.

The type of information that may constitute "sensitive information" could include state or corporate classified or sensitive material, information on staff, financial transactions, or sexually explicit material.

NOTE

When there is a possibility that the laboratory will be dealing with sensitive information, plans and procedures should be in place to address the problem. If the issue has been considered in advance, then these plans and procedures can be put in motion so that when the sensitive material arrives in the laboratory, it can be dealt with without any disruption. The type of measure that can be considered includes a separate processing area, the logging and audit of access to the material, a "two-man rule" (where one person never has sole access to the material), and separate secure storage for the material and any documents or data files produced from it.

The laboratory will need to be located and equipped so it has a suitable level of security for the work it will undertake. This will vary from organization to organization and may also change over time as the laboratory gains credibility and becomes more "trusted."

In a typical laboratory you will need to make space for the following functions:

- Reception area with storage
- Waiting/meeting area
- Rest/refreshment area
- Storage for personal possessions and equipment
- Viewing room
- Dismantling area
- Secure storage
- Sensitive investigation area
- Imaging area
- Analysis area
- Management office

> **NOTE**
>
> A significant number of power points will be required in each work area. A number of network ports will also be needed for the laboratory network, but these should be carefully considered and controlled.

The laboratory will need to have adequate security and in most organizations there will need to be space for a reception area where non-laboratory staff can be dealt with, without them having to gain access to the processing area of the lab.

Space will also be needed within the facility for office accommodation for staff and also for relaxation and refreshments. Always remember that a digital forensics laboratory is an environment where there is normally intense pressure and where there is a need to work unsociable hours.

Depending on the type of organization you belong to, some of these issues may already be catered for by the wider organization. Many organizations already have facilities that possess some level of security which, if available and suitable, can be modified to meet the security needs of the laboratory.

Depending on the configuration of the working areas within the laboratory, consideration should be given to the separation of the workstations into cubicles separated by privacy screens to prevent inadvertent visibility of material on the screen of one workstation by anyone using the other workstations. Wherever possible, the monitors should be positioned to face away from the access point to the laboratory, for two reasons: the first is to prevent anyone entering the lab from having a view of material on the analysis workstation monitors, and second, that the analyst cannot see any persons entering the laboratory. While positioning of the monitors to prevent inadvertent overlooking is important, it is also important that, whenever possible, staff are not working in isolated environments.

Three distinct types of storage are required. A significant volume of storage is needed for the evidence (it is normal that material be stored for a period of weeks, months, and even years), and there is also a need for storage of the images created and any product of the investigation, both documents and digital media. Consideration should be given to a fire safe for the storage of the images, products for onsite storage, and a backup system of offsite storage should also be arranged. Within the work area there will also be a need for space to store all of the cables, connectors, attachments, and tools required in the process of digital forensic investigations.

Other Issues to Consider in the Development of the Laboratory

The lab will be a high-tech environment with lots of sensitive electronic equipment in use. In the plans, make sure suitable anti-static material is used wherever appropriate.

The laboratory should have a network that is isolated from all external connections. You will need to consider the type of server, communications bandwidth (go for the fastest you can afford or justify—you will be moving large volumes of data to the storage array and this can become a significant bottleneck), storage media (again, think big—current workstation disks are now up to 500GB, so your online storage media will need to be on the order of at least 10s of terabytes).

In addition to the network, you will also need a stand-alone Internet connection within the laboratory to let you check information and download tools, patches, and updates. This computer will need to be carefully positioned and managed to ensure appropriate usage and to be certain there is no cross contamination. You will also need to make sure that if this computer is part of a corporate network, that the system administrators are aware of the use it is put to and ensure it has sufficient access privileges to achieve this. All activity on this system should be recorded and regularly audited. It is suggested that the system use a fixed IP address that has been made known to the appropriate local authorities, so that, if it should cause any interest as a result of the subjects being checked out or the sites being accessed, they will be able to contact the head of the laboratory.

One aspect often overlooked is that the staff will need a work area where they can dismantle and rebuild computers and other devices, and the laboratory will also, from experience, need a very efficient air conditioning system.

NOTE

The laboratory will also require a storage area for documents, clean disks, and other disposable items, as well as an area for the short-term storage of equipment.

An Example of a Digital Forensics Laboratory

Figure 3.1 shows one layout for a laboratory that encompasses space for all of these functions. This would be adequate for a reasonably sized, commercially based digital forensics laboratory.

Figure 3.1 One Laboratory Layout Option

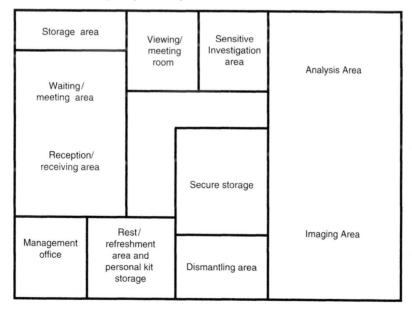

The laboratory will need to have suitable fire, intrusion detection, and motion sensor alarm systems installed, and these should be integrated into the systems of the parent organization if there is one.

For security there will, ideally, be no windows in the laboratory since the site selected for the lab should be at the core of the building so as to offer additional security. If the laboratory does have windows, the security of these should be given careful consideration, even if the laboratory is situated on a floor some distance above the ground. Measures that might be considered include bricking them up, employing bars and grills to prevent entry or exit, and opaquing the glass to prevent observation. This may seem a paranoid approach, but you should always bear in mind that the material that will be processed in the laboratory is sensitive and, as a result, will be of interest to others.

In Figure 3.1, there is no dedicated room for the servers. This is because the location of the servers is subjective, with some organizations preferring to have them located in view in the main analysis and imaging area (this is also the authors' personal preference), while others prefer to locate them in areas such as the secure storage or sensitive investigations rooms.

Identification of the "Customer" Base

One of the most important issues you will need to resolve is who the laboratory will be working for. Put another way, who is the customer base for the laboratory? Is the customer base going to be the corporate investigation team, the audit department, the IT department, the legal department, law enforcement, or commercial customers? When you have determined who the laboratory will be working for, you will be better able to identify the way in which the laboratory and its staff will interact with them and the type of interpersonal skills required. In reality, in most cases, high-tech crime investigators are your usual customers, but there must be a clear understanding of the boundaries of responsibilities between the different roles.

In the hierarchy of the organization, it is sensible for the digital forensics laboratory to answer directly to the manager of the high-tech crime investigative unit or the Chief of Security, whichever is suitable. If it is possible to avoid it, the laboratory should not be placed under the authority of the IT department or the audit department. While investigations carried out may be in support of investigations by either of these groups, and some of the skills and knowledge required may be common to them, the laboratory must retain its independence from them.

If the ground rules are not established from the very start, and preferably documented in the terms of reference for the laboratory, there will be an inevitable expansion of the role or "task creep" of the forensics laboratory. This will almost certainly happen anyway since departments start to realize the range of skills and knowledge that the laboratory staff possess. After all, you will have highly trained staff that are extremely technically competent, and there will always be a call for their skills to "help out" on system and network problems, and investigators will nearly always want "whatever is on the disk" or everything that is "relevant."

Prioritization of Cases

Before the laboratory becomes operational, the type of task that will be accepted into the laboratory and the priority with which different types of cases will be given should be determined. If priorities are set and incorporated into the procedures from the beginning, it will prevent arguments and undue pressure from being placed on the staff by investigators who are only concerned with getting their work carried out and being top priority. The acceptability of tasks and their relative prioritization will need to be regularly reviewed and adjusted as necessary. The role of the triage officer or unit manager, if created, will handle the day-to-day acceptance and prioritization of jobs that come into the laboratory and will normally handle any conflicts in requirements that occur.

Quality Review Procedures

It is essential that procedures to monitor the quality of the work undertaken by the laboratory are established and implemented from the very beginning. This will ensure that an appropriate quality of service is established and maintained and that the procedures are understood by the staff working in the lab and by the management. The quality review procedures will not only support the integrity of the work carried out by the laboratory, but will also be essential in supporting any external certification and will have to be agreed upon by the relevant authorities.

Standards

Standards are essential in any type of laboratory undertaking investigations, particularly when the outcome of the work may be scrutinized in a court or where the livelihood of an individual may be affected. Complying with standards, either within an organization or a community, aids both communication and understanding. Depending on the type of organization you belong to, there may well be national standards as well as local and organizational standards to achieve and maintain. If the procedures to be followed address these standards and are addressed from the start, your staff will have confidence and pride in working for an organization that works according to recognized standards. Two of the best-known standards that should be considered are ISO 9000, which is a set of quality management standards, and ISO 27000, which is a comprehensive set of controls comprising best practices in information security.

Equipment Testing

The digital forensics laboratory will contain a significant quantity of electronic and electrical equipment that will need to be tested at regular intervals for electrical safety. Equipment used for forensic tasks should also be regularly tested to ensure they are "sterile" and carry out their function (and only those functions) as expected. Other equipment in the laboratory may also need to be regularly calibrated. These tests should be carried out at scheduled periods or when there is any doubt about safety, calibration, or effectiveness.

Equipment and Software

Once the role and scope of work for the laboratory has been established and the customer base it will service has been agreed upon, it will be possible to work out what equipment and software you will need. Due to the specialized nature of both the hardware and software, and the nature of digital forensics, a range of tools will probably be required. It is normal to have more than one tool capable of carrying out any of the digital forensic tasks. This way, the results of one can be compared with the results of another to ensure consistency.

Equipment Selection

The selection of equipment, will, in part, be determined by whether you belong to a law enforcement or a commercial organization. A number of companies that produce digital forensic tools will only supply their products to government and law-enforcement agencies or organizations that do work for them and that are vouched for by them. This does not prevent the acquisition of tools to carry out any of the tasks forensically necessary, but it may reduce the number of alternatives available, depending on the type of organization you belong to.

At a bare minimum, you will need a workstation of a type suitable for the task for each analyst, and sufficient space to work with all of the peripheral equipment, tools, files, and other paraphernalia required during an investigation. In addition to the equipment needed to allow each staff member to carry out their tasks, there should also be at least one spare set of equipment, to allow for maintenance and failures, and an additional terminal available in the lab dedicated to Internet searches.

You must also decide how the workstations should be networked and the capacity of the networking interfaces and capacity of the digital storage. From experience, any savings made from buying on-the-cheap in these areas always prove short-lived, since you will end up spending far more in upgrades shortly thereafter. When deciding on your hardware requirements, you should consider that the workstations you create will probably need to:

- Have 5.25 drive bays that are easily ejected to enable the swapping of drives.

- Support fast imaging of the evidence disks.

- Support IDE, SCSI, laptop and micro drives, and a card reader facility.

- Support a range of removable storage media, including tape drives, Zip drives, LS120 drives, JAZZ drives, floppy disks, and USB drives, either through external drives or in the exchangeable bays.

- Have a DVD writer.

- Be capable of supporting PCMCIA drives and devices.

A number of hardware and software options can be employed to ensure "write" protection when imaging systems to ensure there is no possibility of contamination of the evidence from the system. Your choice of "write protection" system may be influenced by the imaging system you have chosen, or by local best practice or local availability and support. Some of the more commonly used hardware and software write blockers are:[4]

Hardware

- Guidance Software Fastbloc[5]

- Tableau forensic bridges (hardware write blockers)[6]

- ForensicPC Mini-Digidrive write-blocking device for reading up to 12 different common Flash memory media

- Drive Lock Serial-ATA DriveLock Kit[7]

- Digital Intelligence UltraBlock and Firefly devices

- ICS ImageMasster DriveLock IDE
- Paralan SCSI Write Blocker
- MyKey Technology Inc. NoWrite
- WiebeTECH Forensic Drivedocks
- LCTechnology International Firewire Second Generation Read Only Removable IDE Bay

Software

- PDBLOCK[8]
- Royal Canadian Mounted Police Hard-Disk Write Lock

Digital Forensics Software

A number of widely used and accepted digital forensic imaging and analysis software suites are currently available. The software ranges in cost and capability, and in addition, you will normally need a range of single task tools to carry out specific tasks. When you have decided on the software that best suits your requirements and have purchased and installed these products, you must also test them to make sure they work on the systems as you have configured them. It is essential you ensure that the software works in the manner advertised since the functionality of the software may become an issue in any disciplinary or judicial proceedings if it has not been tested.

As indicated in the last paragraph, given the wide range of crimes, both high-tech and other types, that you will investigate, you will need a vast array of software tools to look at different aspects of the data you uncover. When selecting these tools, it is sensible to take advice from the relevant professional and forensic associations and also the self-help groups available to find the tools most suitable, those that have received peer approval, and, where possible, have been accepted in cases that have already appeared in court.

As a forensics laboratory, the output of which will always be scrutinized and challenged, it is essential you be scrupulous in ensuring that any licenses for software you use or hold in the laboratory are valid and up-to-date. In addition to it being illegal, it would be unethical and negligent to use software that was not properly licensed and would totally undermine the credibility and integrity of the laboratory. In addition, it would undermine any evidence it was used to produce and could prejudice any cases that such tools had been used on. It would also have a significant negative impact on the credibility of the laboratory and may result in the loss of any certification, and possibly even cause the lab to close if its reputation were lost through the use of such software.

Digital Storage

The volume of storage you are likely to require will be influenced by a number of factors, including the type of work and customers for the laboratory, legislation, and industry best practices. These will all need to be considered before you can make a decision about the volume of storage you require and the location where it is stored. Active cases being investigated and cases that have not been fully resolved either through the courts or tribunals will also need to be stored either on a live server or in some other way that make them easily and quickly available. Completed cases need to be stored against the possibility of further investigation or an appeal, but do not need to be stored on the live system. Instead, they should be stored in a manner that ensures their integrity and future availability. While digital forensics is still a young science, the type of media used to store the large volumes of data necessary has not yet proven to be a significant issue, but it will doubtless be one in the future, given the periods of time that forensic records must be retained. Who remembers the 8-inch floppy disk, and more to the point, who has the drives capable of reading them anymore? Other issues concern the lives of various storage resources. CDs, which were selected as the storage medium of choice a few years ago by a number of law-enforcement agencies, have a limited life before they start to degrade and potentially delaminate, and must be stored in a controlled environment. Consideration should also be given to the storage of software used to create images and analyze them. As software develops, it is possible that new software incarnations will not be able to interpret the files from systems used a number of years ago.

You will also need to consider how to store your backups and arrange for an offsite backup location that can protect them with the same level of security as the laboratory, and do so in a manner that will not degrade the media.

Crime Scene Equipment

You will need to decide what types of equipment are required for "crime scene" forensic work. This will include the type of portable workstations and imaging equipment required and the quantity and type of equipment necessary to hold (and store) systems seized at the scene of the crime (covered in an earlier chapter). When building your crime scene kits, remember that you will potentially be working on a contaminated crime scene and should therefore include protective equipment, not only for the examiner, but also to ensure that the integrity of the physical scene is not compromised and contaminated.

In addition to your imaging tools, the sort of equipment you should consider for your crime scene kit includes:

- Sterile gloves
- Sterile overalls
- Flashlights
- Screwdrivers
- Bags
- Tags
- Sticky tape
- Communications devices
- Devices to test for Bluetooth and WiFi connections
- Cameras
- Mirrors (for looking into spaces you cannot easily see into)
- Pens and permanent markers

- ■ Notebooks

- ■ Forms

- ■ Containers and a cart to transport material

- ■ Power extension leads and adapters

This list is not exhaustive, but is provided as a prompt to stimulate thought on the equipment you will need to carry with you in your environment.

Also remember that you will need storage space in the laboratory for the crime scene equipment in addition to the storage space you will need for seized equipment (remember that you may need to hold equipment for a considerable period of time, and as a result, you may have to allow quite a bit of space). It is worth considering from the outset that as you process more and more cases, the volume of equipment you will need to store will grow rapidly.

Information Resources

Earlier in this chapter, reference was made to the range of hardware- and software-related issues that must be considered during an investigation. In order to be able to carry out there role, the staff in the laboratory must maintain ongoing knowledge of developments in their areas of competence and increase their knowledge to address issues that have not been encountered before. In order to do this, they will need to have access to a wide range of information resources. This will include subscriptions to journals and magazines, the purchase of books and subscriptions to online listservers, and so on. The majority of these must be paid for and the cost of them should be factored into the lab budget.

Another invaluable source of current information and knowledge can be peer organizations— other digital forensics laboratories and associations. Other sources of information will be organizations such as the National Institute for Standards and Technology (NIST),[9] the national white collar crime center,[10] and the FBI.[11] You may also need to look at universities involved in law or digital forensic research and the sites of forensic software and equipment manufacturers or service providers. As the discipline of digital forensics becomes more widely accepted, the number of sources and repositories of digital forensic information will continue to increase.

Health and Safety

The whole digital forensic environment is potentially hazardous to one's health. Staff are using and working on high-tech equipment, are dismantling computers and other devices, and potentially visiting crime scenes. Staff are working in what is, at times, a high-pressure environment, and because they do not know the history of the equipment they are working on, they will need to take care against it being contaminated.

The issue of counseling has been addressed earlier in this chapter, but wider issues related to health and safety must be addressed from the very start. Staff should be trained and briefed on health and safety measures and the briefings should be reinforced at regular intervals. There should also be a strict regime of electrical and chemical safety testing within the laboratory. Regular health and safety checks should be made of the whole environment to ensure there are no unsafe practices or procedures.

Data Retention and Storage Policy

A digital forensics laboratory that does not have a well-defined data retention policy will very quickly run out of storage space. There is also the likelihood that unnecessary retention of data will be illegal in the majority of jurisdictions. A policy for the retention of data should be established and implemented in advance of the laboratory becoming operational and this should be validated with the legal authorities. The data retention policy should then be rigorously applied with periodic checks made to ensure that the laboratory is still compliant.

The Reporting of Findings

Once the role and customer base for the laboratory has been established, decisions must be made about the types of reports to be produced, who they are to be supplied to, and the timeframes for their production. This policy must be a living document that changes as experience is gained and as the pressure of work and delegating tasks develop.

Plans

Before the laboratory starts operations, you must develop a range of plans to ensure the lab is compliant with organizational policies and procedures (if this is applicable), and with regulations, standards, and industry best practices. The plans you will need to produce will include laboratory health and safety plans, contingency plans, incident handling plans, disaster recovery plans, and operational plans, and these must be established and kept current in order to ensure an effective and efficient digital forensics laboratory.

Communications

It is a sad reality that many of the people who have outstanding technical and software skills do not have the same level of communications skills. Communications are fundamental to the success of the laboratory. The forensics laboratory works for customers and there must be a dialogue and procedures for ensuring that the needs of the customer are satisfied and that the customers' requirements are transmitted to the staff. If the investigators do not understand the capabilities and limitations of the forensics laboratory, they will not be able to undertake tasks effectively. The last thing anybody working in a digital forensics laboratory needs is to be asked to "tell me everything that might be relevant to the investigation that is on the disk," without being given some indication of the type of crime suspected, as well as some guidance with regard to what the investigator is hoping to find.

On the other hand, if the customer (the investigator), who may well not understand what is possible for the forensics laboratory to achieve, or what might be recovered from a digital device, is not informed and educated as to the lab's potential, they will not know what to ask for. As a result, it is essential there be a regular and ongoing dialogue between the "customer" and the "service provider." Clearly defined and easily understood protocols for the tasking of the laboratory must be established and agreed upon, together with procedures for the handover of material and the acceptance of various tasks in the laboratory.

Summary

This chapter has examined a range of issues that must be considered in order to develop the business case and obtain the necessary support and funding required to establish a digital forensics laboratory. It has examined a number of factors that must be addressed to ensure the laboratory, once established, will be capable of operating to its full potential, and that the work it will produce will be of an acceptable standard. Issues relating to the recruitment of staff, the allocation of duties, and the subsequent training and welfare of lab employees were also examined.

Notes

1. American Society of Crime Laboratory Directors, www.ascld.org.

2. Association of Chief Police Officers (ACPO), www.acpo.police.uk/asp/policies/Data/gpg_computer_based_evidence_v3.pdf.

3. See Chapter 19 for information relative to outsourcing.

4. The authors do not recommend any specific product but only provide such lists to help you get started in determining what equipment and software is right for your environment. A selection of the relevant URLs are shown in the following paragraphs.

5. Guidance Software Fastbloc FE, www.guidancesoftware.com/products/accessories/FastBloc/fastblocfe.shtm.

6. Tableau Forensic products, www.tableau.com/index.php.

7. DriveLock Forensic Products, www.datadev.com/hd-forensics.html.

8. PDBlock, www.digitalintelligence.com/software/disoftware/pdblock/.

9. National Institute for Standards and Technology (NIST), www.nist.gov/.

10. National White Collar Crime Center, www.nw3c.com/board_contact.html.

11. Federal Bureau of Investigation (FBI), http://www.fbi.gov/.

Chapter 4

Scoping the Requirement for the Laboratory

Introduction

This chapter draws upon the experience of the authors to provide guidance on how to scope out the various requirements of a laboratory. This will include guidance on the potential throughput, the number of staff, and the quantity and type of equipment required to satisfy the anticipated workload.

The first assumption that can be made is that no matter what type of laboratory is being set up, the overriding need to maintain the forensic process is paramount. If you are thinking of setting up a laboratory that aspires to anything less than this, you are not setting up a digital forensics laboratory. Ultimately, even a routine compliance case may yield illicit materials or illegal activities that may see the light of day in court.

In Chapter 2, four common types of investigation, namely criminal investigations, civil litigation investigations, data discovery, and data recovery were defined. For the purposes of scoping the laboratory, however, delineation along these lines is not largely warranted until you are conducting an investigation. For example, if you are undertaking an acquisition task for presentation in court or, at the other end of the scale, to recover data, then the process undertaken should follow the best forensic practice to achieve the maximum potential for outcome.

The forensic process breaks down into three main stages: acquisition, investigation, and presentation. Each stage in and of itself, whilst atomic, relates to the next one by way of continuity. It is feasible, and is often the case, that the acquisition of evidence may be carried out by a different team in a separate location. However, that does not obviate the need for the best and most suitable equipment and processes within the laboratory environment.

High-performance hardware and software are only two thirds of the required equipment for a laboratory. The vital and final third is that of wetware, otherwise known as the suitably qualified expert personnel, the most complex pieces of equipment in any laboratory.

Resourcing should be undertaken with respect to the workloads that have been predicted as a result of the accurate monitoring of the throughput capability of the laboratory. This is often a very complex balance between being overworked and under-resourced and underworked and over-resourced. Whether the laboratory is law-enforcement centric or a fully commercial fee-for-service establishment, prudent resource allocation and usage is critical to success.

Throughput

How much throughput can be expected in a given year is typically the age-old "How long is a piece of string?" question. In a perfect world, humans would work at a consistent rate on every task and use the same amount of resources, effort, time, and energy every time to accomplish the task, making resource allocation and throughput prediction a trivial task.

A correctly set up laboratory should be using standardized devices and processes. In Rumsfeldian logic, we use known-knowns. Humans are notoriously bad predictors or estimators of the time or effort required to complete tasks. One of the redeeming features of digital forensics is that it is a machine-centric and -intensive process, allowing for a *more accurate* prediction of task timelines. The human interactions in the digital forensics process are the abilities to analyze, report, and present the facts.

The following are a few examples to illustrate the known-knowns. Firstly, the cleansing of data from a hard drive of a particular make and model is achieved using a standardized machine, which runs standardized software, and has physical or finite limits. So the cleansing time for this hard drive can be accurately predicted to within plus or minus a small margin of error and placed inside a project/job critical path.

Likewise, other tasks that are undertaken—such as the time taken to create cryptographic hashes for the same hard disk—should also be predictable within given limits. It should also be possible to predict the time it takes to carve the data on a hard disk to recover deleted files when you have collected sufficient data. In fact, very little except the actual human interaction with the analysis process cannot in some way be measured or predicted due to the finite state automata used in computer processes when examining digital data.

The key to accurate prediction is having sufficient data on which to make the forecasts. For existing practitioners, much of this data is operational and most is probably embedded in documentation that has already been produced. What you need to ensure is the overt capturing and recording of this type of workflow information since it is of vital importance to effective human resource management. The following is a list of the rudimentary tasks that should be tracked, which will help in future job estimation and timeline prediction:

- **Media Cleansing:** Erasure of media prior to their use in imaging
- **Media Forensic Imaging:** Imaging of original evidence
- **Forensic Media Replication:** Creating validated copies for analysis
- **Media Indexing:** Indexing of the media for keyword searching
- **Data Carving:** Extracting deleted files from the media
- **Standardized Searches:** Searches involving date and time or targeted keywords
- **Case Archiving:** Archiving of the case and all files to suitable media

Collecting and analyzing this workflow data will provide accurate ways to estimate costs or be used for quotations for jobs. This workflow data is crucial to running a laboratory efficiently in terms of cost and throughput. Information gleaned from the time taken for automated tasks that are necessary as part of the forensic process can be used to help in the estimation of project timelines, which are a critical element in the digital forensics arena. This established datum can also be used as part of the justification for extra personnel or equipment, which will be reassuring when you are up against deadlines for things such as discovery investigations with court orders or Anton Pilar orders to satisfy.

An additional use for the workflow information can be as an effective performance measure for staff. The collected workflow data may demonstrate, for example, that one member of the staff takes, say, 40 to 60 percent longer to complete tasks of a similar quality when compared to others on the team. This anomaly would then point to some form of required intervention, such as retraining, reassignment, or retrenchment.

Yet another use for this collected workflow information from the human resource point of view is that it can be used as a further operational validity check. For example, if a task involving a hard drive is completed in three minutes instead of the long established benchmark of 30 minutes for that type of drive, it is likely trouble is afoot—for instance, the process has terminated early, or a software fault exists, or the hard drive has failed.

The "Job"

One of the major elements that impacts the human factor in the forensic process, other than the actual capability of the staff member, is the burden of proof associated with the task at hand. The level of proof required for some criminal cases can be significant due to the concept of the proof having to be beyond reasonable doubt. Anecdotal stories from law enforcement investigators indicate that the drawing out of the analysis phase is often a method employed by defense lawyers to slow down the process of the prosecution of a case. This is in stark contrast to a civil investigation or a data discovery task, which may hinge on the location and recovery of a single file from media on which there may be literally hundreds or thousands that relate to the same incident. What matters in these cases is that the sought behavior or evidence has been found and it is not the depth or severity of the incident that is important since often only one exposure is severe enough.

The Hardware and Software

The paragraphs below address a number of the issues with regard to both the hardware and software that must be considered when making decisions on the equipment that will be used within the laboratory.

Forensic Analysis Workstations

As mentioned before, digital forensics is a time-sensitive enterprise and consists of a number of computer-resource intensive tasks that are governed by the finite nature of the machines they run on. Tasks such as the keyword indexing of hard disk drives or the cleansing of the same consistently push modern hardware to its finite physical limits, which sadly often fall short of the theoretical limits. A paper by Valli and Patak (2005) that examined the secure erasure of hard disks indicated that the times taken were impacted by both the CPU speed and RAM in terms of available RAM and also the physical configurattion of the system. Little argument exists that the speed of the task is heavily dependent on the processing capabilities of the hardware you purchase. Essentially a dollar saved at purchase time can amount to tens of thousands of dollars lost over the lifetime of the system as a result of losses and delays. Therefore, it is critical when you are setting up a laboratory to use the fastest available systems and to review their performance on a timely, usually quarterly, basis.

The selected equipment should also be on the approved vendor listings for whatever operating system you will be running. If it is not certified, do not purchase it, since you are already introducing a polemic point. At all times you should be using certified drivers for peripherals such as video cards. By using certified drivers, you are eliminating risk and also building your machines to known standards or performance criteria.

Table 4.1 shows a generic outline of a forensic workstation.

Table 4.1 An Outline Specification for a Forensic Workstation

Mainboard (Motherboard)	This should be a vendor-approved list item.
	It should have a suitable number of peripheral slots available.
	Avoid single-slot cases that have a large on-board component for common peripheral devices.
	The mainboard should support high-speed USB and FireWire connections.
CPU	The fastest money can buy; preferably with multiple processors.
	Preferably 64-bit.
Hard Disk Subsystems	The highest speed possible that will allow multiple read/ writes. It should be tested for sustained transfer rates and bursting.
	IDE, SATA, SCSI.
	The ability to handle RAID and large disks.
	Where possible, a hot swap capability will improve throughput.
RAM	The memory should be certified to the mainboard.
	The fastest speed that can be purchased for the mainboard. Install the maximum possible for the operating system.
Hard Disks	As high-speed as possible.
	Should be tested for sustained transfer rates and bursting.
Case	Should have a powerful power supply with spare capacity and multiple connectors.
	Multiple drive bays. Sufficient cooling.

The number of forensic workstations required is typically dependent on the number of analysts in the laboratory. Space requirements are basically a minimum of 3 to 5 m² per workstation. Each workstation or space should have sufficient power outlets for the connection of the systems and peripheral devices.

All forensic workstations should be running on a validated and verified standard operating environment (SOE). A standard operating environment includes the underlying operating system as well as any of the installed applications being used on that particular hardware.

The operating system should conform to a standard configuration and version used on all computers employing that particular operating system and hardware base. Once this baseline is established, the core forensic applications (for example, EnCase, FTK, Autopsy, Sleuthkit, Xways) should be loaded and tested to verify they work correctly. The resultant final build should then be imaged and its replication should occur via a verified and verifiable imaging process. This entire process, plus any upgrade patches or other changes applied should be fully documented in line with standards such as ISO 17025. Furthermore, any of the changes should be carried out with reference to the appropriate IT change management practices.

Disk Imaging Stations

Disk imaging stations may be either computer-based with forensic bridges, computer-based across a network infrastructure, or be a specialist imaging hardware such as the Silo III equipment. The critical element in the use of disk imaging stations is that the combinations of hardware and software used must be regularly validated and verified. This is essential to ensure and demonstrate the correct operation of the equipment during the acquisition of evidence.

Computer-based imaging stations will require specialist hardware controller cards and connectors to access common hard disk types. For example, they must be able to connect both 2.5-inch and 3.5-inch disk profiles (see Figure 4.1) IDE (PATA & SATA), and SCSI (1, 2, 3, UW, U160, U320) as an absolute minimum, as well as FireWire and high-speed USB caddies. The controllers must be on a vendor-certified list for the operating system(s) on which they are being used. The use of simple converter cables that have no onboard chips are also useful.

Figure 4.1 A 2.5" to 3.5" PATA IDE Conversion Cable

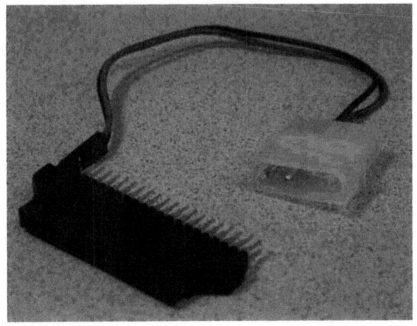

The provision of a high-speed high-quality Ethernet connection is also vital to allow the use of network-based methods of media acquisition and transfer. The author recounts an incident where the particular commercial forensic software employed in a case could not be used to acquire evidence from an old and esoteric network server. The laboratory did not have any suitable hardware to which they could attach and image the network server hard disks. The system, however, was successfully imaged using two copies of an open-source forensic software and a crossover cable, using the UNIX dd and netcat functions. Storage for case files is also increasingly moving towards network-based solutions.

Mobile Device Imaging Stations

This type of imaging station is best suited to a laptop computer for a number of reasons. Firstly, most mobile devices do not have a large internal storage capacity that might outstrip the capacity of a suitably equipped laptop computer. The imaging of the device should preferably be undertaken to media such as a DVD or a USB-attached hard disk. Secondly, the use of a laptop provides a fully portable solution, which given the short battery life left on some mobile devices make it suitable for on-scene triage and evidence preservation. Finally, laptops have their own inbuilt power supply from the battery.

A mobile device imaging station also needs an RS-232 serial connection, Bluetooth, and infrared capabilities to provide connections to a range of mobile devices. Whether some or all of this is in-built or provided by a third-party device is largely moot as long as the drivers and supporting hardware are certified for the operating system. This range of connection methods are necessary in order to cover all the possible ways of connecting to mobile devices, atypically smartphones, BlackBerries, and PDA devices. Older phones may require the use of specialist hardware connections or the construction of a custom cable for connectivity.

This type of imaging solution relies heavily on specialist vendor software solutions such as Paraben Device Seizure, Mobiledit Forensic edition, or EnCase with the neutrino plug-in. In addition to the software, a vast armada of cables, plugs, and power supply alternatives must also be carried. Kits are provided by some of the software vendors for these accessories as an additional cost. The emergent type is the use of phone flasher devices and software such as BK forensics to analyze the resultant device images; however, these types of solutions are currently still in development.

Hardware-based solutions such as .XRY are simply a very specialized, partly siliconized version of the laptop-based solution. This type of equipment is best suited to laboratory bench work rather than on-scene triage. This type of solution also typically requires a large capital outlay to purchase them due to the extensive development, ongoing support, and upgrades needed for such systems.

Two important pieces of hardware for use with mobile devices are those of automated battery reconditioners (discharger/recharger) and variable power supplies. The battery reconditioner is a device that allows even mobile device batteries that have marginal functionality to be reconditioned so they hold a charge longer. These devices are not inexpensive, but due to increasing demand, you would be well advised to include these devices in your laboratory shopping list. The variable power supply will allow a connection, for the purposes of acquisition, via either alligator clips or soldered connections to supply power to a mobile device whose battery may have become depleted.

Finally, for any mobile device analysis system, a network isolation process must be in place. Mobile devices are typically able to connect to multiple network types, including mobile phone networks, Bluetooth, and WiFi. Mobile devices being used as evidence items should be isolated from these networks. Failure to isolate them from a network or communication channel could see any potential evidence being tainted or lost permanently, either by accident or intention. As an example, simply powering on a smartphone or BlackBerry that has been offline for a period of time may result in a flood of e-mail and SMS messages that deletes or even erases items of interest on the device.

One of the significant challenges that this presents is the wide range of frequencies upon which these networks operate: the phones (800MHz to 2100MHz), Bluetooth and WiFi (2.4GHz). The solution to this problem requires the use of measures that provide isolation that stops the egress and ingress of electromagnetic waves. This is commonly called a Faraday shield/cage. A Faraday cage/shield is normally a metallic shell that reduces or ultimately stops electromagnetic fields and frequencies from escaping or entering.

Several options are currently available. One is the use of an isolation bag made out of signal attenuating materials such as the DiskLans Phone-Shield. A more expensive solution could be the installation of a Faraday cage/shield in your laboratory, which allows the operator to work within the shielded environment. If your laboratory will be processing a significant volume of mobile devices, then investigation into the construction of a Faraday cage/shield is warranted.

Software

It is often the case that digital forensics software will outstrip the cost of the hardware it runs on. Traditional computer forensic tools such as the Guidance Software EnCase software fall into this category, but newcomers in the digital forensics area, such as .XRY, are similarly priced. Open source software is free but does require a significant amount of testing and verification to ensure the results obtained using it can be replicated with other tools. Plus, an added disadvantage is that it has no vendor support.

Much debate surrounds open source versus commercial offerings in many areas, and digital forensics is no different. The main difference is that in digital forensics, regardless of whether it is commercial or open source software, the software must be tested to make sure it performs as specified. There have been cases where both commercially supported and open source software have failed to do so, calling into question evidence that has been obtained using them. The argument here is not about support but one of stability and admissibility. The old adage "if it's not broken, don't fix it" should be translated here as "if it works and is validated, do not patch it!"

Whether you use commercial or open source or there are certain function-specific pieces of software needed, the cost of the software and the time for support and maintenance of the same should be factored into your budget. (See Table 4.2.)

Table 4.2 Comparison of Commercial and Open Source Software

	Commercial	Open Source
License to use or operate	$300–$30,000	Free
Product support	Normally included	Time
Bug fixes	Normally included	No imperative
Court support	Normally included	On your own

As mentioned previously, what open source software saves in initial expenditure can often be readily consumed by extensive support costs. Table 4.3 lists some examples of commercial and open source tools.

Table 4.3 Examples of Commercial and Open Source Tools

	Commercial	Open Source
Hard disk analysis software	EnCase	Auditor
	Forensic Toolkit	
	Access Data Forensic Toolkit	
Mobile phone software	MobilEdit	
	Paraben Device Seizure	
	Susteen SecureView	
	Oxygen Forensic Suite	
Virtualization software	VMWare	Xen (Linux)
	Virtual PC	Qemu (Linux and Windows)

Evidence Storage

Evidence storage is an area of the laboratory scoping exercise that is often missed, being included only as an afterthought. This should not be the case. Even small digital forensics practices could, conceivably, within a year, and taking into account current data storage devices, require the capability of storing in excess of one petabyte of live evidence.

Two basic types of storage are required: live and archive. Live storage is required for active cases, while archived storage, by imputation, is material that needs to be archived and preserved, typically for a mandated period of time. The time is largely determined by your recordkeeping and evidentiary requirements, which are typically on a per-jurisdiction basis. For example, within some Australian states, the span can be as long as 75 years, while in other jurisdictions it lasts until the conviction is run or for a period of seven years.

Live storage does not have to be very high speed; however, it does need to be reliable and have good redundancy. Redundancy is essentially how many individual components can fail before a loss or corruption of data occurs. This is typically achieved by using a technology called RAID (Redundant Array of Inexpensive Disks or Redundant Arrays of Independent Disks). What this technology does is combine two or more disk drives into one logical unit. It then applies a combination of techniques—namely mirroring, striping, and fault tolerance (error correction)—to achieve the desired levels of protection versus throughput. One of the key benefits of this approach is that the technology is expandable and uses industry standards for storage. The purchase of proprietary "silver bullet" solutions or the extensions of existing technologies (such as RAID) can be problematic and should be avoided.

The physical size of storage will have a significant impact on your electrical power supply requirements for the laboratory as whole. It should be noted that you must factor in power requirements here for both the storage devices and environmental control via refrigerated air conditioning. This may present significant problems when planning to locate a laboratory within an already populated building or build one that is not near a readily available source of upgradeable power.

Archive Storage

Today, archive storage is typically achieved using DVD-R or CD-R technologies, or large capacity magnetic tapes. It should be noted that this is not a permanent solution but is, in reality, a semi-permanent one that actually requires the data to be re-written to fresh media every five years at a maximum. The space requirement and floor load this can produce can be significant due to the collective weight of large volumes of the media. There is also a need to "archive" the hardware and software that produced the archives for later retrieval. How many laboratories today still have access to 8" floppy disk drives or LS120 or Zip drives, the media that was popular for storage only a few years ago?

A separated storage facility, ideally a room that has a high level of security with physical and logical controls, should be used for evidence storage. Whether the facility is used for live or archival storage is moot; evidence needs protection from not only break-in continuity but also from deterioration as a result of poor environmental control. The facility itself should also have in place barrier controls that allow the monitoring of ingoing and outgoing personnel, and include video surveillance, a fire alarm, and climate control and suppression in addition to the already-stated environmental control via refrigerated air conditioning.

Hardware Work Benches

One of the areas needed is a place for the orderly disassembly or repair of hardware. Ideally, you should have a suitably wide range of tools in the area—for example, screwdrivers, specialist drivers, soldering irons, multimeters, micro drills, and any other paraphernalia required to disassemble or repair electronics or digital devices. This area should also contain a cabinet or workspace that is dust-free for the disassembly and reassembly of hard drives and other dust-sensitive devices. The area should also be free from sources of static electricity and should have fully grounded areas on which equipment can be attended to. In this area, you will position a suitably trained electronics or hardware specialist staff member to conduct the disassembly or repair.

Updates, Maintenance, Equipment Obsolescence, and Retirement

One of the elements of planning that is rarely thought of is that of planning for the ongoing maintenance and eventual retirement of the equipment. Digital forensics is currently a fast-moving discipline that needs state-of-the-art equipment to maintain a competitive edge. The question of whether equipment should be leased or purchased will be addressed in a future chapter, but the fundamental question from a scoping point of view is that of the maintenance, retirement, and replenishment of equipment.

All hardware should be reviewed on an annual basis with the main forensic workstations having a review every six months. Technology advances rapidly—for instance, current quad core CPUs are now available that were not 12 months ago, and eight core CPUs are emerging. This type of advance in hardware can have significant operational impacts, namely the faster processing of tasks, which could result in reduced operational timelines. A simple replacement or upgrade of a CPU may see as much as a 50- to 100-percent improvement in processing power.

All computer hardware should be retired at the end of a three-year term or the cessation of the warranty. The cost of repair of hardware is now largely negated by the purchase of newer faster equipment. Clear and foreseeable problems often arise with sourcing replacement components, such as RAM or video, for devices beyond their warranty. The warranty period is typically there for a reason—that is, the manufacturers' engineers and risk analysts have determined that after this time the risk of failure of the device has increased to a level that is unacceptable.

Summary

In this chapter, the experience of the authors has been used to provide guidance on a number of issues that need to be considered but are often overlooked when scoping out the requirement for the laboratory. The issues that have been examined include the potential throughput of work, the number of staff required, and considerations regarding the quantity and type of equipment needed to satisfy the anticipated workload. Issues concerning the choice of open source or commercial software have been discussed, as well as short-term and long-term data storage.

Chapter 5

Developing the Business Plan

Introduction

This chapter will cover the development of the business plan for the creation and running of the digital forensics laboratory and the unit.

The Business Plan

Developing a business plan is a subjective affair, and considerable advice and examples of best practices are out there for you to adopt. Of course, your own organization will likely also have its best practices and accepted ways of doing things. The material provided here is not intended to be a rigid template, but is offered as an example of a type of business case used successfully by an organization to create a digital forensics laboratory.

As with any good document you want senior management to absorb, there should be an executive summary at the front telling them—in the length of only a page or so—what the document is about and giving them the "elevator pitch" level of information you want them to approve. To provide context, the following business plan has been written as though the digital forensics laboratory would work within the Security department.

- **Executive Summary**

  - This document is the Business Plan for a proposed new activity to be managed by the Security department at the parent Organization.

  - The activity is concerned with the provision of a Digital Forensics Service, aimed at law enforcement, government departments, major corporations, and small to medium enterprises in the high-tech market. The market is ready to explode, and we are ready to exploit it.

  - The market need for these digital forensics services arises from the growth in the detection and pursuit of digital-based crimes and the resultant need to forensically image digital devices for law-enforcement agencies, government departments, and corporations, and to provide individuals who can act as "expert witnesses" in the courtroom.

  - The Digital Forensics Service will provide a low-cost easy-to-understand service, and be a highly effective solution for the current business climate.

  - The purpose of this business case is to present management with the information needed to determine whether or not to proceed with the business. Approval to proceed is sought.

  - Although not without risk, the digital forensics business has both a low technical risk and low financial risk, and is capable of being managed by the Security department.

  - The digital forensics business requires a relatively small investment and has a payback period of less than three years.

  - Income in year 1 will be $250K, rising to $1.4M in three years, and $3M in five years.

The next section of the business plan is the outline of the proposal that gives a short explanation of the purpose of the plan and an indication of the scope.

- **Outline of Proposal**

  - This proposal concerns the establishment of a Digital Forensics Service, to be known as "The Digital Forensics Laboratory." The service will operate on a Monday-to-Friday 9-to-5 basis, with a call out facility for after-hours requirements, and will satisfy a need in the law enforcement and government departments market area for a service that improves the timeliness and quality of evidence for use in prosecutions. In addition it will also provide the same level of quality information for use by corporate customers in industrial tribunals that involve the misuse of digital assets.

  - The business proposed in this "case" represents a minimal viable business, with minimum financial risk, and an expected turnover of $250K, in the financial year 09/10, rising to $3M per annum in year 14/15.

The next section of the business plan describes in more detail the business being proposed and explains what it will deliver.

- **The Business**

  - *The Nature of the Digital Forensics Service Offering:*

    - The purpose of the Digital Forensics Service is to provide clients with a reliable and knowledgeable service that will service the demand being placed on law enforcement agencies and government departments as a result of ongoing operations and new legislation.

    - The law enforcement and government department market for digital device–based investigations is one of the fastest growing markets in the U.S., the UK, and Europe. This has been brought about by an infusion of funds from the government and the creation of a number of high-tech crime investigation units around the country. The creation of these units was a reaction to the increased reporting of digital device–based crimes and the lack of skilled staff to address the issues raised.

  - *The Scope of the Digital Forensics Business:*

    - The business will be a $250k establishment, growing to a $3M turnover business centered in the U.S., from a laboratory located at the corporate headquarters.

    - There will be a number of offerings to clients, all based on digital forensics. The laboratory will provide a digital device imaging and analysis service for evidence to be used in the courts and in industrial tribunals. The laboratory will provide individuals to act as expert witnesses for the courts and, where required, will provide training to organizations in digital forensic techniques.

    - The service offering, known as "Digital Forensics," will be launched on January 1st, 2009.

    - The laboratory will initially utilize industry-standard tools for digital forensic imaging and analysis, but as the requirement for the imaging, recovery, and analysis of particular elements and types of information becomes clearer, tools will be acquired or developed to meet the requirement.

- **Business Strategy for the Parent Organization vis-à-vis Digital Forensics**

  - The principle factors that have influenced the strategy for this business case are investment, staffing resources, and existing expertise and culture within the Organization.

  - Factors that have not influenced that strategy include the organization's desire to be a recognized center of excellence in the computer security and computer crime investigation areas in the future, or the size of the market for such services. The latter is not seen to be a limiting factor to the growth of the business.

  - The strategy for the activity is to establish the parent organization as a premiere center for digital forensics services and digital forensics research in the U.S. This business case, being modest and risk averse, does not seek to establish the parent organization as the market leader.

  - The nonfinancial benefits of this activity are that it will allow the staff involved to become highly proficient in the area, which in turn will benefit the organization as a whole and will enhance the reputation of the parent organization.

  - By undertaking forensic investigations, the staff will gain knowledge and skills in areas that will support the wider organizational infrastructure.

- **Product, Customers, Markets, Channels, Brand, and Pricing for Digital Forensics**

  - *A Description of What Digital Forensics Does:*

    - As digital devices have become more ubiquitous and integrated into ever more aspects of daily business, academia, and individuals' personal lives, so has their use as a tool and as a source of evidence in criminal investigations. Law-enforcement agencies now must consider the role a digital device may play in every type of crime, from murder and drug deals, to blackmail and pedophilia. The digital device may be used as a tool in the perpetration of the crime or just as a repository for information related to the crime. Law-enforcement officials do not have the expertise in sufficient quantity to conduct the required investigations, using their own resources and implementing all of the digital devices and systems necessary. As a result, in many locations, a serious backlog of cases has developed. The services offered by the forensics lab would allow us to be seen by law-enforcement agencies as a "trusted" organization that they could outsource parts of their investigations to.

    - In addition to this type of customer, a number of government departments increasingly require digital forensic services and do not have the necessary investigative or digital forensic skills necessary. This industry need is matched by those of commercial organizations that require these services in order to meet the requirements of increasing levels of legislation.

- **The Need for a Digital Forensics Service**

  - The sheer volume of digital forensics work that has arisen, partially due to the spread in the use of digital devices, and partially as a result of law enforcement and commercial operations to address computer crime issues, has resulted in law-enforcement computer crime units being overwhelmed by the volume of work. The time required to train new staff, and the salaries available for public servants, ensure that the supply of trained staff for law-enforcement agencies will always be less than the demand for their services.

- **Customers**

  - Target customers will, initially, be taken from local law enforcement, government departments, and commercial organizations. As the service becomes established, we will expand this to other law enforcement regions and then to local and central government departments.

- **Markets**

  - We will, initially, target the law enforcement community in the Mid and Southwest portions of the parent organization's operating area. When this customer base is established, other law enforcement bodies will be targeted, and then eventually the government market, banking, and financial services market, health care market, manufacturing and retail market, and telecommunication markets.

  - Research conducted with local law enforcement agencies and feedback from practitioners attending local seminars has demonstrated there is an unprecedented level of interest in the proposed service.

- **Channels**

  - The main channel to market will be via word of mouth through existing customers and contacts. It is not proposed that intermediaries be used. Moreover, it is intended the services will be marketed only in the U.S., under this business case.

- **Pricing**

  - The Digital Forensics Service will be charged on a per-job basis. Fees will be based on the range of services required.

  - Pricing strategy is based on the need to recover, at minimum, all fixed and variable costs with a sufficient margin for profit, while, at maximum, providing a service at similar or lower cost to our clients than our competitors, and at a cost to clients that is consistently less than what they would incur were they to provide such a service in-house.

- **Competitive Strength of the Digital Forensics Service**

  - *Competitor Analysis:*

    - There are three main types of competition, the first being other suppliers of digital forensics services, the second being the suppliers of digital forensics service products, and the third being the customers' use of their own in-house resources.

    - Competitor service providers include organizations such as Digital Forensic Services Inc, Kroll Ontrack, Midwest Forensics, QinetiQ, and International Risk Management.

- Competitor product suppliers are led by Guidance Software, the providers of EnCase Digital Forensics Tools, which is the most commonly used tool in law enforcement for computers and network devices, and Paraben, which is the most commonly used tool for mobile devices.

- The preceding product suppliers are not in direct competition with the parent organization, in so far as they do not supply their customers with a service. However, they are in the business of providing our potential clients with software and hardware solutions, with the intention that their customers operate their own systems, and hence do not need our services.

- **Differentiators**

  - In addition to providing customers with digital forensics services, it is intended that the laboratory will offer them additional services, which, while not unique in the market, will differentiate the offering from that of our competitors.

- **Unique Selling Points (USPs)**

  - The digital forensics service offering is unique in that it is able to provide an independent service using industry-standard software. Initial survey activities have identified a need for this service; however, potential clients are extremely cautious as to whom they will trust to perform this service. The feedback is that the parent Organization is seen to be trustworthy.

- **Key Business Issues for the Parent Organization vis-à-vis Digital Forensics**

  - Several key business issues are likely to impact the success of the Digital Forensics Service business.

  - No known political, economic, environmental, economic, or societal issues are likely to affect the success of the Digital Forensics Service business. However, there may be personnel issues, as well as legal and financial issues, that must be addressed.

  - The Digital Forensics Service business requires a certain level of operational staff in order to maintain its services. This minimal resource level is capable of delivering service to many customers. Thus, sales are not limited to our ability to recruit additional staff, above this "base" level. However, the parent organization has, at present, no difficulty in attracting and retaining suitable staff. If, however, for some reason the Digital Forensics Service business is unable to recruit and retain sufficient key staff, the business will fail.

  - The Digital Forensics Service business will require a limited investment. If, for whatever reason, the necessary funding is not forthcoming, the business will not be viable.

  - The Digital Forensics Service business will need to embrace certain activities such as marketing and customer liaison and entertainment in a manner, and to an extent, that is currently unknown in the parent organization. If, for whatever reason, these activities are not performed, the business will fail.

■ This business case assumes that the business will be conducted from within the parent Organization. At issue is whether or not such a business is best placed to prosper within the parent Organization environment.

■ The investment required to launch this business, while modest by industry standards, is not trivial. The issue for the parent Organization's senior management is whether or not its aspirations for engaging in new business ventures is correctly aligned with the practical realities of doing so.

■ Summary of Compelling Business Proposition for the Parent Organization

■ The Digital Forensic Service business opportunity will establish the parent Organization in the U.S. digital forensic services market. The business requires a modest investment and, with low technical and commercial risk, will produce potentially substantial and continuing profits. the parent Organization has already gained, through its research, a reputation for world-class technical expertise in the field of digital forensics. The Digital Forensic Service business leverages this know-how into a service offering for the U.S. market. The Digital Forensic Service business will provide a platform to enhance the reputation of the parent Organization, both through the exposure to a range of live cases and through contact with potential customers.

■ Management

■ *Organization of the Digital Forensic Service:*

■ Under this business case, it is proposed that the Digital Forensic Service business be operated from within the Security department of the parent Organization. The director of the business will be the head of Security, with Mr. Smith and Ms. Jones responsible to him for the profitability of the venture. Mr. Smith will be the Digital Forensic Service Business Manager.

■ Key Staff for the Digital Forensic Service

■ Mr. Smith and Ms. Jones have the knowledge and expertise needed by the business to deliver in-depth technical advice. They will form the core of the Digital Forensic Service business, and their skills will be needed on a regular basis. Other staff members will require skills in the fields of live forensics and the forensics of handheld devices.

■ Interfaces and Dependencies

■ On the supply side, the Digital Forensic Service business is reliant upon access to the suppliers of digital forensic products. The Digital Forensic Service business must evaluate and select the "best-of-breed" products for use in delivering the service.

■ No known obligations and dependencies will need to be addressed by the Digital Forensic Service in respect to regulatory issues or conflicts of interest with corporate standards or procedures.

- **Resources**

  - The availability of suitably qualified staff is critical to the success of the Digital Forensic Service business. This issue represents the second most important risk to the success of the business. It is not anticipated that the organization will have a problem in the short term. The brutal reality is that, in the long term, if the business is very successful, problems currently suffered by law enforcement agencies may also be encountered by the Digital Forensic Service business. With the level of training and skill required to create an effective digital forensics investigator, the potential for highly paid commercial employment is a reality. There are no known requirements for external supplies of resources, facilities, and materials other than operational equipment, software, and communications services freely available on the open market.

- **Location and Facilities**

  - The Digital Forensic Service will be operated from an isolated accommodation in the Corporate Headquarters facility of the parent Organization.

- **Intellectual Capital**

  - *Intellectual Property of the Digital Forensic Service:*

    - There is no requirement for the acquisition of intellectual property by the Digital Forensic Service business. However, it is anticipated that, over time, the laboratory will develop IPR that will add value through licensing and reputation.

- **Know-How of the Digital Forensic Service**

  - The Digital Forensic Service team has yet to learn how to manage the service in the most economical way. This will improve as experience is gained.

- **Financial Approach**

  - The staffing level is modeled upon the quantity and roles needed to conduct the business. Standard current (parent) Organization rates have been used. Pay levels are allocated to roles. A separate schedule, the effort sheet,[1] identifies the effort needed to perform individual tasks or roles in the business. The model then performs a sanity check to determine whether or not the business has too many or too few staff.

  - Marketing and entertainment costs have yet to be identified. Judgment is required to estimate the level of money needed to generate sufficient market awareness and business generation.

- **Anticipated Revenues and Costs for the Digital Forensic Service**

  - A five-year budgetary estimate of revenues and costs, excluding taxes, with a commentary on the assumptions underlying the projections is provided in the following.

- **Formation Costs for the Digital Forensic Laboratory**
    - The business is scheduled to commence trading on the *Month* 1ˢᵗ, *20XX*. Effort expended by staff has not been included in these estimates. It is estimated that startup costs will amount to $115k.

For a breakdown of proposed costs, see Table 5.1.

Table 5.1 Breakdown of Laboratory Creation and Running Costs

Costs in $	Initial	Post Launch
Time span	To XX/XX/20XX	From XX/XX/20XX
Laboratory Equipment	(48,000)	8,000
Software	18,000	12,600
Training	16,000	12,000
Staffing		
Total	**82,000**	**32,600**
Cumulative	**82,000**	**114,600**

- **Legal and Regulatory Issues Affecting the Digital Forensic Service**
    - Not applicable under this business case.
- **Benefits to the Parent Organization**
    - *Financial*:
        - The potential profitability of the business is high. This is not based on extravagant expectations of a high number of sales. Indeed, the assumptions have been modest as to the likely uptake of new customers. High profits will arise from the fact that the Digital Forensic Service is a service business that lends itself to repeat business, and that the marginal costs of service delivery are low compared to the potential income.

- **Nonfinancial**
    - The Digital Forensic Service business moves the Security Department towards service offerings that complement the current consultancy-based services. With minimal marginal effort and cost, the services can be renewed year after year to produce continuing revenues.
    - The Digital Forensic Laboratory Service can be used as a basis for launching additional services to clients, as market needs change. Once the Digital Forensic Service laboratory is running, sales will not be constrained by the organization's ability to resource them.

Law-enforcement agencies will be able to obtain a service from the laboratory rather than the advice and ad-hoc support they currently receive.

- **Risks and Critical Success Factors for the Digital Forensic Service**
  - *Setup Phase:*
    1. Laboratory not set up and ready for business in time
    2. Insufficient staff trained and in post when needed
    3. Insufficient investment

- **Product Liability**
  - The Digital Forensic Service business will require professional indemnity insurance. The level of insurance required is still under investigation, but will be essential since clients may sue the laboratory in the event of a mishandled investigation. There is also a possibility that a client may go to an alternative supplier if the laboratory is not responsive and does not provide a suitable service offering.

- **Market Development**
  - A number of key issues are likely to prevent the Digital Forensic Service from successfully penetrating the market:
    - A market leader may emerge to dominate the market. This market leader may, through superior technology, smarter working practices, and economies of scale, offer a more attractive offering than the Digital Forensic Service.
    - Insufficient or poor quality marketing may deny the laboratory the success it might otherwise have achieved.
    - The Digital Forensic Service may not be able to "deliver" the level of service expected by our customers, resulting in a loss of reputation, such that it will be more difficult to attract new business and retain existing customers.

- **Management and Service Delivery**
  - There is a risk that the parent Organization may manage the Digital Forensic Service business as a "project" rather than as a "business."
  - There is a technical risk that the Digital Forensic Service analysts may not be able to categorize and prioritize investigation incidents and facts effectively.
  - There is a technical risk that the amount of effort needed to conduct a forensic analysis of a system has been underestimated.
  - There is a technical risk that the software used by analysts in the Digital Forensic Service laboratory will be unable to analyze the material in an effective manner. This could result in ineffective advice to the law-enforcement community.

- **Financial**

  - The most sensitive variables that affect profitability are the number of clients (the sales volume), the selling price (fee rates) for the digital forensic services, and the number of clients the laboratory staff can manage effectively.

- **Legal**

  - No known legal or regulatory factors could adversely impact the business.

- **Exit Plan for the Parent Organization**

  - It is envisaged that the digital forensics business will continue, in one form or other, in perpetuity.

  - Should the business fail, the majority of the staff employed in the laboratory could be readily redeployed within the parent Organization, as could the equipment and accommodation facilities.

- **Responsibilities for Exit Management**

  - The exit will be managed by the head of the Finance department of the parent Organization.

- **Distribution of Assets and Liabilities**

  - The distribution of assets and liabilities will remain with the Security department.

Summary

This chapter has outlined the issues that need to be considered and the arguments that need to be raised in the development of the business plan for the creation and running of the digital forensics laboratory. The business plan is based on one that has been successfully used in the past in a commercial organization and has been modified only to make it as generic as possible. While each environment and organization will have slightly different requirements and will demand that different issues are addressed in the business plan, the one provided should provide a good outline.

Note

1. The effort sheet is the breakdown of time that has been estimated to carry out each of the anticipated tasks. This will need to be updated as experience is gained.

Chapter 6

Laboratory Location

Introduction

This chapter will address a range of issues that must be considered when deciding on the location of the laboratory. These will include the location of the laboratory in terms of the geographic location, the location with regard to the owning organization, and the location of the laboratory within a building.

The location and security of the laboratory is a critical item that is often overlooked or poorly considered. Much of the forensic data stored must have a physical location that is secure, stable, and sterile. Continuity of evidence demands a high level of auditable access control to the data being processed or stored, which can only ultimately be provided in a secure, sterile, and systematic way.

A multitude of guides and manuals, such as the FIPS 31 Guidelines for Automatic Data Processing, Physical Security and Risk Management, are available. Although the FIPS 31 guide was first released in 1974 and finally withdrawn in 2005, it provides a solid grounding for a secure facility with information processing resources. Though much of what is contained in such manuals seems common sense, experience has shown that sense of this type isn't very common.

The Location of a Laboratory

The first critical aspect is the location of the site and its inherent security, which must be balanced against access to the facility. Most of the work, whether slated for law enforcement or a civil matter, normally infers that a "response" will be provided in a prompt and orderly fashion. This mandates that the facility has easy access to major arterial roads or fast routes to the core areas of interest it serves. In some cases, this may mean a facility is not contained within a Central Business District (CBD), but instead is only a short drive from the CBD at peak hours.

Another aspect that affects the selection of the site is the actual site's susceptibility to naturally occurring events that can impact operations, namely fire, flood, storm, and earthquake. It would be unwise, if there were any options, to acquire a building that was known to be:

■   In a flood zone where it might wash away or be unusable due to water damage

■   Close to a fire hazard—for example, a forest or natural grassland, or a facility storing flammable materials such as fuels or solvents

■   Located in a high-wind area

■   Sitting on top of a fault line or an area of volcanic activity

The site should also be located with ready access to services that may be required. In a digital forensics laboratory, this will be access to sufficient power and telecommunications capability. Power availability is a major issue for the establishment of any computer laboratory and many buildings will not have sufficient spare capacity to cater to large computer installations. With computer workstation power demands currently averaging between 700 to 1000 watts for each workstation, it does not take long for this to add up to a significant power requirement. On top of this, a significant load for air conditioning must be factored into the design.

Access to services should also be set up in as physically secure a manner as possible. Security of communications and power is an essential requirement for any well-secured facility. To achieve the required levels of security may involve the installation of specialist cabinets/lockers and doors into the access points used by the building for utilities. The cost of these expenses will need to be factored into the budget for the laboratory. The installation of appropriate alarm controls on these cabinets/doors is also advised in order to trap intentional or accidental incursion into these areas. In determining the requirement of the laboratory and the suitability of the location, where possible, the minimum service/fault guarantees provided by the suppliers should be investigated, as this will enable you to decide whether there is a requirement to seek alternative supplies or install standby facilities on site.

A truly redundant approach to critical service supplies can significantly mitigate operational risks resulting from failures by a third party. The use of two ISPs for the provision of Internet services is one such example. Should the primary ISP fail, the other ISP should be able to cover the base operational load. It should be noted, however, that they must be two physically separate ISPs, both in terms of termination at the building and routing to the Internet, for this to have any value.

In the case of power, the provision of backup onsite power generation may be required, particularly if the digital forensics laboratory is used to analyze devices involved in significant and high-priority incidents such as terrorism or drug smuggling.

The site itself should utilize defense-in-depth principles in its construction of countermeasures, both physical (structures, access ways) and logical (access control, network defenses). The defense-in-depth principle is use of what can be considered concentric circles or layers of appropriate defenses, or barriers to protect valuable assets. This is sometimes referred to as the onion defense. Each layer should be a barrier that must be penetrated before the next can be accessed. (See Figure 6.1.)

Figure 6.1 The Layered-Defense Concept

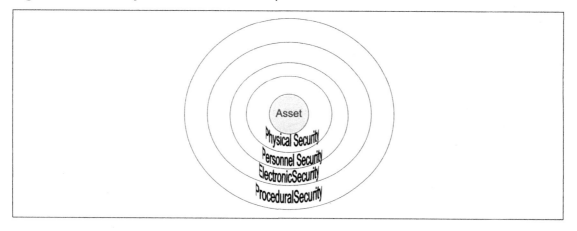

The outer perimeter of the site should be a combination of manmade and natural barriers that controls the flow of material, information, and people into the site. It should have a minimum of egress and ingress points, preferably separated, with suitable access controls installed at each. This could be accomplished through the installation of fences, the effective use of perimeter lighting and cameras, and/or restriction of vehicular access through the use of gates or bollards to control traffic flows. The use of natural barriers such as embankments, tree lines, or large rocks can also be used to create zones of control.

Another measure that can be implemented is the separation of car parking for staff and visitors. Staff areas should, ideally, be controlled via a swipe card entry system and have physical barriers and appropriate controls to prevent tampering, or have covert tracking devices installed. Parking facilities for visitors should have a "standoff," whereby visitors cannot bring their vehicles within close proximity of a building exit. All visitors should have to report directly to an inbound handling area/office area for screening and processing.

The building itself should have a low fire rating. This is normally accomplished through the use of fire-resistant materials. Ideally, the building should be constructed of materials that do not allow it to contribute to the fuel load in the event of a fire and that also enable it to maintain its structural integrity. Low internal loading materials (that is, materials contained within the building) should not be flammable. In areas where regular seismic activity exists, the building should be constructed in such a way (or have a construction rating) that mitigates these effects.

The building perimeter should use appropriate locks on doors and windows, and these should be used in conjunction with appropriate lighting, surveillance systems, and alarms. Window foil should be applied to all windows. This is a metallic tape or skin that is applied to windows so that in the event of an explosion or when someone attempts to break the glass, the skin prevents the glass from shattering. In some security systems, a small electrical current is applied to the foil so any crack or scratch of the window will activate an alarm. Similarly, if the material to be processed in the laboratory is of a high-enough sensitivity, the walls or cavities may use fine wires to detect incursion.

The use of physical locks and keys are normally an essential element in any secured facility. Doors, however, are an often overlooked physical access control measure and too often we see doors employed with expensive locks and swipe cards that utilize half-height glass panels, and as a result, potentially allow for a would-be malfeasant to simply break the glass and circumvent the lock to gain access to the room. All doors (and the frames that they stand in) at any control point should be of a suitably solid and heavy construction, be metal preferably, whose glass panels should be limited to the minimum size allowed to meet any health and safety requirements. All doors should also be self-closing and locking. Any doors to sensitive areas of a facility should be fitted with an audible alarm that sounds if it is left open or ajar for an extended period of time, and procedures should be put in place to ensure such alarms are responded to. This can be accomplished by using magnetic or electrical switches contained within the door frame. Any movement through a key control door or entrance should be designed to eliminate the possibility of "tail-gating," where an unauthorized person follows immediately behind an authorized one.

Doors with locks and keys, however, normally only allow the person that holds them access to the resources and do not normally allow for logging of that access or movements within the facility. Also keys in this instance are hard to revoke—that is, possession is ten/tenths and most hard keys are easy to replicate. For these reasons, swipe technology (access cards) that enable physical access are becoming more widespread in usage. These systems typically use contactless RFID chips in their construction and these allow for the logging of activity that not only includes details of entry and exit from the facility, but can also record movement past other sensors within the facility. In addition, they can revoke access instantly by disabling the access rights of the individual card/token.

A common problem is that, often, the swipe card logging systems are not synchronized or integrated with other security monitoring and management sources within the organization, and the clocks of these systems are also not synchronized—for instance, with the local area network or the security cameras. Lack of time synchronization significantly lowers the value of such security measures. A synchronized clock establishes reliable datum for incident management or investigation and the reliable correlation of events for intrusion detection purposes.

Using Internal Zoning

The internal structure of the building should have control zones implemented, namely general/public access, normal access (escorted external personnel), and restricted access (restricted internal access based on need). The zones should be clearly delimited with appropriate signage, a point that is sometimes overlooked.

All visitors to the facility should present themselves to an inbound office/area located on the boundary of the public and normal access areas. In most laboratories, if they are allowed in at all, visitors who will be moving beyond the public areas, must be escorted at all times. All visitors must sign in and be signed out, and this should occur at a public reception area where the identity of the person is verified, and where the visitor is assigned to a laboratory employee who will be responsible for them as their escort. All staff and visitors should wear an identification badge at all times that indicates both their status and the organization they belong to. The passes for visitors should also show the date of issue and the period of validity. On conclusion of the visit, the visitor should be signed out at the reception area and the identification badge surrendered.

Restricted access areas should not be located near an external exit point and at all times defense-in-depth principles should be used for entry and exit to these areas. The location of critical elements or restricted access areas, such as the laboratory, itself should be behind as many physical barriers as possible. Ideally, they should be located in the center of the building, with each wall and doorway being used as an additional barrier to control the movement of personnel. Any restricted area should be above the ground floor level and preferably not directly below any roof. It also should be away from overhanging balconies or other possible means of physical access.

Power Supply Controls

As mentioned previously, the power source should be secured at the point of connection to supply. All internal power sources should be conditioned—in other words, a power filter should be put in place that prevents spikes (an increase above base power) and brownouts (a decrease in base power). The next step is installing an uninterruptible power supply (UPS) that supplies power in the event of a power failure. The power for the UPS is drawn from standby batteries that are kept at maximum charge by the main power supply when it is available. When developing the laboratory, the minimum requirement for power from the UPS to enable the power down equipment in an orderly and controlled manner should be determined and its cost calculated. This can be readily derived, with any margins of error, and incorporated into the equation.

UPSs are of two main types. For simplicity, these are referred to as active and passive. Active is a type of UPS that is actually a power filter and supplies a constant regulated power supply to the connected devices. These types of UPSs mitigate the damage caused by spikes and brownouts. A passive UPS monitors the line for spikes or brownouts and responds by switching to the battery energy. However, therein lays a potential problem. In a passive UPS, if the switching should fail or only partially respond, you effectively have no real protection against one of the events you were trying to prevent. The net result can be a loss of data, or worse, the complete failure of connected devices, be it the power supply or components such as the mainboard, CPU, or hard disk.

Most UPS systems use a high-capacity battery (normally lead acid– or metal hydride–based) to supply the energy for the standby power. As a result, these technologies, by their very nature, will decay to zero capacity over a given number of charge/discharge cycles or simply because of age. The typical usable life for these batteries is around two to three years, at which point they must be replaced. A regular feature in the IT audit cycle should be routine maintenance and testing of these batteries for both capacity and the ability to respond under a heavy load. Most good enterprise-scale UPSs have management software combined with the physical hardware. This software enables the active monitoring of a battery's condition, and some of the systems have built-in alerting functions based on settable tolerance thresholds. However, the authors cannot stress enough the need to actively audit these devices, since in their experience they have seen the failure of reputable UPSs under loads that were within the functional limits of the software.

As mentioned previously, some operational circumstances will require the provisioning of an alternate reliable power supply via standby generation capacity. This is largely determined by the business need and will be case-based given the laboratory function and purpose. It should be noted that these systems need regular maintenance and testing as well, which should be done by suitably qualified professionals familiar with standby generation requirements.

Cameras

Security cameras throughout a facility allow for oversight of operations, and in the case of a forensic laboratory, you should consider them as almost mandatory. The cameras themselves should have a sufficient capability to allow for the identification of a person within the confines of the area under surveillance. CCTV systems must record and store images of a sufficient resolution to identify persons or actions undertaken over the range of the cameras' area of view. The footage should also be captured at a rate that allows for the accurate detection of behaviors—for instance, only taking a snapshot every five seconds may miss vital evidence.

Any area where CCTV is being used should also have automatic lighting controls installed so a would-be perpetrator cannot simply turn off the lights to avoid detection. The use of motion-sensitive sensors is advised so that any movement within a darkened room will cause the lighting to activate.

Sufficient cameras should be installed to ensure that, without exception, any activity or any person's actions can be recorded and documented fully in restricted access areas. In addition to this, the recorded footage should be archived for a sufficient period should reviewers need to investigate any breaches or incidents. The size and extent of the archive is ultimately a business decision that will be determined as a result of risk assessments and experience. The installed cameras should be a mixture of overt and covert devices in an effort to document all behavior. The camera system should also be factored into loadings for the UPS so camera operation can continue in the event of a main power failure.

Air Conditioning

In the case of computer laboratories, refrigerated dry (zero humidity) air conditioning should be used at all times. Unlike evaporative systems, this type of air conditioning does not put water in the form of vapor into the air. Evaporative systems, while cheaper in per-unit cost, are simply not suitable for installation in an area that uses electrical circuitry or has heat-loaded metallic surfaces. The reason for the exclusion of evaporative systems is that the water vapor used to create the temperature differential condenses back into water droplets, and by the *laws of thermodynamics will condense on a hot element that is cooling.* This state is always present in a computer when it is powered off—for instance, the components, even on a soft reset, will cool for a while, and as a result will build up condensation. Likewise, CPU limiting technologies may cause similar effects on CPU seals and cores.

From a physical security viewpoint, all air-conditioning ducts should be small enough to prevent an intruder from bypassing security by using them as crawlspaces. In the case of established buildings with large ducts, this can be readily accomplished with the installation of grills or suitable restriction barriers. Should this not be feasible for a variety of reasons—for example, heritage covenants placed on a building—then the installation of appropriate motion sensors and alarms should be installed within these ducts and conduits.

The air-conditioning units should be capable of maintaining a constant ambient temperature range. Dependent on your geographical location, this will determine the type of air-conditioner capacity you will need. The heat load for air conditioning also varies because of the different static loads you will create in a particular area or room. Many factors go into the calculation of the heat load—for example, the number of computers and their heat output, as well as the position, location, and size of windows. It is important the job be done professionally and the proper heat load calculations generated by air-conditioning experts.

Emissions Control

Wireless networks (both WiFi and 3G and mobile telephony networks, GSM, and so on) are a modern reality and now saturate most metropolitan expanses. A potential exists for these legitimate signals to interfere with the forensic analysis of suspect devices. This problem is of particular relevance when, for instance, examining mobile phones, PDAs, or wireless-enabled laptops. By simply powering on these devices, they may automatically attempt to connect to a network and begin downloading or synchronizing data in the form of SMS, MMS file updates, calendar entries, task lists, and so on, to the device being examined. This saturation of the airwaves and resultant connections may cause an accidental overwrite of vital evidence stored on the device. Alternatively, at another level, it may allow a savvy offender to remove evidence from the device when it becomes network-aware and connected. The operation of wireless equipment within a building also presents a significant and identifiable problem for the broadcast of transmissions, which may result in the inadvertent leakage of information. The use of a Faraday cage or similar signal-retarding countermeasure is warranted in areas where these devices will be used or examined.

The positioning of computer monitors should be considered when windows and reflective surfaces are present in the laboratory. The incorrect placement of a monitor would potentially allow oversight of the monitor via the naked eye, or even a telephoto lens from some distance away. It should be noted that people pursuing information in sensitive cases are not always the defendants—sometimes the media is.

Laboratories that routinely deal with graphic or obscene material must create a separate work area or cordon off or quarantine the workstation areas involved—for occupational, health, and safety reasons—in order to prevent staff from inadvertently viewing these types of images.

Another emission that should be controlled is the leakage of electromagnetic fields (EMF) from power conduits. EMF can be damaging to anything that uses magnetism for storage. EMF can also affect network transmission, so the separation of power from network cables into separate conduits is mandatory.

Fire Control

Fire control is an example of a service that is sometimes overlooked and can have catastrophic effects for digital equipment. Some of the equipment used in digital forensics is relatively esoteric and may be difficult to replace at short notice.

Most fire control systems in buildings are sprinklers that control a fire by dowsing the general area with large volumes of water. These are effective but are not the best solution for computers and digital equipment. In some cases, insurance companies will not provide cover for water damage caused by fire systems when the risk is a foreseeable one.

A purpose-modified container or room for servers and any evidence storage will need to be built, or an existing room will need to be converted—wherein carbon dioxide or gas can be used to extinguish fires rather than water. These fire-control refits can be nontrivial, expensive, and time-consuming to undertake. So care should be taken to select a system that is not itself damaging to computers or storage media.

Insurance

A well-secured site should also affect the premium rate for insurance applied. The use of some effective and recognized countermeasures can have a significant impact on insurance premiums for a facility. It is worth contacting prospective insurers and asking for a list of preferred locks and other treatments.

Summary

This chapter has discussed a range of the issues that must be considered when deciding on the location of the laboratory. Factors that might affect decisions about the geographical location of the laboratory and its positioning within a building have been examined and various issues addressed. Finally, the services required to enable the laboratory to function effectively have been examined and recommendations made.

Chapter 7

Selecting the Staff

Introduction

This chapter will discuss a range of issues related to the selection of the right staff for the laboratory. This will include assessments of the suitability of staff, their qualifications and experience, their references and, if required, their background checks and security vetting. The chapter will also deal with the requirement for the provision of support for staff that should include access to counseling and psychiatric assessments.

It is assumed at this point that the need for, and purpose of, the laboratory is initially well defined. Why do we say only initially well defined? Well, quite simply the environment in which this operates is one that changes rapidly, and the requirement and purpose will change over time.

There is little argument that the personnel required for a digital forensics laboratory will require a variety of skills and experience. Several key operational roles are, however, required in any laboratory setup regardless of the type of digital forensic tasks undertaken. These roles may be substantive full-time roles in a large laboratory or in a small laboratory, one member of the staff may perform a number of different roles within their job.

Roles within the Laboratory

Detailed below are the main roles that will need to be undertaken within the laboratory. The size of the laboratory, the type of organization that it belongs to and the type of work that it will undertake will affect the decision by the management as to whether one of more of these roles are combined or whether there are multiple members of staff appointed to carry out one role. If the laboratory is large, then other roles may need to be created.

The Laboratory Manager

The laboratory manager will be responsible for the day-to-day running of the laboratory. This would include such duties as job scheduling, continuity management, document management, the quality management and review processes, human resource management and safety management. In addition, the laboratory manager is typically charged with responsibility for financial management for the operation.

Digital Forensics Examiners/Analysts

Digital forensics examiners and analysts are competent in the use of one or more digital forensic tools and processes at an expert level. This role will typically have, at minimum, a forensic tool vendor certification for the particular product they are using, or significant and documented training and experience on the job. Preferably, these individuals will also have some tertiary qualification in a suitable discipline—for example, computer science or digital forensics.

Case Investigator/Managers

The case investigator/manager may not be a digital forensic expert, but will be a trained investigator in cybercrime and digital forensics issues. They will be the person who acts as the liaison or interface to the outside world and to other agencies. The person will be responsible for the day-to-day running of the case, which would include interaction both within and outside the laboratory.

Laboratory Technicians

A laboratory technician has a skill level that allows them to confidently and effectively perform a set of basic laboratory tasks well with regard to defined standards, procedures, and metrics. The type of task typically carried out by a laboratory technician will involve underlying knowledge that is tacitly embedded in the logic of the device or process being used. A good example of this is the operation of an imaging tool such as Rimage or Silo 3, where much of the interaction is simply verifying menu selections and attachment of hardware.

These technician roles are performed in support of tasks that require higher levels of expertise or cognitive understanding—for example, the examination and analysis of data contained on a Windows NTFS formatted hard disk. While an experienced examiner would be capable of generating or replicating images of the media, it is not the best and most productive use of their time.

Overall, the number and specification of these technician roles are typically dependent on the focus and workload of the laboratory. The one exception is that all laboratories will have a need for an imaging technician. An imaging technician is responsible for the acquisition of data from devices into validated forensic images for which the continuity of evidence has been maintained and documented. This can only be achieved using validated methods and tools that could subsequently be analyzed by any digital forensics examiner for correctness of operation of the tools and the process.

Staff Selection

The effective selection of staff is critical in any work domain; however, within the area of digital forensics, poor selection as the result of poor processes can have catastrophic results. Staff who are found to have used poor processes, or been deliberately malfeasant or lax in their application of prescribed minimum standards could render all evidence they have been involved with inadmissible. Even if the evidence is not declared inadmissible, it will bring into question the credibility of the laboratory and lead to the questioning of all results produced by it, or cause of loss of work coming into the laboratory. The possible negative outcomes for dilettante behavior are potentially catastrophic when compared to mainstream IT—excepting, of course, those staff involved with the critical national infrastructure. It is therefore imperative that the selection of staff be a well-considered process that offers up the best available candidates.

Qualifications vs. Experience

In a forensics laboratory that is employing sound scientific processes to capture, identify, and extract data for subsequent presentation in a court of law or tribunal as evidence, the use of suitably qualified staff is essential. Staff who supervise or perform an analysis on the processing of evidence should be able to present their findings in court. With sufficient experience, they should also be able to act as an expert witness (this will vary depending on the jurisdiction). The staff member should be able to talk and present cogent arguments, both at a high technical level and also to explain complex issues in layman's terms, in their recognized area of expertise. The processing of evidence that any digital forensics specialist has followed should use sound scientific principles, again with the staff member being capable of describing coherently and accurately every process undertaken. Conversely, a staff member should also be able to expertly critique or defend claims made by opposing experts.

For staff to be recognized as being able to give evidence in a court of law as an expert, there normally must be a significant external validation of that person's skill base. Traditionally, this has been accomplished through well-established recognition of formal education and scientific scholarly processes, normally requiring, at minimum, the completion of a university degree within a relevant discipline. This degree is then normally coupled with subsequent further study and validated research within the area of chosen specialization before recognition as an expert witness occurs. This is an appropriate and recognized pathway within the area of traditional forensic science; however, due to its very short history and the rapid developments in the area, digital forensics has some current issues.

One of the key problems with selecting staff is the evaluation of their competence or expertise in digital forensics. Currently, no mandated competency standards are in place for digital forensics examiners, whether by a government organization or a recognized professional association. The emergence of specific digital forensics degrees and courses of study in universities are recent. Most of the vendor training available has typically not been around for longer than five years.

Current university degrees in IT and computer science provide a solid grounding for digital forensics examiners at a technical level. However, significant on-the-job training will need to be undertaken in the specific forensic tools and processes, in addition to a degree or significant certification. Furthermore, a computer science degree rarely deals with legal and evidentiary issues—for example, the continuity of evidence. The legal concepts and issues encountered in this area will either be learned on the job or require further external training and validation.

Vendor training is one aspect of the skill set that is a potential filter for a digital forensics examiner competency and level of expertise. It should be noted that vendor training typically only provides certification of proficiency in the use of that vendor's specific packages. Having undertaken vendor training is not, of itself, normally strong enough evidence that a person is a qualified digital forensics examiner. It is eminently plausible that a person who has no in-depth knowledge of computer science or forensic science could complete the vendor training successfully and achieve certification in the use of a particular package or software suite. However, in the current absence of established standards for presentation of evidence by an expert that exists within other science fields, they can add weight to the determination of technical expertise or proficiency for the area.

Some work has recently been undertaken by a group in Australia that was drawn from national and state law enforcement, academia, and the commercial sector to develop a framework for assessing the competency of digital forensic practitioners. The framework that has been developed breaks competency down into three main areas of skill. The first of these is evidence acquisition, which is concerned with the acquisition and preservation of the original evidence, either in-situ or in-stream in a sound forensic manner using appropriate tools and techniques. The second area deals with evidence analysis, which is the production of a scientifically replicable analysis of evidence using sound forensic processes and validated technology and techniques. The third is evidence report and presentation, which is the presentation of evidence to external third parties and courts of law through cogent presentation of the facts that have been revealed by an investigation. Within each of these areas of assessment there is a further refinement of the areas, and then a layered assessment regime based on Bloom's Taxonomy (of learning behaviors) to assess competencies. Frameworks such as these that are being developed are comprehensive, and while good for assessing competence internally, they may not be suited for a pre-employment screening process.

Pre-Employment Screening

There is no doubt that psychological and organizational testing are imperfect sciences; however, they are still good for detecting potential employees who may prove difficult to manage or who are not suitable for appointment. Psychological tests can detect staff that have potential issues with integrity and honesty and subsequently may be open to bribery, corruption, or other unsavory practices. Digital forensics deals with issues that can be distressing and disturbing on a range of levels. Psychological testing can be used to filter candidates who are more likely to be prone to, or susceptible to, the effects of such stresses. The use of this type of testing allows an employer to make an informed decision about job placement. It would be foolhardy, for instance, to task a staff member to investigate a case of spider smuggling if they had arachnophobia. Some testing can be used to reliably determine problem-solving abilities, which are a crucial skill for any digital forensics examiner.

Organizational tests such as Myers Briggs and similar personality trait testers may also prove useful in the staff selection process. These types of tests can be used to create a more optimized mix of personality types for your particular organization. This is most appropriate in an investigative laboratory since not all probable solutions are suited to one particular personality type or trait, and too many of the same personality type in the one organization can be counterproductive.

Teamwork is an essential element of working in a digital forensics laboratory, even if the laboratory is a team of two people. Psychological and organization testing systems can readily identify staff that are not suited to group or teamwork. This is one attribute that needs serious consideration—for example, do you employ a team of technically brilliant isolates who have problems interacting and communicating, or a competent team who can communicate and express ideas and problems and work together to solve such problems?

Background Checks

Another important aspect of pre-employment screening is that of performing standard background checks for potential employees. This would include, but not be limited to, financial checks, previous employers' references, police or agency clearances and the substantiation of claimed qualification or certification.

Financial checks are important to verify the soundness or highlight potential problem behaviors in staff. An example of an issue that may be a cause for concern would include the discovery of multiple short-term loans or large credit card debt, possibly indicating a gambling problem or other personal issues other than poor fiduciary management that may have an impact on work. Recurrent debts of this kind are excellent vectors for persons seeking targets for bribery or corruption either by enabling further compromise or extending bad behaviors.

Previous employer references are the most obvious form of screening available to employers, but many employers fail to verify the veracity of those references presented by prospective employees. The verification of a reference can be readily achieved by communicating with the party that provided the reference and asking questions relevant to the information presented in the reference. This can often reveal the "golden handshake" or "thank God we can get rid of them" style of references that can hide or obscure the reality of the employment situation or circumstance.

Police or agency clearances are one way of making sure the prospective employee has current and satisfactory police clearance and no known criminal record. While these clearances are not perfect, they at least provide an indication of any serious criminality that may have occurred in the past. Some jurisdictions, however, have significant limits on the amount of information they can provide in this style of clearance. For instance, in some jurisdictions there is a limit imposed on the type of conviction that can be listed. There are often limits on the number of years one can go back on matters that may be recorded and reported. Furthermore, if at any stage a prospective employee has held external agency clearances and these clearances are now rescinded within normal expiration limits, then the reasons for this should be ascertained.

Substantiation of claimed qualifications is another important process in the initial pre-employment screening of prospective employees. This is particularly important in the current digital forensics arena due to the lack of established and readily identifiable certifications and qualifications within the discipline area.

For industry certifications claimed by a person, most vendors have services that can be used to verify an individual's certification status. This verification process sometimes requires that the candidates provide their testing IDs. It should be noted that many industry certifications expire after relatively short periods and verification of currency is an important aspect of validating industry-based certifications.

For qualifications such as degrees or diplomas issued by statutory or accredited authorities like polytechnics, technical colleges, or universities, these likewise need verification. There have been numerous cases worldwide where individuals have claimed to hold degrees they do not actually possess. Incidents such as these make it essential to verify with the certifying institution that the person has in fact completed the degree or diploma in question. It is a requirement for most organizations of this type to use a person's full legal name on the testament, and to have a date of graduation and normally a graduation number. It should be noted that the quality and type of university degree also varies greatly, and if the university is unknown or unfamiliar, it would be worth verifying its degree's standing.

While the execution of the basic human resource policy is not a complete mitigation of this type of risk, it should be used as a minimum to weed out the inveterate liars.

Security Clearances

Security clearances are important and mainly have an impact on the private sector. The normal digital forensic investigation sectors (for example, law enforcement, military, or secret government organizations that deal with classified or restricted material) will normally already have well-established procedures and systems in place for the completion of security checks. Typically, if private enterprise or private individuals are being contracted to work by an agency that requires security clearance, this is typically provided or sponsored by the requesting agency. The clearances are normally completed as part of the recruitment and approval process. Often, many tenders for work will specify the level of security that must be observed.

Support for Staff

Unfortunately, there is still a high proportion of case loads in digital forensics investigations that deal directly with the possession and distribution of illegal images. These images and movies are typically sexual in nature, and involve children, minors, bestiality, or murder (snuff films). These images and movies are graphic, often violent, and ultimately disturbing in nature.

Long-term exposure to material such as this could cause desensitization at best. It is more likely that staff could develop psychological damage as a result of long-term exposure to this type of material. Even staff that may seem unaffected for a considerable amount of time may possibly develop post-traumatic stress disorders well after the incident or the material being viewed. Anecdotally, the possibility of this is formally recognized in most systems in the world, and so staff members, whenever possible, are rotated through jobs to minimize the level of exposure. There has been very little in the way of research into the impacts of prolonged exposure to these types of images and movies, mainly due to the recent nature of this type of material on the Internet. Reasonable parallels can be drawn from other areas where long-term exposure to traumatic events has resulted in the need to monitor such stress on a firm's human resources.

Most established management systems for computer crime or digital forensics teams require the regular psychological testing of staff. However, the period of review varies greatly, with some organizations requiring monthly checks, while other systems can be as long as 12 to 18 months before retesting. This interval will be largely dependent on the type and level of cases undertaken during the period for the particular staff member. It is also important that staff time with respect to the amount of time spent on these cases, or within these areas, be recorded accurately.

The provision of counseling services to staff can readily mitigate some of the risks involved with long-term exposure to this type of graphic material. The provision of counseling services can prevent or mitigate a relatively minor issue from turning into a major problem with respect to the ongoing mental health of an individual involved in this type of work. Alternatively, counseling can assist in the ongoing evaluation of issues and problems encountered within the workplace. These ongoing evaluations provide an insight not normally obtained by standard management practices and structures into the health of the team.

The establishment and use of a mentoring program where the more senior staff provide support to the more junior employees can also provide an additional support mechanism for coping with issues that may arise. Most senior staff will have experienced many of the issues junior workers may be encountering and some of the latter may feel more at ease expressing themselves to senior staff members rather than an external party.

Ancillary and Contract Staff

Ancillary and contract staff are not the people that actually perform the processing or analysis of material within the digital forensics laboratory. These types of staff are the ones who perform ancillary tasks, such as cleaning or plant or site maintenance, within the laboratory facility. The staff may not actually be directly employed by the laboratory itself but may be part of third-party arrangements for resources that may come with the building occupancy or contract. This may present further problems for having a secure facility and is one of the aspects sometimes overlooked because such staff are seen as "someone else's problem."

Others that should be included in this grouping are external contract IT staff that may be brought in for site business or brought in for working on a contract basis. In the case of contract IT staff, there is often little need to let them enter a restricted area with the use of appropriate VLAN (virtual local area network) and VPN (virtual private network) infrastructure. These categories of people can be contained in a physical DMZ, as it were, within the building, restricting their access to some areas. This may have cause significant impacts on network design and space requirements; however, this can be readily counterbalanced by the increased physical security alone. Some financial managers may see the "extra" space for this sort of containment as an expense. This cost, once compared to the provision of an escorting staff member for each external person working onsite, will rapidly become agreeable.

Such ancillary and contract staff are often given higher levels of access to a facility than a full-time laboratory staff member. This typically occurs as a result of flawed security evaluations and subsequent rights allocations. These staff, at minimum, should undergo the same security screening and vetting procedures that the internal laboratory staff goes through. Staff who need access to restricted areas or areas that require external security clearance should have their vetting at the same level as regular vetted users of this space.

Summary

This chapter has looked at a range of issues that relate to the selection of the right staff for the laboratory. It has looked at the selection of the right mix of staff and the measures that can be implemented to ensure they have the skills, qualifications, and experience that they claim, and that they are suitable for the post. It has addressed some of the issues related to the employment of ancillary and contract staff and their access to the laboratory, and the control of their movements when they are in the laboratory. The chapter also looked at issues relating to the provision of support for staff, including access to counseling and psychiatric assessments.

Chapter 8

Education and Training

Introduction

This chapter will address the requirement for staff training and achieving the balance between enough training to create and maintain an effective unit and excessive training, which is likely to cause unnecessary costs and leave the organization vulnerable to the poaching of staff by rival companies or organizations. It will also address a strategy for the development of specialist areas within the teams.

Most professional bodies have a minimum education standard, and many now have ongoing training and education requirements so members can stay current. Well-established professions have ongoing peer training and professional development that is seen as part of their vocation. The digital forensics area currently does not have any overarching body for professional representation that requires minimal professional educational standards in order to become a member.

External Factors

The IT and communications industries continue to grow at near exponential rates and are producing new technologies, devices, and systems at a similar pace. This rapid growth impacts significantly on the need for ongoing training of digital forensics practitioners. The following is a timeline of 32-bit Windows operating systems that a current digital forensics examiner should examine.[1]

Table 8.1 Windows 32-Bit Operating System Timeline

Windows 98	Windows 98 Second Edition	Windows 2000 Professional	Windows Millennium Edition	Windows XP Home and Professional	Windows XP SP1	Windows XP Media Center 2002	Windows XP Tablet PC Edition
June 30, 1998	June 30, 1999	March 31, 2000	December 31, 2000	December 31, 2001	September 8, 2002	October 27, 2002	February 11, 2003

Windows 2000 SP4	Windows XP Media Center 2004	Windows XP SP2	Windows XP Media Center 2005	Windows Vista Beta 1	Windows Vista	Windows Vista SP1	Windows XP SP3
June 23, 2003	October 27, 2003	August 6, 2004	December 30, 2004	July 25, 2005	January 30, 2007	February 4, 2008	April 29, 2008

While there are only possible file systems for these variants (FAT16, FAT32, and NTFS), the structure of the Registry may vary considerably. However, the Registry has similar principles of operation across the different versions of Windows.

Similar types of timelines are available for other common operating systems, which include, but are not limited to, the Macintosh OS, Unix, SCO Unix, Linux, IBM AIX, HP/UX, SunOS, and Sun Solaris. However, due to Microsoft's dominance in the operating systems market, a digital forensics practitioner who is trained and competent in these operating systems will be able to address more than 90 percent of the installed computers they will likely encounter.

Similar patterns emerge in the mobile device area. As an example, the timeline for the ubiquitous Apple iPod is shown in Figure 8.1.[2]

Figure 8.1 The Apple iPod Timeline

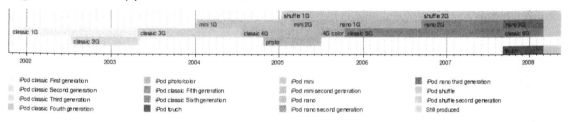

Each of these iPods, while similar, contains a number of differences. They utilize a system on a chip designed by Apple. The iPod devices are commonly partitioned either as a Windows-based iPod using a FAT32 partition or as a Macintosh-based iPod using an HFS+ file system. Each of these file systems requires different toolsets and knowledge bases for the forensic examination of what externally appears to be the same device.

Other mobile devices such as cell phones and PDAs have as many potential complexities in the selection and use of memory, file systems, tools, and techniques.

Forensic Software

The forensic software tools (and suites of tools) released by vendors have similar discrepancies and differences in the way they operate. While a forensic specialist may understand the processes and procedures to be undertaken during the forensic process, operating the software required to achieve this is sometimes an entirely different issue.

Software vendors often derive much of their revenue from the training and certification of individuals. Said vendors generate revenue by releasing new and improved versions of their software to address new technologies or new issues that have been discovered with existing technologies. One has to question spending in excess of $2,000 for a license and then spending from between two and five times that to undertake training to a certified level on each release of the vendor's software tool.

Training: The Good, the Bad, and the Ugly

There is little question that digital forensics is a fast-moving area when compared to what are considered more mature traditional forensic areas, where changes occur at a much slower pace. Traditional forensic areas also require that any staff member remain competent in their area of expertise and that they receive training in the tools and techniques needed for their daily work. However, because the pace of change and development of tools and techniques takes place over a longer period, the overhead cost of the training and skill maintenance is significantly lower.

The approach that is currently adopted in digital forensics revolves around the provision of vendor-based training—regarding any new versions of software that may be released—for a least one staff member, preferably the training officer, or if possible the entire team. Either method has a large cost associated with it.

The training officer model would then allow the training officer to construct and document a process to upgrade the software and training and assess the skill sets of existing staff in the new system or technique. Some vendors also have schemes such as certified instructors or train-the-trainer programs where suitable staff can become qualified in delivering training.

This training officer/certified trainer system requires considerable effort on the part of the training officer in learning the content and developing a suitable curriculum. This often incurs significant cost and would need to be factored into any decision to deviate from vendor-based training. Delays in the provision of training may occur as a result of the learning cycle required for the training officer to acquire the necessary skills.

Although the course that is developed may be tailored to meet the requirements of the organization, it may in fact introduce issues with regard to the competency argument because of the in-house nature of the training. Consider the position that a member of staff would face if the opposing counsel in a case came out with the phrase, "I put it to you that both your expertise and the evidence are in question since you did not receive training in EnCombobulator 2008, Menu Option 12. Can you enlighten us as to what is in Menu Option 12?" Even though it may only be the Help menu, if the staff member is unable to answer this, it could be detrimental to their credibility. Thus, it is important that whenever possible any in-house training be subjected to peer review or some external process of validation to ensure the completeness of the course content.

The vendor-based model has a number of benefits for the organization. The first benefit is that it is an external validation of a practitioner's skill level by a third party. Another is that they are normally well documented and may be supported by textbooks. While this is itself not without problems—for instance, some courses are viewed as "textbook certification," it is at least perceived to be independent to your organization.

Secondly, the vendor training is based around a developed curriculum that would be delivered to all parties wishing to be certified in the same manner. This potentially reduces the likelihood of any dispute about the competency of a particular individual who has undertaken the training and achieved certification. It also provides a baseline measurement of competency for the expert.

Finally, the examinations that many of these certification systems utilize are run by independent testing organizations that are separate from the vendor of the software or hardware. This again confirms and validates the independence of the process. However, this external certification of skills may give an internal staff member an opportunity to exploit that externally recognized certification in their curriculum vitae and use it when looking for employment with another organization.

Higher Education

Digital forensics is an emergent discipline that has its basis in both forensics and computer science. Many of today's most competent and experienced digital forensics practitioners come from a law enforcement or military background, and have not until recently developed careers in academia. Most of their expertise has been learned on the job, often with very little traditional educational qualifications to back up their claimed level of expertise. However, many of these experts are presently undertaking courses in higher education as a result of suitable courses now being offered and available.

The higher-education sector now has a significant set of course offerings in digital forensics at the undergraduate and postgraduate levels; however, only a few institutions actually offer a complete degree in either computer security or digital forensics. An undergraduate degree typically takes three to four years of full-time study to complete. These courses typically consist of a common first-year in which students learn the theoretical underpinnings and rudimentary concepts for use in second- and third-year specializations, or "majors" as they are often referred to. Majors typically constitute a year's worth of study in a particular specialization, such as computer security, digital forensics, information security, or computer science.

A postgraduate qualification is normally completed after an undergraduate degree or equivalent full-time work experience (typically, five to ten years) for a coursework-based Master's qualification within the given area. Postgraduate degrees also have a further distinction between the research-based degrees, which has a substantive thesis of typically 50,000 to 70,000 words and a coursework-only course where the degree is obtained by the completion of coursework units/content only. The research Master's degrees are normally completed after a full undergraduate program within a given discipline. For instance, a person completing a Bachelor degree of Computer Science would then typically go on to complete a Master's of Computer Science by research. The postgraduate coursework degrees are essentially the minimum units needed to achieve understanding in the core concepts in the degree from the undergraduate degree, and then the major or core units that relate to a specific discipline within the title of the degree at a Master's level. Within a coursework Master's degree, there sometimes exists levels or stages—these are normally Graduate Certificate, Graduate Diploma, and the Master's. The distinction is that the Graduate Certificate represents the study of the core concepts from an undergraduate degree and is typically six to twelve months in duration if undertaken as a full-time student. A Graduate Diploma incorporates all the content of the Graduate Certificate and typically a further six months of study in the specialization. The Master's degree includes all of the previously mentioned parts, along with an additional 6 or 12 months of further specialization.

The completion of higher-education degrees is a significantly slower process for achieving a qualification when compared to vendor-based training. It should be noted, however, that the benefit from this form of training can be realized as the completion of a subject of study within a degree. For example, a unit in the degree may be called Mobile Forensics and be used to educate students in the examination of mobile devices, such as cell phones. The skills and knowledge attained in this unit can be used almost immediately and are not constrained to the operation of a specific vendor's tool, but will include a wider understanding of the underlying issues.

Depending on the country in which you undertake your studies, they may be no-cost, low-cost, or full fee–based; however, the money paid is not a determinant of quality. Other more significant factors must be taken into account when selecting higher-education options. Firstly, is the actual provider accredited by the government, a professional body, or some other recognized independent arbiter? Secondly, what is the level of qualification and experience of those running the program? In a university environment, this would typically mean the staff should have a degree of equal standing, and preferably a doctoral-level qualification. Thirdly, the relevant university staff should be active in research in the appropriate subject. They should be publishing articles in scholarly journals and presenting at conferences relevant to the subject area. Finally, they should have an understanding of the requirements and constraints of part-time mature students, and the appropriate supporting systems, to enable and support success at this level.

In addition to educating you within a specific discipline and enabling you to become a lifelong learner, higher education is typically more demanding than training. In particular, it is demanding in terms of the time required to achieve qualification milestones. This must be factored in when deciding which staff members are appropriate for this type of development. To highlight the level of commitment, a three-hour attendance at the university for a lecture and tutorial on a particular topic should typically result in the attendee having to do two to four times this amount (six to twelve hours) in out-of-class activity in the form of skills practice, reading, and self-directed learning activities to achieve successful completion of the topic.

One of the other key differentiators with higher education is that there is a higher level of intellectual engagement and subsequent understanding of the subject matter when compared to training. A somewhat simple differentiation between an educated person and a trained person is that while a trained person knows which buttons to push (apply a principle), an educated person knows why, can *explain* why, and most probably can build you a better button (apply, describe, and critique).

Many experienced practitioners unnecessarily discount themselves from taking higher education as a valid path of training because they believe they will not satisfy the entry requirements. Currently, most academic institutions offering university-level qualifications have programs that recognize prior learning as an entry pathway into these programs. This prior learning can include:

- Attainment of industry-based certifications, such as EnCase EnCE, Microsoft MCSE, and Cisco CCNA

- Actual relevant work experience—for example, presentation in courts—acting as a considered expert, that is normally completed over a substantive period of time

- Attainment of promotion within a documented structure that has competency as its basis for promotion

- Recognition of professional standing—membership in professional associations that have professional competency requirements, the presentation of papers or keynote speeches at significant events such as industry-based, national, and international conferences.

- A portfolio of work that demonstrates significant competency or achievement in the discipline, normally demonstrated over a number of years of achievement

Some higher-education programs will also provide subject exemptions or credits on the basis of prior training and experience, thus shortening the length of the degree program. These exemptions are sometimes subject to the candidate completing a challenge assessment that is typically in the form of an examination the candidates would normally have taken at the end of a course. This is done to certify the person gaining the exemption has a sufficient grasp of the concepts and content.

Balance

There is little argument that digital forensics practitioners should receive training to retain competency. There are, however, substantive problems in trying to determine the appropriate level of training to give to a staff member. The digital forensics arena currently has a lack of suitably qualified people, and a competitive edge may be gained through training in a particular tool or technique.

Developing Specializations

In the opinion of the authors, the most effective way to obtain training, if it is for more than one person, is normally the team-based approach, and because most teams do not run by consensus, it is important to have team leaders. These leaders should be the person(s) recognized for their expertise or specialization in a given area of the discipline. It is not expected that staff will be experts in all aspects of digital forensics, and with the growing diversity of electronic devices, this is simply not possible anyway. By training together as part of a team, it is possible to give staff a sense of worth to the team, a place in the organization, and a feeling of belonging. Studies such as The Hawthorne Plant study where workers were subjected to a series of experiments demonstrated that regardless of the conditions applied—whether negative or positive—a positive increase in behavior resulted. This has become known as the Hawthorne Effect (Mayo, 1932). What the study proved was that there is an increase in worker productivity and well-being when staff are made to feel important and part of a team.

Development of specializations can be a double-edged sword. Digital forensics by its nature almost demands the development of specialists; however, this very act of specialization develops differences, and these can be used as a leverage point for more reward, or as a pathway to exit from an organization. Specialization done well, however, can give a well-balanced team a significant advantage over competitors.

A learning organization is one that values its staff and the intellectual capital they possess. Companies such as Nokia, Shell, BP, and other notables have used this approach with their executives and teams for years. The basic concept is that to get a promotion or reward, an individual must demonstrably increase the skill level of subordinates or actively pass on knowledge to the team. The same approach should be used with a digital forensics team. This approach not only drives diversification but also spreads specialized skills among your staff and becomes a self-replicating system of expertise spreading and development. This type of stewardship of intellectual capital is vital if your digital forensics team is to be successful in the long term. Such an approach also buffers the organizational turmoil that can happen when one of the "stars" leaves.

Certain basic core specializations are required in a digital forensics team, and these can form the basis for a framework of expertise.

- **Acquisition:** Skills in acquiring evidence from devices is becoming highly specialized in order to meet the demand of an ever-wider range of devices. There is generic training in the tools, methods, and computer file systems that all forensic investigators should undertake. In the mid-1990s, for the most part, this would have been adequate for most sources of data encountered during data acquisition. Now, however, due to the explosion of sources of digital evidence, unique skill sets in this area must be fostered. Some of the emergent devices that may be encountered include 3G cell phones, PDAs, embedded devices (iPods, USBs), firmware, networks, and GPS products to name but a few.

- **Analysis:** Analysis of the data of interest is a core skill. There are, again, a number of generic skills that all examiners must have with respect to keyword searching, indexing, and data extraction. However, there are also specialist skills that can be developed with respect to search, file carving, extraction, and reverse engineering.

- **Presentation:** The presentation of data in the form of report writing and the oral presentation of content is a skill in itself. Just because a person is technically brilliant and, for instance, is an expert in the dissection of malicious code, does not mean they are an expert at presenting it.

Planning and Budgeting

Most releases of vendor-based software are carried out to a schedule that is published well in advance. This forward publishing of expected release dates allows an organization to effectively plan and budget for vendor training requirements. In turn, this allows for proper management of the human resource. Good management occurs by making sure the relevant staff are available to attend training as it becomes available, and that it is tailored to their skill set or needs and the needs of the organization.

In order to estimate the budgeting requirements, you should take into account the current skill levels that exist within the organization. For example, if you have eight staff who are certified version 3 examiners of a vendor's product and the organization trades on this as a key selling point, then it is important that competency in the product is maintained. So when version 4 is released, it would be foolish not to have sufficient resources put aside so these staff can obtain competency in the minimum time possible with the least amount of disruption to the business process. The cost of obtaining the training is not only the raw cost of the training. The full cost of training will also include the cost of replacing the person who is receiving the training, provision for travel, accommodation, meals, and other expenses should they be warranted. In addition, it is unrealistic not to factor in lost business or operational capacity as a result of the person not being able to execute their normal duties while involved in the training. In university-based training, although there may be little or no direct cost burden placed on the organization as a result of the fees for the courses, other matters must be considered when planning and budgeting. This is increasingly true, and there may be no immediate direct impact on the person's work timetable since many of the current courses are offered on a part-time basis, often in after-hours modes or through online provision that allow study at any time. However, in most organizations people undertaking this type of study are given some relief during the workweek, in recognition of their need to attend lectures, tutorials, and other study-related activities. This has impacts on operational capacity that must be factored in.

From the authors' experiences, most organizations that do not provide logistical and organizational support for training and education over time will breed resentment from their employees. On the positive side, organizations that do provide support tend to engender loyalty, and if not loyalty, they present a significant opportunity/cost decision for employees considering switching to an alternative employer.

Assessing Training and Competence

Many institutions send staff to training with good intentions and hopes that the staff will gain the necessary skills. Unfortunately, there is often very little assessment made of skills transferred beyond a simple static test taken within a given time period at the conclusion of the training. This is not the most satisfactory outcome. One of the best ways for the organization to benefit and to demonstrate competence is to ensure that the recipient of the training teaches and transfers that skill to other team members. As mentioned before, an organization that adopts a learning organization approach will engender this.

Currently there exists little in the way of coherent educationally based frameworks or training curricula for digital forensics. Although the discipline is relatively new in the computer science area, many of the principles of operation and theory are the same as existing science disciplines.

One of the other dangers currently with training in the digital forensics domain is that much of the "education" is vendor-driven training. This form of "education" being offered is, in reality, specific training about a vendor's product and the execution of the same to achieve forensics outcomes with that given product. While it is essential for the effective and proper use of the tools, this is not really education. It is training, and as such should be sold as that. Education is about theories and principles of operation to enable lifelong learning, whereas training is given to achieve an end goal with a given tool. Furthermore, by developing skills using a vendor-centric approach, a professional will tend to see solutions to a problem that may not be the most expedient or efficient and will end up being tool-centric rather than problem-centric.

Many attempts in the past at creating frameworks of education and validating skills in a particular area have been technology- and process-centric, which is not ideal for the construction of a framework in an area that is rapidly evolving. One of the major problems is that a professional will become aligned with a particular solution or process, which will inevitably not be the best approach or solution for every case. By being process- or vendor-bound, examiners may also be less inclined to try alternate avenues of investigation for a particular case, with the end result being there could be a loss or failure to discover critical evidence. Furthermore, aligning a framework with a particular process in an area that is changing as rapidly as digital forensics has at best tenuous credibility. As processes evolve in a science, those things that are held to be true must be reexamined and realigned to better fit the changing knowledge landscapes.

Two overarching principles for the framework are 1) that the framework should be vendor-neutral and skills-centric, and 2) that the framework should employ educational theories in the development of the framework. Educational learning theories can aid in the structuring of learning targets and outcomes and are valuable tools in the construction of a skills matrix that addresses competency or learning. Most skills are learned through example, training, or education; very few are innate or intrinsic to a person—the concept of *tabula rasa*. Even the simple ability to dodge a flying object such as a fast moving baseball is too often a painfully learned behavior.

One of the major educational frameworks used is Bloom's Taxonomy. This is a well-established learning taxonomy in learning artifacts and objects. Bloom's Taxonomy consists of six levels of abstraction applying to the categorization of skills and the development of appropriate evaluation mechanisms. These levels are Knowledge, Comprehension, Application, Analysis, Synthesis, and Evaluation. The concept of this taxonomy has been adjusted to match the requirements for digital forensics.

There are six levels of expertise for rating skills (numbered Level 1 through 6). The use of the levels is intended to demonstrate a progressive hierarchy of skill or achievement of process execution ability. These levels are then used to generate activities or performance criteria for attaining certification of a core competency at a particular level. The use of the six levels borrows heavily from Bloom's Taxonomy of Learning that describes a progression of knowledge and skills acquisition. The six levels presented in this framework are constructed so that each level provides the requisite skills for further levels. Progression or certification to a level is only made as a result of achieving mastery of the prior levels of expertise. These levels are intended to be discrete and it is expected that even highly knowledgeable and experienced people may only achieve level 6 competency across some domain areas within the matrix. The competency levels are described as:

- **Level 1 – Define:** This level indicates the lowest level of competency. A person would be able to define what an activity, process, or concept is—for example:

  - Define a forensic image.

  - Define a cryptographic hash.

- **Level 2 – Apply:** This level indicates the ability to apply an activity, process, or concept. For example:

  - Apply a cryptographic hash.

  - Apply a procedure to attain an acquisition of a forensic image.

- **Level 3 – Explain:** This level is indicated by the ability to apply an activity, and explain the process or concepts. For example:

  - Explain how a cryptographic hash is created.

  - Explain how a forensic image is acquired.

- **Level 4 – Evaluate:** This level is indicated by the ability to critically evaluate an activity, process, or concept. For example:

  - Evaluate cryptographic hashes for suitability to a task.

  - Evaluate various methods of forensic image acquisition for a given scenario.

- **Level 5 – Critique:** This level is indicated by the ability to critique an activity, process, or concept using a sound scientific process. For example:

  - Critique the use of cryptographic hashes by another examiner, using a variety of methods to conduct the evaluation.

  - Critique another examiner's acquisition procedure using appropriate methods.

- **Level 6 – Synthesis:** This level is indicated by the ability to synthesize relevant material to produce an expert report or a validated solution for an activity, process, or forensic concept using a sound scientific process. For example:

  - Produce an expert report on another examiner's hard disk acquisition procedure.

  - Produce an expert report for the court on the MD5 hash collision issue.

  - Solve a multi-partite forensic issue, such as the acquisition and verification of a live RAID system.

As an example in this chapter, we will provide a breakdown of one stream of the framework based upon evidence acquisition as the core competence. The outcomes are the end goal or skill base that a digital forensics examiner should aspire to attain to demonstrate competence. It is expected that a competent digital forensic examiner should be able to:

- Acquire an exact or best possible copy of digital evidence from a digital device or appliance with minimal disturbance of the original evidence.

- Explain the fundamental principles of computer and forensic science as they apply to the acquisition of digital evidence.

- Apply valid forensic processes and principles to acquire digital evidence.

- Apply appropriate technology to acquire digital evidence in a forensically sound manner.

- Validate the forensic acquisition processes and outcomes using sound scientific methods.

- Validate forensic acquisition technology using sound scientific methods and principles.

- Cogently communicate either verbally or in a written report a process or technique related to the acquisition of digital evidence.

From these outcomes, the generation of skill levels or target behaviors can be generated. As an example, detailed in the following are the outcomes for Evidence Acquisition at Outcome 1 at Skill Level 1, 2, and 3. Again, the lists of competencies are not complete and are meant only as an example.

Outcome A-1

Acquire an exact or best possible forensic image of a digital device or appliance with minimal or no disturbance of the original evidence.

- **Level 1:** This level is demonstrated when a candidate can:

  1. Define a forensic image or bit level copy.

  2. Define a simple procedure to acquire a forensic image of a computer hard disk or USB memory stick using suitable forensic imaging software.

  3. Define a cryptographic hash.

- **Level 2:** This level is demonstrated when a candidate can:

  1. Apply a simple procedure to acquire a forensic image.

  2. Apply a cryptographic hash to verify a file, directory, or image.

- **Level 3:** This level is demonstrated when a candidate can:

  1. Explain how a cryptographic hash is used to verify a forensic copy.

  2. Explain a procedure to acquire a forensic image from a digital device.

  3. Explain the concept of a partition and how it relates to an image of a disk.

Assessing Competence

One of the key elements of the framework is structuring the assessment of the skills in the framework. Table 8.2 gives indicative methods of assessment.

Table 8.2 Suitable Assessment Types

Level		Suitable Assessment Type
1	Define	Multiple Choice Test Written Test – Short Answer
2	Apply	Practical Test
3	Explain	Practical Test Written Test – Essay, Short Answer
4	Evaluate	Written Test – Essay, Short Answer Case Analysis
5	Critique	Written Test – Essay Case Analysis/Defense
6	Synthesis	Written Test – Essay Practical Test Case Analysis/Defense

To demonstrate competence at Level 1 typically requires the rote learning of basic facts relating to the relevant outcome. Mastery of this level can be adequately demonstrated by using multiple-choice or short answers, as outlined in Table 8.2 as the primary assessment mechanism.

Level 2 is the application of rudimentary concepts and processes learned from the attainment of Level 1. Demonstration of the mastery of this level is best assessed by the practical application of the concept/process under test conditions. In the example Table 8.2, one of the Level 2 outcome indicators was "*Apply a simple procedure to acquire a verified forensic image.*"

To test this skill, a person could be tested in a practical manner in their ability to apply a given procedure to the acquisition and verification of a forensic image. The actual procedure could be of the candidate's choice, or be based on a departmental or standard process used by the validating organization. It is critical that the acquisition and verification of the forensic image be closely observed and assessed in the evaluation process.

Level 3 is again progressing from previous levels and the examiner must now combine and use their knowledge of the area by demonstrating the ability to explain a concept or process. It is considered that this stage would represent the basic level of competence for a digital forensic examiner capable of presenting material to a court or tribunal. In the earlier example, "*Explain a procedure to acquire a forensic image from a digital device*" would mean that an examiner could explain the underpinning concepts, processes, and procedures required to acquire a forensic image either orally in a court of law or in a written report. Assessment of this skill can be undertaken in a written test or peer evaluation of the oral presentation abilities of the candidate using the subject matter. Practical demonstration with dialogue and instruction would also demonstrate mastery at this level.

By using a framework such as this, a digital forensics organization can program effectively for the acquisition and evaluation of skills.

Protecting Your Investment

Businesses expend large sums of money in keeping their staff competent and qualified, particularly in the area of digital forensics. As previously mentioned, one of the easiest ways to retain staff is to make sure the organization is supportive of staff who are undertaking training and rewards them. This environment then creates a significant opportunity/cost situation of obtaining and maintaining skills for the employee who is considering switching to an employer who does not offer the same. Another way is to contractually tie the staff to the training expenses. By using a formal contract that makes staff acknowledge that should they terminate their employment and be employed within the same field with another employer within a given period of time, they will be responsible for pro-rata payment of the training.

By spreading your risk and making sure that as many staff as are applicable and affordable be trained or educated to the same level of expertise, you lessen the impact of any potential loss of a staff member. It is far cheaper to send an extra staff member on a training or educational course than to recover the costs associated with loss of income as a result of a loss of niche expertise, or someone having to play catch-up. This is one of the decisions regarding when and how much to invest in training that the manager will need to make. Too much would be wasteful and inefficient, too little will leave the organization exposed to a level of risk that might be unacceptable.

Another important aspect that is often overlooked is that of the assessment of the training that has been delivered. The fundamental question that must be asked is, "Is the organization getting value for money from a particular type of training?" The organizational impacts of these courses are considerable when you take into account course fees, time lost, any accommodation or other expenses incurred as a result of the training, and potential additional salary to reward the increased level of skill. Very few organizations actually take time to evaluate the training given by the various providers. Your staff are your best asset in this regard. They are experienced, reasonably good assessors of value, and hopefully excellent critics. The assessment does not have to be overly formal and a simple documented debriefing session should be sufficient, or at least highlight potential problems—for example, if six people are trained and four say it was subpar. Moreover, if your staff are failing to achieve certification, it could be a result of poor training and have nothing to do with their skill, which likewise may be discerned in a debriefing session.

Summary

This chapter has looked at a range of issues that must be considered with regard to staff training, education, and staff retention. It has looked at the issues with regard to vendor-provided training and academic education, and the validation and certification of staff skills. The chapter also looked at the issue of staff development, motivation and retention, and the development of specialized skills to meet the role of the organization. The chapter has highlighted a number of considerations and decisions the manager must take to make the most effective use of the available finances and resources.

Notes

1. http://bravotech.us/info/msos-timeline.htm
2. http://en.wikipedia.org/wiki/Template:Timeline_of_iPod_models

Chapter 9

Legislation, Regulation, and Standards

Introduction

This chapter will look at a range of international, national, and local legislation and regulations that must be addressed if the laboratory is to fulfill its role and be credible and efficient. The chapter will also look at issues such as data protection and human rights laws and the impact these may have on the resources and methods used to carry out investigations.

The Doctrine of Documentary Evidence

Arguably, the most important area for the manager of a digital forensics laboratory is the maintenance of the integrity and continuity of the evidential chain, sometimes called the chain of custody. If this is not maintained, or if it is compromised, then any evidence produced may be excluded from a courtroom.

The United Kingdom Association of Chief Police Officers' (ACPO) *Good Practise Guide for Computer-Based Electronic Evidence* describes the Doctrine of Documentary Evidence. This is explained as the requirement for a piece of evidence, when presented to a court, to be no more and no less than it was when it first came into the possession of law enforcement.

That requirement remains constant whether the evidential item in question is a physical piece of paper or digital media, and it is for that reason that the examination of digital exhibits is, unless compelled by circumstance, carried out using an image of the original exhibit.

The ACPO guide details four principles that guide the collection of digital exhibits and are pertinent not only to law enforcement officers but to any private investigator working within the forensic computing arena.

- Principle 1:
    - *No action taken by law enforcement agencies or their agents should change data held on a computer or storage media which may subsequently be relied upon in court.*

- Principle 2:
    - *In circumstances where a person finds it necessary to access original data held on a computer or on storage media, that person must be competent to do so and be able to give evidence explaining the relevance and the implications of their actions.*

- Principle 3:
    - *An audit trail or other record of all processes applied to computer-based electronic evidence should be created and preserved. An independent third party should be able to examine those processes and achieve the same result.*

- Principle 4:
    - *The person in charge of the investigation (the case officer) has overall responsibility for ensuring that the law and these principles are adhered to.*

Increasingly, as the software used in the process of imaging digital exhibits has been tested and found to be of a standard acceptable to the judicial process, and therefore not capable or worthy of challenge by the defense, in attempting to show that the evidence found is unreliable, the focus of attack has shifted to the exhibits themselves.

If the investigator does not properly record the seizure and later storage of exhibits, then the defense will highlight the discrepancies and claim that the evidence could have been tampered with and seek to have the evidence excluded.

All exhibits on entry into the laboratory must be photographed and their condition recorded, including, for example, how many hard disk drives were present in a seized computer, and even whether or not a hard disk drive was present on receipt of the seized item. This is of importance in preventing later allegations that seized items have been either damaged or parts lost while in the custody of the laboratory.

While it is appreciated that the laboratory manager has no control over the actions of independent investigators, it is vital that his staff are instructed and understand the need to keep records and to correctly document the seizure and handling of exhibits at all stages of the process, from seizure during the course of search, to passage through the laboratory, all the way up to the eventual presentation of the evidence in a court of law.

In particular, notes of the steps that have been taken and the decisions made when examining seized digital material are of vital importance, as is their retention in a format that is non-editable (cannot be changed). The requirement to create an audit trail of activity that allows a third party to be able to re-create the steps taken and arrive at the same result cannot be overstated. If the notes fail to record vital steps and decisions, then the whole process is open to challenge and may result in the "smoking gun" evidence being ruled inadmissible.

A similar focus for challenges by the defense is of any post-seizure activity on a computer system. The mere act of switching on a computer or laptop, without going further, results in changes to the time and date stamps on several hundred files. Should documents be accessed or searches performed, then potentially many crucial dates of creation, last access, and last written data may be changed and evidence overwritten.

The examiner has no choice but to "tell it as it is" in relation to their findings when examining digital media. Unexplained activity after the date and time of seizure of the exhibit resulting from overzealous or well-intentioned personnel is, or can be, the subject of challenge and result in the entire exhibit being excluded from trial.

The United Kingdom Section 78 Police and Criminal Evidence Act (PACE) 1984 gives judges a wide discretion to review the fairness of any evidence presented and exclude any evidence they feel is unfair to the defense in any respect.

The Computer Misuse Act (CMA) 1990 (as amended by the Police and Justice Act 2006) under Section 1, makes it an offense to cause a computer to perform "any" function with intent to gain unauthorized access to any program or data held in any computer. However, Section 10 of the act makes clear that this excludes any activities that involve lawful inspection, search, or seizure.

Prevailing Health and Safety Laws in the UK
The Health & Safety at Work Act 1974

The Health & Safety at Work Act of 1974 puts the duty of care upon both the employer and the employee to ensure the safety of all persons using the work premises. This includes visitors and contractors.

The Management of Health & Safety at Work Regulations Act 1999

The Management of Health & Safety at Work Regulations Act of 1999 requires employers to conduct a full assessment of:

a. The risks to the health and safety of his employees to which they are exposed whilst at work, and

b. The risks to ensure the health and safety of persons not in his employment arising out of or in connection with the conduct by him or his undertaking.

The Electricity at Work Regulations Act 1989

The Electricity at Work Regulations Act of 1989 requires that all systems shall be constructed and maintained so as to prevent, so far as reasonably practicable, various dangers:

- "'System' means an electrical system in which all the electrical equipment is, or may be, electrically connected to a common source of electrical energy and includes such source and such equipment."

- "'Electrical Equipment' includes anything used, intended to be used or installed for use, to generate, provide, transmit, transform, rectify, convert, conduct, distribute, control, store, measure or use electrical energy."

The Provision and Use of Work Equipment Regulations (PUWER) 1998

The Provision and Use of Work Equipment Regulations 1998 states that "every employer shall ensure that work equipment is maintained in an efficient state, in efficient working order and in good repair."

- PUWER 1998 only applies to work equipment used by workers at work. This includes all work equipment (fixed, transportable, or portable) connected to a source of electrical energy. PUWER does not apply to fixed installations in a building. The electrical safety of these installations is dealt with only by the Electricity at Work Regulations (see earlier).

All the legislation mentioned earlier has an impact on digital forensics laboratory in a number of operational areas and ensured that work practices are carried out with safety in mind.

- The safety of all electrical items and connections used in the laboratory must be confirmed by a suitably qualified operative prior to commencement of any activities, and at regular intervals thereafter.

- The testing of seized computer equipment and peripheral devices prior to their being activated, but not until all removable media has been taken from the target machine and imaged, is a necessary procedure to prevent examiners from receiving electrical shocks. At least one member of the laboratory staff should be trained in Portable Appliance Testing (PAT).

- Examiners will, as a consequence of their employment, spend long periods of time sitting and working in front of, and looking at, computer screens. It is of vital importance that the configuration of their work area, from the type of chair to the size and height of the screen, be checked to ensure the best possible working environment. They must be encouraged to take regular breaks from the screen, and consideration should be given to paying for yearly eyesight tests.

- There must be a suitable first-aid kit on site, and a member of the staff (or an entity nearby) should be trained in first aid.

In the course of their work, examiners will inevitably come into contact with material that is unpleasant and can cause stress and discomfort. In particular, pedophile images, some adult pornography, and written material detailing pedophilia, incest, or rape and torture fantasies can potentially affect examiners.

The taking and distribution of indecent images of children under 18 years of age is governed, in the United Kingdom, by the Protection of Children Act (England and Wales) 1978 as amended.

In the case of *R v. Bowden* 1999,[1] it was established that the act of downloading a photograph or pseudo-photograph from the Internet was an act of "making" an indecent image of a child, which consequently triggered the more serious offense, and brought with it the liability to up to ten years imprisonment.

More worryingly, for those involved in the investigation of such offenses, whether as investigators or forensic analysts, it meant that the examination of seized media and the viewing of such photographs implied that the examiner also committed offenses under the act.

This brought about an amendment to the Sexual Offenses Act of 2003 and the creation of a statutory defense for those professionals working in this arena, whether in law enforcement, government, private forensic laboratories, or the communication service provider industries.

The act also created a Memorandum of Understanding between the Crown Prosecution Service (CPS) and the Association of Chief Police Officers (ACPO), which clarifies the position of these parties and describes the circumstances in which written authority may be given to those professionals who may, in support of the legislation, need to frequently "make" images of child abuse.

Laboratory managers should familiarize themselves with this legislation, and in particular Section 46 of the Sexual Offenses Act of 2003 and the strictures inherent in the statutory defense and memorandum of understanding.

A regime of referral to a psychology practitioner should be in place to ensure that support is available. The scheme should be mandatory, with at least one visit per year and more considered if the laboratory processes this type of material on behalf of law enforcement. Arrangements should include employee-initiated telephone or other support in the intervals between the mandatory visits.

The Data Protection Act (DPA) of 1998 and the European Data Protection Directive (94/95/EC) of October 24, 1995 impacted the operation of forensic computing laboratories.

The Act requires that personal information, meaning data that relates to a living individual who can be identified…

- from that data, or

- from that data and other information which is in the possession of, or is likely to come into the possession of, the data controller

…is dealt with in a manner compatible with the act.

In particular, the act identifies a number of areas of sensitive personal data:

- The racial or ethnic origin of the data subject

- A person's political opinions

- A person's religious beliefs or other beliefs of a similar nature

- Whether a person is a member of a trade union (within the meaning of the [1992 c. 52.] Trade Union and Labour Relations (Consolidation) Act 1992)

- A person's physical or mental health or condition

- A person's sexual life

- The commission, or alleged commission, by a person of any offense

- Any proceedings for any offense committed or alleged to have been committed by a person, and the disposal of such proceedings or the sentence of any court in such proceedings.

The conditions for processing these data sets is described in Schedule 3 of the 1998 Act,[2] and data controllers must be aware of this.

The forensic analysts within the laboratory will, under the 1998 Act, be considered data processors rather than data controllers, and therefore not require registration. If the laboratory is part of an organization that has a data controller then that person has a responsibility for ensuring that the strictures of the data protection legislation are complied with.

If the laboratory is independent, then it will be incumbent upon the data controller for the contracting organization to ensure that any personal data is dealt with in a manner compatible with the act. However, a contract should be in place that deals with the issue of data protection compliance, as well as its commercial aspects. In the absence of such a document, the organization may breach the requirements of the data protection legislation.

If data is to be transferred from within the European Economic Area (EEA) to other countries, then special rules apply and care must be taken. The transfer of personal data to those countries not considered to have an equivalence of protection to that subsisting within the EEA is forbidden within the UK 1998 Act and the European Community Directive.

A list of those countries considered to have the equivalent data protection is published on the Information Commissioners Web site[3] and, at the time of this writing, June 2008, included the following countries: Argentina, Canada, Guernsey, Isle of Man, and Switzerland.

The European Commission and the United States of America created a "Safe Harbor" agreement that incorporates an agreed set of rules for dealing with personal data in July 2000, any firms signed up to the agreement are considered to have equivalent safeguards, and personal data may be passed to them.

Alternatively, model contracts are available that have been created, together with binding corporate rules, for internal use at multinational corporations. All can be found either on the Web site of the Information Commissioner,[4] or the Web site of the European Commission.[5]

The European Convention on Human Rights and the Human Rights Act of 1998 bring with them a requirement for courts, whether civil or criminal, in the United Kingdom to have regard to the effect of both the Convention and Act.

Whether or not the laboratory is part of law enforcement or a private company, their output, the results of the examination of digital media, will impact those courtrooms; therefore managers must ensure that working practices take into account the requirements of the act.

Of the various articles within the Human Rights Act of 1998, the two which the Laboratory Manager will most often need to observe are:

- Article 6—The right to a fair trial, and

- Article 8—The right to privacy and private family life

Whether within law enforcement or the commercial field, both articles and their effect must be considered when dealing with seized material.

Consider the following scenario: A couple is divorcing and the husband has left some old computers, which he used in his business, in the custody of the wife. She knows little of his business dealings or his real net worth and so hands the computers over to a forensic laboratory so they can image the computers, examine the contents of the hard disk drives, and enable her and her legal advisors to gain intelligence and evidence as to the husband's monetary position.

The examination would, potentially, reveal details of private correspondence (e-mail traffic) and private correspondence detailing business dealings, banking details, and so on.

Has this breached Article 8—The right to privacy—and is there a potential breach of Article 6—The right to a fair trial?

Under the terms of Article 8, there has almost certainly been a breach, and it would be for the courts to determine whether the wife's rights were being subverted in the absence of this knowledge.

As regards Article 6, if the policies and procedures of the laboratory are sufficiently robust, then the evidence produced should be acceptable to the court, whether it is entered in evidence is, of course, a matter for the rules governing that court and the judge's discretion.

The case of *Nuemeister v. Austria* 1998 brought about the concept of "equality of arms" in judicial proceedings. In short, if the policies and procedures of the laboratory are not sufficiently robust and clear so that another forensic analyst could not follow the steps taken and re-create the result, then the evidence obtained may be ruled inadmissible.

There are currently no licensing requirements for forensic investigators in the UK, nor are there formal qualifications required before an analyst can set up shop. The Council for the Registration of Forensic Practitioners[6] (CRFP) in the UK has created a peer-reviewed registration process for forensic analysts; however, the take-up rate has been slow. There are moves by the Security Industry Authority, under the Private Security Industry Act of 2001 in the UK to license private investigators; however, the full extent of those to be licensed is, as yet, unclear and may include forensic practitioners. The consultation phase closed in 2008 and the licensing regime is unlikely to commence before 2010.

These moves in the UK are being paralleled in the U.S., where a number of states are now seeking to restrict forensic computing activity to licensed private investigators.[7] A report from U.S. Government Computer News in February 2007 stated that the U.S. had only 12 accredited computer forensic laboratories. The criteria for accreditation had only been agreed upon in 2003, which enforced the vision of a relatively new branch of forensic science and tried to establish a set of rules to enhance the value of practitioners, weed out the incompetent, and give the customers a base line from which to decide who or which organization is best suited for their needs.

The Sarbanes-Oxley Act created two new offenses, codifying the destruction, concealment, falsification, or alteration of any record or document for the purpose of obstructing or influencing any "official proceedings" of a federal agency or in relation to the "contemplation" of any such matter as illegal.

While it is not suggested that forensic analysts or their laboratory managers must be clairvoyant, they still must be aware that the focus of an investigation where data has been deleted may well be a timeline of activity that proves or disproves an offense under this act.

The issue of "expert" evidence is a matter that has tasked courts at all levels within the criminal justice systems of both the UK and U.S.

In the U.S., the case of *Daubert v. Merrell Dow Pharmaceuticals* (92-102), 509 U.S. 579 (1993)[8] dealt with the effect of Rule 702 of the Rules of Evidence, which provides:

> **If scientific, technical, or other specialized knowledge will assist the trier of fact to understand the evidence or to determine a fact in issue, a witness qualified as an expert by knowledge, skill, experience, training, or education, may testify thereto in the form of an opinion or otherwise.**

As in the UK, the onus of deciding whether or not a witness may give evidence as an expert—that is, evidence of opinion as opposed to fact—is that of the trial judge.

The Daubert decision has also affected the software tools used in a forensics laboratory. For instance, have those tools been subject to a scientific review? If not, or if there is any uncharted area, then the tools are not fit for the job and should not be used in the laboratory unless first tested and validated.

For the laboratory manager, this battle must often be fought. Analysts, by their nature, are innovators; however, innovation or use of tools that are "cool" and/or cut down the time taken to complete a particular facet of the examination of digital material may be superb timesavers, but they may also ultimately deny admissibility of the evidence found. Thus, the laboratory manager must rule on whether or not these tools are used in the lab.

In many cases, the "Pop Up or Trojan Horse" defense is raised by defense experts. The laboratory manager must ensure that his analysts are fully aware of the latest defense gambits in use, and that they, during the examination of the media, record and report any such items.

NOTE

A Trojan horse is a piece of malicious software which appears to perform a certain action but in reality is doing something totally different. A Pop Up is normally a web page that appears on the screen without being requested and happens when certain web sites open a new web browser window to display material that the user did not request. A pop-up window is usually generated by using Javascript, but they can be generated by a number of other tools and applications.

It is not suggested that pop-ups or Trojan Horse software should be routinely reviewed to test functionality; however, their presence should be recorded so prosecutors are aware of the potential threat, and so such items can be reviewed in greater detail later.

In conclusion, many similarities exist between the requirements placed on UK and U.S. forensics laboratories, and the awareness of the same required of the manager. Both must be alert to the skill set, technical knowledge, and training of their staff, and ensure that they are kept up-to-date with recent legal decisions that affect their environment.

The managers' knowledgebase, however, needs to extend beyond that point and encompass the wider issues of health and safety at work, human rights, data protection, and associated legislation. The successful manager will be one who can juggle these responsibilities together with the workload balance and financial viability of his laboratory.

Summary

This chapter has examined a range of international, national, and local legislation and regulations that must be addressed to ensure that the laboratory is credible and efficient and able to fulfill its role. The chapter has also looked at a range of other issues, such as data protection and human rights laws, and the effect they may have on investigations.

Notes

1. http://www.iwf.org.uk/police/page.22.36.htm
2. http://www.opsi.gov.uk/acts/acts1998/ukpga_19980029_en_10
3. http://www.ico.gov.uk/what_we_cover/data_protection/international/international_transfers.aspx
4. Ibid.
5. http://ec.europa.eu/justice_home/fsj/privacy/modelcontracts/index_en.htm
6. http://www.crfp.org.uk/specialties/specialties/computers/computers.htm
7. http://www.hackerfactor.com/blog/index.php?/archives/137-Digital-Forensic-Investigators.html
8. http://www.law.cornell.edu/supct/html/92-102.ZO.html

Digital Forensic Incident and Crime Investigation Management

This section addresses the digital forensics management issues related to digital forensic incidents and crime investigations. It looks at how investigations are carried out, what needs to be considered in the planning of an investigation, and the conduct of the investigation including the collection and storage of evidence. The section also deals with the vitally important issue of quality assurance so that the efforts and risks taken are not wasted, and the organization gains and maintains a good reputation. The section finishes with a number of case studies to highlight how things can go well if they are done properly and how they can go wrong if they are not.

Chapter 10. Responding to Crimes Requiring Computer Forensic Investigation. This chapter talks about what actions are required, the management considerations, and just as importantly, what should not be done when responding to a high tech crime scene. It deals with the differing requirements that must be considered for the range of types of investigation in which the unit may be called upon to take part, including standalone PCs, servers, networks, live acquisition, and wireless, and discusses the management issues that relate to the use of function specific tools.

Chapter 11. Management of the Collections of Evidence. As the title states, this chapter talks about the management issues that relate to the collection of high technology crime scene evidence, a crucial part of any high technology investigation. It also deals with issues such as continuity of evidence and chain of custody.

Chapter 12. Management of Evidence Storage. This chapter addresses the issues that relate to the storage of evidence and the management issues that need to be considered to ensure that it is carried out effectively and meets the relevant rules and legislation. We also address the difficult question of long-term storage periods, a particular problem for law enforcement.

Chapter 13. Quality Assurance. This chapter addresses the vitally important issue of quality assurance, and describes when it should be carried out, by whom, and to what standards.

Chapter 14. High Technology Crimes: Case Summaries. This chapter gives a range of cases that illustrate the types of incidents that may be encountered under the general grouping of high technology crimes. There are examples of cases that have been successful and other examples that highlight how a lack of good procedures can lead to considerable expense, loss of credibility, and embarrassment.

This section of the book looks at the issues that affect the underpinning reason for the existence of the laboratory by addressing the management issues that relate to the investigation of digital forensic incidents and investigations. The laboratory must be competent at the tasks it undertakes and significantly, be able to demonstrate that it has the procedures, training, and quality assurance measures in place to ensure this; otherwise the management of the laboratory will not have been successful. In order to explain and highlight a number of the issues raised, a number of case studies are detailed.

In having an understanding of these issues, the manager will be able to ensure that the appropriate processes and procedures are created and implemented to enable the lab to carry out its function properly. This section is focused on the management of the investigative process in order to give the manager an understanding of the issues needed in order to ensure that investigations are carried out in an efficient and testable manner.

Chapter 10

Responding to Crimes Requiring Digital Forensic Investigation

Introduction

This chapter will look at what actions are required in digital forensic investigation, as well as various management considerations, and (just as importantly) what should *not* be done when responding to a crime involving artifacts that possibly contain digital evidence. It will deal with the differing requirements that must be considered for the range of investigations the unit may be called on to take part in, including items such as stand-alone devices, servers, networks, live acquisition, and wireless, and will discuss management issues relating to the use of function-specific tools.

Capabilities

This chapter is about how the digital forensic investigator should respond to a request for input to an investigation, and the management issues that must be addressed. This is not just about "high-tech crimes," since the skills and experience that the digital forensic investigator possesses may be required to support a whole range of investigations, from hacking to fraud to murder. This, in turn, will mean that the people who the digital forensic investigator is working with will have a wide range of levels of previous knowledge and experience regarding digital forensic investigations and investigators. This is something the digital forensic investigation manager can influence as a part of the management process by developing the appropriate relationships and briefing investigators in a range of other disciplines (the TV series, *CSI*, is exceedingly good, but the authors are still looking for, and have yet to meet, an investigator who has such a wide range of skills and who can solve a case in less than an hour).

In doing this, there are potentially two main advantages for the digital forensic investigation unit. The first is that when an investigation is being conducted into a non-computer-based crime, such as murder or blackmail or fraud, investigators are aware of the possible sources of evidence they may encounter. They may also have an idea of the actions that must be avoided if that source of evidence is to be preserved. The second advantage is that these relationships can be used to educate other investigators about the capabilities of digital forensic investigators, the time and effort required to recover digital evidence, and the contribution they might be able to make to an investigation.

In addition to the range of crime types that the digital forensic unit may be called upon to get involved with, the different kinds of devices that may be encountered often require specific skills. In the following paragraphs, various device types and issues are addressed. From the digital investigation management perspective, this is important since it will be relevant to the selection and training of staff and may affect the types of devices the unit can, and should, acquire.

Stand-Alone Devices

While addressed as a single topic, stand-alone devices essentially fall into a number of subsets. The first of these subsets is the PC and the laptop. This is probably the least problematic for the digital forensic manager since it has the most established history in digital forensics, in that it was really the advent of the PC, together with its wide acceptance by all types of users, which created the need for the capture of evidence.

The digital forensic capture of data from a desktop PC or laptop computer has had the advantage of them being "self-contained" with a finite volume of storage, although with disk sizes of

750GB and 1 terabyte now widely available, the digital forensic examiner may not agree! The various issues the manager must resolve are items such as ensuring that the investigator is properly briefed as to what's required of them, and making sure the staff member is appropriately trained, certified, and experienced in the use of the chosen tools and their proper procedures. The next issue the manager must address is making sure the analysis of the captured data is carried out in the most cost-effective yet competent manner, while simultaneously meeting the evidential requirements of the investigation.

The capture of data from a desktop PC or laptop computer has become increasingly complex in recent years with the advent of wireless devices. The investigator must now also take into account the fact that an apparently unconnected device may actually be networked and connected to a range of devices. This should be covered by the manager in the task briefing. Another issue the manager must address is that of health and safety, and the investigator must be trained and briefed about any potential problems before each task. If the device is a laptop computer, additional consideration should be given and research undertaken into the make and model since access to the hard disk is becoming increasingly complex in some laptops. An example of this can be seen in the Apple range of computers.

The next subset is the range of handheld devices. These are addressed as a separate group since the significant characteristics of many of these devices are similar and the approach and the tools and techniques that need to be used are common.

Again, in the past, while this group of devices had some additional issues that had to be addressed, they could be relatively easily understood and defined. As the devices have become more intelligent and the memory size has increased, they have also become more feature-rich, and there is now a much greater diversity of devices. This has all resulted in a much more complex environment in which the digital forensic process must take place. A number of the major issues that relate to this type of device and that must be considered include:

- **The volatility of the data.** Unlike desktop computers and laptops, handheld devices do not normally have hard disks. On these devices, data is normally stored in volatile memory, which will be lost if there is a partial or total loss of power. Recovering data from volatile memory and preserving it in a state in which it can be analyzed can present significant problems. If the device is reset while being stored or imaged, there may be a loss of data. A loss of battery power, either through it becoming drained or being removed, will cause a hard reset, and care should be taken to ensure that the battery power level is regularly monitored. A hard reset will purge all of the data stored in the RAM. A soft reset will reinitialize the dynamic memory, and any records marked for deletion will likely be removed.

- **The dynamic nature of the data.** Data can easily be altered either knowingly or by accident. The data stored in the memory of a handheld device is likely to change dynamically even when the device is left idle. As a result, they can be difficult to image and it is unlikely that a hash signature that can be replicated can be produced for the entire device. This is partially a result of things like the system clock, which forms part of the data stored and is constantly changing. Because of this, it will be necessary for the manager to decide on the approach to be taken and then determine how to preserve the data and related hashes.

- **The generic state of the device.** Even when a device appears to be in the off state, it may not be entirely inactive and may have background processes running. Any sudden change from one state to another may cause a loss of data. It will be necessary to try to determine the current state of the device and the state it should be kept in.

- **Associated accessories.** Most handheld devices support a range of devices that can be associated with them, from external keyboards and speakers to additional memory storage such as MMC, SD, and CF cards. It is essential that during the seizure process, all associated devices are also collected.

- **Synchronization with other computers and handheld devices.** Potential evidence on handheld devices could include data such as e-mail, text or voice messages, an address book, a calendar, multimedia files, documents, and passwords.

Issues that the digital forensic manager must take into account for this group of devices include:

- **The availability of the appropriate tools.** With the increasing range of devices that may be encountered during an investigation, an increasing range of tools is required in capturing the available data in a forensically sound manner. On each of the devices, the data may be stored in different locations and formats. In some cases, such as satellite navigation systems, research is still taking place to determine the best methods for the collection, storage, and ways of interpreting and presenting the data. The challenge for the manager is the selection of the most appropriate tools for the laboratory and the balance between investing in what are normally very expensive tools that may never be used and not having available the tools that are required. This can be solved in part by the acquisition of tools required to meet the needs of the organization's environment and an understanding of where the other tools can be acquired, on short notice. This can be achieved by researching a wide range of the devices before deciding which tools should be purchased. The manager must also ensure that once the tools that are identified for the toolkit are purchased, that members of staff are trained, certified, and experienced in their use.

- **Knowledge.** With the range of devices and suitable tools to address them, it is essential that the manager ensures that the required knowledge of the devices, how they operate, and any known problems in capturing data from them is obtained and kept up-to-date. The same must be done for the appropriate tools.

- **Experience.** With the complexity of the devices and the range of devices that may be encountered, it is essential that the manager makes sure a sufficient range and depth of experience exists amongst the staff so any data capture is effective and credible.

- **Procedures for the collection and storage of the devices.** With the ever-increasing range of devices on the market, it is essential that suitable procedures be in place for the collection and storage of the devices. To be clear, what is being referred to here is the actual device, not just the data it contains. Issues that the manager needs to consider include equipment and procedures for the collection of the devices. This will consist of signal suppression boxes or bags for the containment of the device on site, and for shipment back to the laboratory and the accepted and agreed upon procedures for their use. It will also include various equipment and procedures to ensure that, once in the laboratory, the devices are stored in an environment that suppresses any communication, but also allows for them to be kept charged to ensure there is no unnecessary loss of volatile data.

- **Data connection cables.** With the range of devices that will potentially be encountered, it will be unlikely that the laboratory will have all of the data connection leads it requires. The problem here for the manager is to understand what connection leads are required for each device and where they can be obtained, at short notice, when needed.

- **Cables for charging the devices.** The problem for management here is exactly the same as that regarding the data connection cables.

The range of devices that should now be considered in this group is continuing to expand as digital processors and memory are put to an increasing number of uses. The range currently includes:

- Personal digital assistants
- Mobile phones
- iPods and other MP3/4 players
- Digital cameras
- Satellite navigation (satnav) systems
- Printers
- Photocopiers
- Car engine management systems
- Domestic devices (washing machines / refrigerators)
- Games consoles
- Personal digital recorders (for satellite, terrestrial digital, and broadband TV)

Additional issues that the digital forensic manager must take into account include:

- **Servers.** Some of the considerations that need addressing in the acquisition of data from a server include the potential volume of data that may be encountered and the probability that it may be difficult or impossible to turn the server off in order to create an image of the storage. A clear understanding of what information may be stored on the server and what evidence is required for the investigation will help the manager in developing a plan for the recovery of the required data. Even if it was possible to obtain all of the data on a server, the time that would be required to carry out a thorough analysis must be factored into the cost of the investigation.

- **Networks.** The logical acquisition of selected files can be used on networked systems to copy logical files from a remote device. Tools are available that are capable of copying files in a manner that preserves the settings for both ownership and security. When considering this approach, the manager should take into account that even though the data can be recovered in a forensically sound manner, there are occasions when the data is of no value as a result of it being dependent on the hardware or software of the system it was collected from. In addition, in some cases, it may not be possible to gain access to the target system without access to the administrator's password. If this technique is used, it is important to check the data recovered and ascertain that it is in a readable form as soon as possible so that if the data cannot be successfully read, alternative steps can be taken to gain physical access to the system.

- **Acquisition of live data.** This is the process of acquiring information contained in the memory of the device. This process is often referred to as a random access memory (RAM) dump and is used to copy the data that is residing in the system memory. This is a process that has a number of limitations and the manager must take these into account when deciding whether the risk and cost are justified. Some of the limitations include the fact that the date and time information related to the data will not be included, nor will it necessarily be possible to determine the ownership of the data recovered. It is also possible that some, or all, of the data recovered will not be in a form that is readable and may not be recovered in the order it was entered or used. It may be necessary to process the data further to present the data in a format that is of use for the investigation. When deciding whether to attempt to recover live data, consideration must be given to the possibility that the data recovered may include system settings, passwords, documents that had not been saved, and a range of other information that would otherwise be lost. Data recovered from memory can be saved to a storage device for later analysis. The manager must ensure that if live data recovery is undertaken, the documentation is complete since it will not be possible to re-create the environment in a manner that another investigator could verify. Consideration should be given to using a video camera to capture the steps taken by the investigator.

- **Full system capture using live acquisition.** A number of potential benefits exist to carrying out a live acquisition of the full system rather than the live acquisition of the RAM and the conventional imaging of the static files. One of the benefits may be the capture of additional data that might not have been obtained when the logical files were acquired.

The manager must balance the benefits and shortcomings of the approach before adopting it since the data that is ultimately recovered may be more difficult to prove on a forensic level and be more liable to challenge in a court of law. However, the benefits of this may be the capture of data that would otherwise have been unrecoverable or unreadable. The type of additional information that may be recovered using this approach includes files that have not otherwise been saved, information on the processes that were running at the time of acquisition, users that are connected to the system across the network, and shared network resources such as folders or drives.

Again, the manager should ensure that if a full live system capture is undertaken, the documentation is comprehensive and complete since it will not be possible to re-create the environment in a manner that another investigator could verify. Consideration should again be given to using a video camera to capture the steps taken by the investigator.

Wireless Device Issues

The forensic seizure, transporting, analysis, and storage of wireless devices poses a number of problems that the manager must address. The first is that, before any devices are touched, the scene of the incident must be thoroughly checked to ensure they are not connected to any other devices. It would be unfortunate (or even incompetent) for the investigator to seize one device but not get the device it was connected to that actually contained the evidence sought. The next issue is ensuring that the device, if it stores data in volatile storage, is handled appropriately to preserve the evidence. Next is the management of the transport of the device(s) to ensure that they do not communicate with any other devices once they have been seized since this could contaminate or destroy any potential evidence. The last of the major issues that the manager must address is the actions that need to be taken to store the device in a safe and secure manner. Good briefing of the staff, together with well-practiced processes and procedures, will help in managing these issues.

While the following is relevant to all devices, it is particularly relevant in the investigation of handheld devices. A number of problems that arise from the requirements caused by the range of ways in which digital information can be stored and transmitted have resulted in tools being developed that address specific issues. Examples of this are tools such as the Access Data Forensic Toolkit, the Prodiscover tool, and the Guidance software EnCase tool, all of which have been developed to deal with single computers. Then there is the tool produced by Guidance software, the EnCase Enterprise tool, which is used for the remote collection of evidence from computers connected to a network within an organization. The system works by downloading an applet to the target computer that then allows a forensic image of it to be taken across the network. When dealing with mobile devices, another group of tools is available, such as the Paraben Device Seizure tool and the Datapilot Secure View Kit for Forensics.

In addition to this, a range of single-function tools have been developed to assist the analyst in their task. All of these tools have their own strengths and weaknesses, but the reason that the digital forensic investigation manager must give consideration to their selection and use is because a number of issues will need to be taken into account. When selecting the suite of tools to be used in the laboratory, the range of tasks envisaged for the laboratory must be carefully thought through to ensure that the correct set of tools are obtained and that the staff are adequately trained. In addition, the manager must also take into account issues such as the "industry standard" in their particular environment and the available experience of the staff. It is sensible, wherever possible, to standardize the toolsets used in order to ensure that the procurement and maintenance costs, as well as the training bill, are controlled.

Health and Safety

Health and safety is a subject that must be taken seriously in all areas of the digital forensic investigation process, and the manager must consider a number of health and safety issues when digital forensic investigators are deployed in support of investigations. First and foremost, the manager must ensure that a comprehensive and effective health and safety policy is in place for the unit. This policy must take account any other policies in place for the rest of the organization and any relevant government regulations or rules issued by environmental and safety authorities. It is important that the manager make certain that not only does the unit have a policy in place, but that the members of the staff have read it!

Health and Safety Risk Assessments

Both in the laboratory and when attending the scene of an incident, it is essential that health and safety risk assessments are carried out. A health and safety risk assessment consists of a number of steps that must be covered in order to understand any potential issues that may create hazards for staff members.

The health and safety risk assessments must not only be carried out for the laboratory itself, but also each time its staff is deployed from it. While this may seem to be "over the top," it does not have to be particularly time-consuming or laborious. It simply must document the fact that any potential problems to staff health have been considered and that the risks have been minimized. In addition, such assessments cause the staff to consider the environment they will be working in and think about the potential hazards.

The risk assessment process consists of the following steps:

- Identification of all hazards that might be encountered in the area that staff are being deployed to.

- Identification of the staff that may be exposed to the hazards.

- Evaluation of the significant risks to which staff may be exposed.

- The probability of foreseeable accidents or injuries.

- Practical precautions and control measures that can be implemented to reduce risk.

The risk assessment should cover the environment in which the staff are to be deployed, the working procedures, and the equipment to be used. A separate health and safety risk assessment should be carried out for each deployment, and the staff to be deployed should be involved in the process. An example of a template for a risk assessment form is at Appendix B.

Because of the nature of the work and the explicit nature of the material the investigator may be exposed to, it is essential that access to counselling sessions be available to staff on request and that there is a program of regular compulsory counselling sessions in place. The manager must also ensure that any early signs of distress or unusual behavior amongst the staff are referred to the counsellor.

Another health issue that must be managed is that of the long-term use of computer monitors and keyboards. Digital forensics require intensive use of this type of equipment and the manager must ensure that the equipment is set up correctly and that staff operate them in a sustainable manner and take regular breaks from the computer. This is normally mandated by legislation in what is often referred to as "Display Screen Equipment" regulations.

Within the laboratory, which will inevitably contain a large quantity of electrical and electronic equipment, the manager must ensure that suitable anti-static matting is placed under workbenches to prevent the buildup of static electricity or grounding. The use of wristbands to ground the operator should also be mandated in laboratory policies. Other issues that must be considered for the laboratory include fire prevention and suppression systems and access control override systems for emergency escape from the laboratory. Circuit breakers for use in case of an accident should also be easily accessible.

The electrical safety of equipment should be tested at regular intervals. It is normal for this testing, often referred to as portable appliance testing, to be conducted upon receipt of the equipment, then on an annual or biannual basis (in accordance with organizational, local, and national policies and regulations), and then finally when the equipment is disposed of. This is important not only for the safety of the staff, but also to ensure the equipment is operated correctly.

Security Issues

Physical issues regarding the security of the laboratory premises were dealt with earlier in this book. However, the security of the staff, both in the laboratory and when deployed to the scene of an incident, must be considered and reviewed at regular intervals. Whenever an investigator is working outside the laboratory, a security risk assessment should be carried out.

Security Risk Assessment

The security risk management process is made up of four main phases, which are normally listed as:

1. Security Risk Assessment
2. Decision Support
3. Control Measure Implementation
4. Program Effectiveness Measuring

The security risk assessment phase represents a process identifying and prioritizing security risks that will pertain to the deployment. The security risk management process provides detailed instructions on how to carry out a risk assessment and should break down the risk assessment process into a number of steps. The first step is planning, which will create the structure for a successful security risk assessment. The second step is that of data gathering, where the information required is collected in order to facilitate the process. The third step is that of prioritizing the security risks in a way that is both consistent and repeatable. As with the health and safety risk assessment, this does not need to be time consuming or a major burden, but should be carried out in order to ensure that the investigator is conscious of the environment they are about to deploy to and also to make certain they have been briefed on any potential security issues.

In addition to the security of the staff both in the laboratory and while deployed, the manager must ensure that adequate security is provided in a range of other areas. These include:

- **Any property or exhibits that have been collected or are being stored.** To ensure the security of these items, a system must be put in place to make certain they are dealt with in a manner that maintains their integrity and the chain of custody for such exhibits. The system must also ensure that the items are held in a secure store when not in use.

- **Data.** Security of the data falls into two separate areas. The first area that management must consider is to have in place processes and procedures to ensure that the data captured and created remains confidential—that is, it is only available to those who have a need to know and the clearance to access it. This is normally achieved through good physical and logical security, good physical and logical access control, and the use of encryption where appropriate. The second area is that of resilience. This involves making backup copies of the data and software on the workstations and servers and storing them in a secure location offsite to allow for disaster recovery. In the event of an incident, the hardware can be easily replaced, but the data that has been captured and the working files and research cannot. One special case the manager should develop procedures for is that of sensitive or illicit material. Copies of this type of material should be kept to a minimum. If it is necessary to make copies of them, the production, handling, and storage should be tightly controlled and arrangements made for their destruction at the earliest possible opportunity.

- **The Internal Laboratory Network.** This should be isolated and not connected to any network outside the laboratory. There will inevitably be a requirement for a system to be connected to networks external to the laboratory and the Internet to enable communications with other parts of the organization and with other organizations. External connectivity will also be needed for the investigators to carry out research and to download software tools and information. The external communications requirements might be satisfied by one system or two separate systems, but must be isolated from the systems that the investigators use for imaging or analysis. Due to the type of material and subject matter the investigators may be researching, the manager should consider registering the IP address of any externally connected system with the relevant authorities so its use does not cause undue alarm to the organizations' system administrators or other authorities. The main management issue that must be addressed is ensuring that policies and procedures are in place to ensure that staff are aware of the requirement to keep systems, and the data they contain, separate.

Record Keeping

The creation and maintenance of records is of major importance in the digital forensic process, and its importance cannot be overemphasized. It would be unforgivable to put staff at potential risk and to invest significant time and effort in the collection and analysis of data only to have it made unusable because the records of the actions taken were incomplete or wrong. The value of keeping records becomes apparent in large or complex investigations, and also when there is a long period between the capture and analysis of the data and its subsequent use.

The types of records that must be maintained with regard to the items seized might include a copy of any legal authority required, the chain of custody, a description of the evidence items to be examined, details of the packaging and condition of the evidence when it was seized, and all communications relating to the case.

The types of records that must be maintained during the analysis of the data should be detailed enough to allow another competent forensic examiner to be able to understand what has taken place and be able to re-create the analysis and obtain the same findings independently.

Once the analysis is complete, a report must be produced that details the findings of the investigation in a clear and concise manner.

The issues for the manager with regard to this documentation start with ensuring that the investigators are briefed and conversant with the documentary requirements. A second issue is ensuring that, when the documentation has been completed, it is checked for completeness and any errors are corrected. This can best be carried out when the details are fresh in the minds of the investigator and the manager. The third issue is that of ensuring that the investigation report provides answers to the questions asked and is clear and error-free.

Summary

In this chapter, a range of management issues related to the deployment of staff at digital forensic investigations were discussed. While much of this may seem mundane, it is all essential for the proper and efficient running of the laboratory, and is ultimately important to the lab's credibility. The manager must ensure that health and safety and security risk assessments are carried out and that the staff are aware of any issues. The manager also needs to ensure that staff have been given a clear understanding of the role they are to perform in the investigation and that they have the suitable skills and equipment to conduct the tasks at hand. The manager must also make certain that the documentation produced is of a high quality and that when reports are written they are done so in a manner that makes the information they contain clear and understandable and show evidence of quality control.

Summary

Chapter 11

Management of the Collection of Evidence

Introduction

This chapter will talk about the management issues that relate to the collection of high technology crime scene evidence, a crucial part of any high technology investigation. It will also deal with issues such as continuity of evidence and in chain of custody.

The maintenance or lack thereof of the chain of evidence is one of the biggest single causes for the inadmissibility of evidence. Evidence needs to be handled in a manner that allows for full auditing and review of the processes, possession, and what testing or examination has been undertaken since it was secured and extracted from the crime scene to its eventual presentation at a hearing. The integrity of the complete record is also important and checks and balances should be incorporated into the system to ensure that this can be proven beyond any reasonable doubt.

There are existing standards and handbooks such as ASTM E 1492 – 05, AS/NZ HB 171, IOEC 2002 that are relevant to digital forensic issues, and these will be used as the basis for this chapter.

Collecting the Evidence

Collection of evidence of value within a digital forensics context is increasingly challenging with the range of devices that may contain potential evidence constantly expanding. In addition, data that the devices contain is becoming increasingly volatile and disconnected.

The traditional sense of computer forensics was about the examination of a computer hard disk that typically was located at a suspect's place of work or domicile or one the suspect had on his or her person at the point of the incident (i.e., the laptop he or she was operating). This is no longer the case because data is becoming increasingly mobile and separated from the offender.

The example in Figure 11.1 of a teddy bear–based USB storage key that potentially could contain its own execution environment and several gigabytes of data highlights this issue.

Figure 11.1 Teddy Bear USB Device

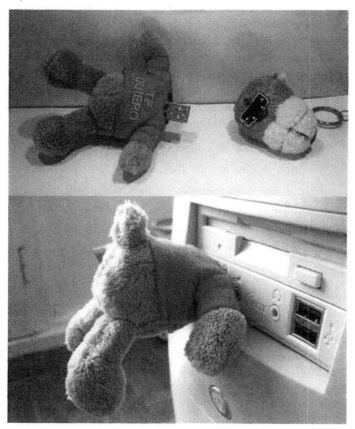

In addition, the use of personal computer networks also is becoming increasingly problematic with criminals using WiFi-based embedded storage systems that are covertly stored within a property limit to access materials. There are also systems that allow for the storage of material on the Internet, which brings in jurisdictional issues. Each of these will have impacts on how we search for evidence, but this should not largely affect the processes we should undertake to collect the evidence. Fundamentally, all these sources will result in an examiner reviewing and interpreting a binary bitstream whether it is, at seizure, stored semipermanently on Mylar on a hard disk's surface or as a network bitstream of a network communication.

The most crucial element is the production of a robust collection system to record the collection of items of interest/evidence. The collection system is not typically a complete IT system per se, but a systematic and well-thought-out series of procedures, processes, and records that document what happens to the items of interest. Ultimately, the system should be able to be fully electronic as technologies such as RFID tags mature and their adoption is more widespread.

Designing the Collection System

When items of interest that are processed and eventually admitted as evidence from an incident are first collected there are steps that must be undertaken to ensure continuity, whereby the uniqueness of the item/record and the ability to track it can be demonstrated, verified, and easily maintained. The correct selection of unique identification and a sufficiently rich metadata makes it easier to facilitate the searching and indexing of items for the purposes of later cross-referencing and investigative needs. Various standards and handbooks describe requirements to maintain continuity or the evidentiary weighting of items that relate to the management of the evidence. These requirements are summarized into:

1. Authority identification—Who has accessed, changed, or created records.

2. Authority verification and validation—Verification of the authenticity of changes, access, created records, and that the recording processes themselves are validated and reliable.

3. Availability and archiving—The records are available and stored in a format that is useable and accessible and can be reviewed at any time.

Identification

One of the first crucial design points is that each particular piece of evidence and its possible subsequent parts can readily be identified within each case. These parts may take many forms within one item of evidence. For example a computer system may be seized that has an internal RAID array of eight hard disks. The record should allow for the RAID to be recorded and examined as physical parts (hard disks) as well as any logical parts (partitions, volumes), and of course, the RAID controller itself.

This mandates the use of sufficiently rich, unique, extensible identifiers in the construction of this record as well as complete as possible metadata. The choice of identifiers should be such that within the given context there is sufficient "key space" to handle all potential workloads or situations that would exist within an organization. For instance, if an organization processed in excess of a thousand cases per annum, it would be foolish to select a three-digit case number as the unique case identifier. Likewise the use of an eight-digit case number would be excessive in most contexts.

A generic record format that would work is:

```
Case Number - Item Number - Part Number - Description - Timestamp - Creator
```

A sample records detail might look like this:

```
00003 - RC001 - HD001 - Scene Notes, Serial Numbers - 200803121732 - CTV
00003 - RC001 - HD001 - Initial Disk Hashes - 200803121821 - CTV
00003 - RC001 - HD001 - Disk Analysis Report - 200803190944 - PRK
```

Case Number—A 5-digit integer incremental.

Item Number—A 5-character string. The first two letters identify what it generically is; for example, DC—desktop computer; LC—laptop computer; RC—RAID case; MP—mobile phone. The last three characters are digits 001–999

Part Number—A 5-character string. The first two letters identify the part generically; for example, HD—hard drive; MS—memory stick; SD—SD card; FM—flash memory; UI—unknown item; etc.

Description—A self-evident description.

Timestamp—In the format YYYYMMDDHHMM.

Creator—In this example, the full initials of the person creating the record. It could be a service/badge number, network login, or some other unique identifier.

The nomenclature for naming items or identifying them typically is tied to the organization producing the records. The important part is that the schema or nomenclature is designed and declared.

Time and date stamping is a critical issue in the creation, retrieval, and storage of evidence, and in particular, digital evidence and related records. Time stamps allow for the accurate reconstruction of events that have occurred to the items of interest or records about them. All computer systems within the laboratory should use a centralized time server that itself uses external time clocks to synchronize time. The common protocol for this is NTP (Network Time Protocol), whereby the main lab server would contact, on a regular basis, an external time clock that is maintaining UTC (coordinated universal time) or GMT (Greenwich Mean Time) via an atomic clock. All these interactions on the main server and clients where a change in time occurs should be logged and secured. One way to ensure that time is synchronized is to ensure that all client devices on the system query the central server when they log in and have their clocks synchronized to the internal source. In the case of workstations that are not network connected this will have to be done manually, recorded, and documented.

Within the case itself a three-pronged approach should be taken to verify all items of interest. For items of interest that are digital, cryptographic hashing is the commonly used method to verify and uniquely identify digital evidence artifacts. The use of a single hashing function is not best practice and the use of two sufficiently strong hashing algorithms such as MD5, SHA256 should be adopted. This process is required to ensure that the items of interest are uniquely verified and identified. For physical items the storage within an appropriate receptacle that can be sealed is required, and it also must have a physical log sheet or RFID tag or barcode (or similar electronic enabler) associated with it.

This process for identifying a human mandates the use of a user authentication system that validates and identifies that a user is, in fact, who they claim to be. This can be via a strong password, strong PIN (personal identification number), a biometric identifier, a smart card, digital signature, or multifactor authentication, which is a combination of two or more of the techniques to provide access. Multifactor authentication is best practice, and is easy to achieve with modern computing systems. The key is that the authentication does not become so cumbersome that is affects the productivity of the processes being undertaken.

The system should have sufficient levels or granularity to record the cause for a change in the state of a record. It would also be prudent to track who has read any record in the system, and any access to any record or item should be able to be traced. Where possible the use of an authentication system should be corroborated with, for instance, video surveillance footage of the laboratory area. Furthermore, the file system or system on which this record is stored should be able to identify who created the file and also who has accessed the file. On most file server operating systems such as Windows Server or Novell Server, file auditing should be enabled and archived. File auditing within these systems tracks all interactions with the files. Similarly if the computer-based record is held within a database structure, for instance, on a database (SQL) server, then likewise all relevant auditing should be enabled with the application, because typically these are run via a web interface that talks to the database system. One of the traps here is that the web server will write files to a storage drive normally with the privilege and identity of the user on the system who has permission to run the web server, which is unitary and universal for that web server.

Authority Verification and Validation

One of the most important concepts is the verification of authority within the chain of evidence/ continuity. A process or separate record should be able to demonstrate who created the initial record and any persons or processes that have since accessed or changed the initial record. Furthermore, the processes that do this must be validated and tested to ensure completeness of record and also integrity of process and the record.

The record itself should be stored in a system that makes it difficult to modify, change, delete, or even view a record without causing a logging or recording of this activity. This can be achieved by stringent file locking; that is, when a file is rewritten to disk a record is produced that stores the new filename. As mentioned before, modern network operating systems have the capability of tracking documents and changes and they also have well-established methods for stringent file locking. It is imperative that the systems that create, store, and maintain the records are not able to change or modify the audit trails; these should be stored securely on the originating device and also on a separate logging system/device. These methods of time stamping, auditing, and control are well established for systems that are connected to the network. However, much of the initial acquisition of potential evidence is undertaken off site.

For items of interest that are collected off site, the use of standardized and validated forms for entry of evidence is needed. The forms should be witnessed and provide as much detail as practicable and reasonable about the items of evidence. The use of a video or still camera to capture images of evidence within the scene is crucial.

Archiving and Availability

This is an increasingly complex and difficult process in the IT domain. Not only is the volume of information increasing but also the multitude of devices and formats in which it is stored. As mentioned previously in this book, evidence in some jurisdictions has to be preserved for a period of up to 75 years.

For physical artifacts such as paper, there are established standards and methods for ensuring preservation of the record. The technology to read paper, however, has not changed much (i.e., the eye). The storage medium is known and standard, typically cellulose-based paper, in both standardized sizes and weights (e.g., A4 80gsm). The format (i.e., the language) changes slowly. Compare this to digital evidence, which can be stored in a variety of formats and stored on a variety of media.

Magnetic-based media will decay over time. Also the media on which it is stored can also physically decay. For example magnetic tape will oxidize over time. The mechanisms such as the bearings within a drive mechanism may seize or fail to spin, capacitors or circuitry may fail. These issues will be dealt with in more depth in the next chapter.

Collection of Evidence

The previous sections dealt with the necessary systems and systems design requirements for the collection of evidence. This section will deal the actual physical collection of the items of interest that hopefully will become evidence. The process of collection is undertaken in several separate yet connected stages. These are known as on-site triage, transit, receipt, storage, and archiving.

On-Site Triage

On-site triage is involved with the collection of evidence from a crime or incident scene. One of the key methods to document actions taken is known more formally as contemporaneous notes. Contemporaneous notes are the complete, systematic, and chronological recording of any actions on the original electronic records or evidentiary copies. Individuals must make contemporaneous notes of any decision-making process, including information available, persons consulted, authorities sought, and reasons for the decision. These notes must record just the facts and not opinions or conjecture; it should be a true and accurate record of what has occurred. These notes can be either in paper-based form or in electronic form. The important fact is that the authenticity and authority of the record can be proven. For on-site triage, paper and photography is still an effective form of recording scene evidence in a fast and efficient manner. The resulting paper documents and scene photos can then be an evidence datum.

The collection of material should be done on paper-based forms that are consistent with the electronic record of which they are to be entered. For instance it would be ill-advised to omit critical elements that uniquely identify the evidence being collected. Similarly correct use of photography that includes numbers that uniquely identifies each item of interest is also required. Any photographs taken should also be linked to the item of interest on the form.

All items of interest should be stored in an appropriately labeled or identified receptacle or conveyance that uniquely identifies the item of interest and that clearly identifies the person creating the record and the person witnessing the record with the placement of a binding seal that protects the item of interest. The purpose of the seal is to ensure and also demonstrate that the item of interest has not been contaminated or corrupted during transit or storage, hence maintaining the continuity or chain of evidence.

The receptacle or conveyance should be sufficiently robust to protect the item from environmental extremes, physical damage, or from disintegrating in transit. As any of the items of interest that are acquired are typically subject to interference that can corrupt the state of the item, there is a need to ensure that the item is stored away from strong electrical currents, radio frequency emanations, or sources of magnetism. Environmental control is also important as extremes of temperature can also cause severe degradation of material of interest. The insides of automobiles can reach temperatures of 70°C or more in a matter of minutes on a summer day in the southern states or in the Mediterranean. Likewise extracted hard drives that are left exposed to the sun will also significantly increase in temperature, or conversely, ones exposed to subzero temperatures will freeze. It is worth noting that the casings of hard drives are typically aluminum, which is an excellent conductor of heat and electricity, both of which can affect the stability and integrity of magnetic fields and media.

Physical damage is an issue that must be also mitigated. Hard drives and many other digital components are susceptible to damage by shock that can result from dropping them onto a hard surface or some such similar event where a significant force is imparted on the item of interest. Where possible any drive or device being handled by an investigator should be secured at all times by placement and affixing it to a stable surface.

Evidence Transit

This is an important process in the life of any item of interest and one of the common instances where continuity can easily be broken. It is important that at no stage during the transit that intercession by a third party is possible. At all times the items of interest should be sufficiently supervised. As mentioned previously in this chapter the items of interest should be secured so as not to allow collisions or movement of items, and it should also be ensured that they are protected from high power electrical currents, radio frequency fields, or magnetic fields, and have appropriate environmental controls to regulate temperature.

In some cases it may be necessary that the device is connected to an external power source (e.g., a mobile phone, PDA, or similar mobile device that has finite power). In this type of case, it may mean that the power has to be self-contained within the receptacle or provided in the vehicle of transit. The powering of the device should be done again with due deference to not interfering with other items of interest as a result of production of electrical or magnetic emanation, and care should be taken that any mobile device that is turned on cannot receive a radio frequency signal.

Evidence Receipt

The receiving of the items of interest is one of the most crucial activities that will be undertaken. Improper or inaccurate receipt of items of interest at this stage can invalidate their presentation as evidence.

It is assumed that the building has a separate evidence receiving area. The receiving area, for want of a better description, is the organization's DMZ (demilitarized zone) or holding area between original inbound evidence, the evidence store, and working forensic copies for laboratory use. It is important that this organizational border is strictly secured and separated in both a physical and logical sense. This enforced separation allows greater control of continuity, reduces the margin for error, and should circumstances or events become a matter of dispute, audit and resolution of continuity issues should be easier to achieve.

All items of interest should be logged and receipted at this logical and physical border. Items should not move through to any other part of the business process until proper receipt of the items has occurred. For the purposes of this book, management of evidence collection "proper receipt" will include the processing of a record or item to produce an evidence copy or forensic copy of the original item. Collection is complete when there is a viable working forensic copy of an item for use in the laboratory that has full audit trail and chain of authority.

In an ideal world, we would like to verify hashes and apply forensic process to verify the integrity of items before accepting the goods; however, this is simply not practical or expedient in reality. However, we can control the process by which evidence crosses the "border" from one entity to another. The following is an outline of processes that should occur to ensure continuity and orderly collection of items of interest while maintaining separation. At this point it is assumed that the items of interest have crossed the physical threshold of the organization and are "in the building" at a physical manned receiving area.

1. **Verification of Ownership**. This process relates to the verification and validation of the identity of the person(s) submitting the items of interest, or the "who are you?" This process should as a minimum use one form of photographic identity and signature for a physically present individual. If the items are being couriered, make sure that you identify

the courier by full name, the courier company, and that the dispatching company or person is correct. Items should have a tracking number as well, which should be recorded. As tiresome as it is, even for internal staff, the process should ensure that correct identification and verification occurs every time.

2. **Checking of Items**. Substantiation and checking of the items presented is vital to ensure that you are taking receipt of the correct number of items and that they are uniquely and appropriately identified. Assurance should be undertaken to verify that the descriptions provided are a true and accurate record of the items presented. This should be contained in documentation about the items in question. Continuity seals should be checked for integrity; any breaks or abnormality should be recorded and documented via photography and contemporaneous notes. In the event of a break in a seal or any other abnormality, the matter should be escalated as a matter of urgency to the Laboratory Manager or relevant Case Manager.

3. **Item Reconciliation**. This is the process of entering the items into the internal system where the details of the items are recorded onto the system for use by the receiving organization. If the items are from your own organization, a simple yet necessary verification process should be undertaken to ensure that all details needed are recorded. In the case of paper records these should be used as the datum for all records. If the items are from an external organization, there has to be a reconciliation of the external record with the internal record details and requirements. In some cases this may involve further tagging or production of a new record(s); for instance, to uniquely identify each item. One such case could be that the organization delivering the items may have tagged a RAID box containing 15 drives as a single item. Your organization may wisely require that each drive is accounted for separately. Another example may simply be linking the existing case/item identifier to your records. These instances will really be uncovered only as a result of established custom and practice, however it is very important they are addressed. Organizations that exchange this sort of information will often do so on a regular basis. It is therefore a good idea to develop standard processes and procedure sheets in order for this reconciliation process to occur in a consistent and orderly manner.

4. **Processing of Items**. This requires that items of interest now should be initially processed where forensic copies of the original items are created and verified through standard forensic practices such as disk imaging, file copying, or photographic reproduction. Upon verification and logging of a forensic copy, the original item is logged, resealed, and secured in the evidence storage area. The forensic copy then can be fed into the normal investigative processes of the laboratory.

Procedural Documentation

Finally, procedure plays a large part in making sure that no errors or omissions are made. Standardized operating procedures should be developed for each common instance of evidence collection that is encountered. The use of standardized procedures reduces the possibility of an error occurring through the constant reinforcement and repetition of the process; that is, you are less likely to forget or omit steps in the process. The following are basic procedures or forms needed for the orderly and proper collection of evidence.

1. On-site triage/crime scene procedures:

   a. Initial Scene Documentation—A procedure to initially document the site prior to collecting evidence. This involves the use of notes or video and photographs to document the scene.

   b. Tagging of Items—A procedure to initially tag and identify items of interest. This involves the production of a procedure that identifies the items to be labeled in a manner that is consistent and relates directly to any systems in use at the laboratory.

   c. Initial Processing (Scene/Site)—Procedures to allow for the orderly removal of items from the scene. These will be different for each generic device found. As a minimum the following should be covered:

      - Desktop computer
      - Laptop computer
      - Mobile phone
      - PDA
      - USB memory devices
      - Embedded devices (iPODs, MP3 players, routers)

This should include the procedure to securely package each of the devices for transport.

   d. Transportation Protocols—The procedures for transporting the items to the laboratory facility. This should cover the minimum mandatory requirements for secure/escorted transportation back to the laboratory to maintain continuity.

2. Laboratory procedures:

   a. Receiving and receipt—Procedures to ensure the correct receiving of items from the site or external party.

   b. Reconciliation—This should be done as a separate process to reconcile the items into the internal system.

   c. Creation of forensic copies and storage of original items—These procedures are how to deal with each item to create a working forensic copy for laboratory use. Again as a minimum, the following should be covered:

      - Desktop computer
      - Laptop computer
      - Mobile phone
      - PDA
      - USB memory devices
      - Embedded devices (iPODs, MP3 players, routers)

The final phase is the secure storage of the original item in an evidence room or safe.

Conclusion

The collection and management of items that eventually become evidence is a complex task and one that is demanding and exacting. The basic tenet of forensics is the preservation of the original evidence with minimal or no change to its state. If any change has occurred, then the why, who, and when should be recorded. It is imperative that any procedures or processes developed to handle potential evidence must ensure that each event, process or change that has occurred to the item in question can be audited, authenticated and established. These processes and procedures must also be able to be accounted for within an accurate chronology of events within the context of the case and beyond a reasonable doubt. Failure to do otherwise may see the evidence dismissed from court.

Although the staff within the laboratory must be involved in the production of the appropriate policy and procedures, it is the responsibility of the manager to own them. The manager must decide which of the options (and there will normally be several) is the best and must ensure that all staff follow the policy and procedures. If you don't, you do not have either policy or procedures, you have anarchy and the laboratory will not maintain its credibility for very long.

Management of Evidence Storage

Introduction

This chapter will address the issues that relate to the storage of evidence and the management issues that need to be considered to ensure that it is carried out effectively and that it meets the relevant rules and legislation. We will also address the difficult question of long term storage periods, a particular problem for law enforcement.

Cyber crime or electronically initiated crimes are merely streams of bits of data that may or may not be physically recorded. Unlike conventional crime artifacts like a crowbar, handgun, or knife, digital artifacts are readily changeable, volatile, and easily destroyed. To obliterate an incriminating file is relatively easy with the use of an erasure program or a strong magnetic field. Even more sinister is that digital evidence can be modified or tampered with little trace being left. Evidence storage and in particular preservation is one of the areas that often remain unaddressed even in established organizations dealing with electronic evidence. For traditional crimes there are established procedures for dealing with the physical evidence, and these systems and methods apply to confiscated hardware but rarely are translated to electronically stored evidence.

One of the problems with electronic evidence and its processing is its seemingly unquenchable thirst for secondary memory storage. Take for example a one-terabyte hard disk; the item itself is physically small, but its digital equivalency is by current standards not a small or trivial task to process, move, and store. There will typically be as many as two or more instances of the image of the drive being available on the digital forensics laboratory evidence storage system. There would be the original forensic copy that is verified against the physical device (which would be stored in a physical evidence locker, room, or vault) and any subsequent validated working copies of the original forensic copy. The original forensic copy may be burnt to DVD using a Rimage or a similar imaging device. In the case of a 1TB drive this would mean that now there would be in the region of 250 DVDs associated with this one case. Even as newer technologies such as BluRay emerge at around 50GB burn size per disk, this would still mean around 20 disks that have to be verified, catalogued, stored, and archived.

The next issue is that of the analysis of the forensic copies themselves. Efficiently moving and monitoring the movement of large quantities of data pushes modern computing systems, including the personnel that are part of that system, to their limits. The example previously given of a 1TB drive would have to sit on a 1TB or larger mechanism and be accessible in a timely fashion to team members for analysis. This has significant impact on capital investment in terms of hardware, management, and the personnel to carry out the analysis of the data. Finally, on completion of the analysis, the disposition or archiving of the material must take place and this again can be a complex and involved task. These issues will be examined in the following section.

Management of Evidence Storage

As mentioned in the introduction, there are well-established guidelines and standards for this type of evidence and the type of security that is required for such a facility. The American Society for Testing and Materials (ASTM) E 1492 – 05 *Standard Practice for Receiving, Documenting, Storing, and Retrieving Evidence in a Forensic Science Laboratory* contains a short section on the storage of evidence. This can be summarized as follows:

- A storage area should provide the ability to protect and store evidence in a manner that is orderly, traceable, and retrievable while preserving the integrity of the evidence.

- The evidence storage areas must be secured from unauthorized entry or tampering.

- A proper accessible and accurate record must be kept for evidence egress and ingress into the storage area.

- A routine maintenance system for the contents of the evidence must be established.

- A documented disposal regime is also to be put in place for evidence in the storage area.

Many of the aims and requirements of the standard can be replicated with electronic evidence by the application of logical and physical controls to the storage facilities used for electronic evidence. Logical access controls can be provided by most modern operating systems through the access rights or ACL (access control lists). Further logical control can be provided by the incorporation of biometric identification methods into these access control measures provided by the operating systems. Physical controls are the traditional barriers that we commonly use, such as locked doors.

In addition to the requirements of ASTM E 1492 – 05 and other established storage protocols for digital media (electronic evidence) facilities there are additional specific requirements for the protection of evidence. These requirements are as follows:

1. The facility should use environmental controls and have an ambient temperature of between 15 and 20°C. This should be refrigerated air-conditioning, not evaporative, and have 0% humidity.

2. It should have a dust-free environment.

3. It should be well away from large electrical conduits or magnetic fields.

4. Fire control should be by oxygen deprivation, not a sprinkler system.

5. It should not be located near any source of vibration (on the edge of the building near a busy road).

6. The facility should be not near sources of direct ultraviolet light (e.g., the sun). This is because ultraviolet light can rapidly degrade some optical and magnetic media.

Electronic evidence that currently is being examined may actually be stored in large disk arrays that are normally mounted in 19" computer racks, but access to these arrays should be restricted. Where possible these racks should be separated from the other operational areas of the digital forensic laboratory IT infrastructure and in their own separate room. Access to these racks should be through several physical barriers, of which at least two should have strong authentication and authorization controls. These controls can be swipe card access, punch codes on doors, biometrics, or controlled conventional hard keys. Access to the data in these racks also should be managed by running it on a physically isolated internal network.

The other type of storage area is the more traditional evidence storage area. This ideally should be fitted with industrial strength shelves, and racking should be provided because physical computers, RAID hard disk packs, or even CD and DVDs packed densely can have a considerable weight. These shelves also preferably should have lockable doors or gates on them to prevent removal of evidence items. The keys for these doors or gates should be security controlled and logged at all times. This room should have the same stringent authentication and authorization controls in place. Both types of facility should also have CCTV and automatic lighting that is activated as someone enters the area.

Managing Electronic Evidence Storage

There are distinct phases in the life of electronic evidence that each have specific storage requirements. The management of the collection of evidence has been dealt with in Chapter 11. This chapter is concerned primarily with the management of electronic evidence within the analysis and archiving stages of its lifecycle. There is a significant and sustained trend of increases in the volume and size of evidence artifacts as computing and associated technology continues to advance. Principally, digital forensics involves the analysis and interpretation of data that is stored on secondary memory devices, for example hard disks, USB thumb drives, floppy disks, and flash memory cards. The capacities of these devices has been seen to increase markedly within a five-year time span. To illustrate this fact, it was in 1980 that the first gigabyte capacity drive was produced by IBM. It was the size of a refrigerator, and when Seagate released the ST506 drive for microcomputers it was a whopping 5 Megabytes. We now have 1.5 Terabyte drives, which represents three orders of magnitude of change in the size in less than 30 years. A parallel for this, using the modern automobile's fuel tank and economy as an analogy, would mean that a 1980 car that consumed two gallons to travel 60 miles now, for the same two gallons, would be able to travel 6000 miles.

Electronic Evidence Management for Analysis

In this section, we are dealing with an item of evidence that has been entered into the case management system being used by the organization that is live or active for analysis/investigation. As explained in the previous chapter this means that a forensic copy has been taken from the original evidence, which is now stored in a secure evidence facility. What we are addressing in this phase is what will ultimately become the complete electronic record for the presentation of evidence in court. This complete record incorporates the physical evidence copy and any associated contemporaneous notes, details of the analysis, any findings and tests that have been undertaken on that particular evidence copy during the time it has been held as live evidence.

As mentioned in Chapter 11, much of the auditing that is necessary to track who has opened, viewed, saved, edited, or modified the file in any way is capable of being competently undertaken by the modern operating systems used by the client PC and network devices such as servers and network accessible storage (NAS). The major requirement for the laboratory manager is to ensure that this auditing is enabled and that it is periodically and systematically checked for compliance. It is also important that the ability to uniquely identify each person who accesses the material must do so through the proper authentication methods and that a record of this is maintained.

Movement of Electronic Evidence

One of the more demanding and computing resource intensive activities is the movement and processing of electronic evidence throughout a digital forensics laboratory. Conventional network bandwidth currently has a theoretical limit of 1 Gbit per second, but the reality of modern Ethernet networks and the de facto standard of the TCP/IP protocol suite means that the transfer rates are at best 30 to 40% of this 1 Gbit per second limit. This means that an effective optimal transfer rate is between 30 to 40 MB a second. Add to this the fact that this is a shared resource among all the analysts and you start to see some of the problems associated with moving large amounts of data around the organization using the network conduits.

Even when moving data from hard drive to hard drive, some of the volumes of data that need to be copied are considerable, and it will take a relatively long time to complete the process due to machine-based performance bottlenecks. This movement of evidence within the laboratory is not simply a matter of copying from one drive to another because there are intensive computing tasks required between each copy in order to maintain continuity. This includes the hashing, verification, and logging that prove that the copy itself is a complete, accurate, and true record of the original from which it came, and all this takes time. None of these issues are trivial, and they must be taken into account when processing evidence and more importantly when planning the supporting infrastructure for the analysis of digital evidence.

Policies and procedures will need to be developed with respect to the movement and access to artifacts within the organization. The procedure(s) in particular will take refinement within your organizational context to find an optimized outcome. There is no one golden solution and much of this will be determined by the business need. Some generic points to consider are:

1. How do you account for copies of copies? Is there a limit on the number of working copies?

2. Who is responsible for creation of copies, logging of copies, distribution, and eventual deletion?

3. How are these copies transported? Via network file transfer? Hardware transfer?

Intraorganizational management is also an issue. From time to time it will be necessary to surrender copies of analysis material to other organizations or individuals either for further investigation, peer review, or analysis by an adversarial expert. There is little except nondisclosure forms and tracking details that can be used here to protect the data. It is advisable however to securely package the evidence and preferably hand it over to the other party at your laboratory. A signature and demonstration of photo identification (which should be copied) should also be taken. Wherever possible you should avoid delivery of the material via third person.

Availability versus Viability

In an ideal world, high-speed access to data would be cheap, commonplace, and limitless, but sadly we don't live in an ideal world! High-speed devices are expensive and will rapidly become obsolete, however they are a necessary evil if you want your laboratory to process and manage evidence effectively and profitably. Forensic workstations are the best place for these devices, although to place high-speed drives and controllers in all workstations can be an expensive exercise. However, the cost of your competent forensic analyst being unproductive should not be underestimated. If your teams are delayed for 15 to 30 minutes every working day due to slow equipment this equates to 10 hours a month per person downtime. If you calculate the revenue loss this represents, the price of high performance computers that could reduce this by even 30% starts to seem attractive.

A further element in the solution to this problem is the use of a network-based caching system whereby data that is needed for active analysis is stored on high-speed, cutting edge devices where there is the least amount of latency for availability. Other queued materials are placed on cheaper, lower speed devices and can be copied to the high-speed devices during operational downtime. Further refinement could be achieved by placing intensive tasks such as disk indexing onto the high performance machines and leaving lower powered machines for review or lighter tasks. This approach will involve active case management and planning on the part of the laboratory manager and the team but will result in higher productivity with lower financial overheads.

Archival Phase

Once the case has concluded, the evidence can be moved from a live system to an archival storage facility. It may seem a relatively simple process to copy data to some permanent media, catalogue it, place it in a receptacle, and switch off the light on your way out of the room. This is an all-too-accurate record of what already occurs in certain organizations and hence why they end up with a deteriorating digital archive. Archive management is a continuous and ongoing process that needs to be integrated into the complete business plan for a digital forensics laboratory.

Computing and the arena of digital devices is moving at an almost geometric rate in terms of change. The first problem that this presents for a digital forensics laboratory is that of obsolescence or the ageing of the technology. The following section will address solutions that commonly are used for archiving digital media.

Magnetic Tape

Tape drives were some of the first types of secondary memory systems ever used for computer systems. Tape drives today are still used for large scale archival storage due to their relative low cost and good working speeds. One of the strategies for archival material that you might employ from an IT perspective is the archiving of material to comparatively large backup tapes. The problem with this approach is that every three to five years a newer technology arrives, with greater capacity and better speeds. This normally means that the new drives are purchased when server rollout or replacement occurs. This now presents the organization with the problem of what to do with the petabytes or pentabytes of archival tapes sitting on the shelf in the old format. Most organizations do not currently think in those terms, but for a digital forensics laboratory this is not an option as the preservation of evidence is paramount. There are two obvious options available, the first of which is to archive the backup system hardware and supporting software with the old media. The second option is to transfer all the backed up data to the new system and media. The correct option for a digital forensics laboratory is the second option. The reason that the first option is not a good alternative is that, over time, magnetic media will decay through the process of oxidization and other chemically induced breakdowns. This deterioration of the media itself can be in either the actual magnetic/storage layer or the supporting substrates of plastic film on which the data is stored. Also, over time the hardware itself will start to deteriorate and eventually fail through lack of use, possible as a result of poor maintenance or simple component tolerances.

Given the long times that are mandated during which the evidence has to be maintained, the only current option for a digital forensics laboratory is the transferring, verification, and logging of its existing data on a given tape platform to new media. This is one area where the constant changing of computing and IT capacities in storage make it actually cheaper to store evidence. There is, however, the cost in terms of hardware for the new tapes and also the labor for the transferring, validating, and logging of the evidence.

Optical Media: CD, DVD, BluRay

When CD technology first came out it was reported as being indestructible and a permanent solution for storage. With the passage of time, as with all new technologies, there has been an intersection of sales hyperbole and physical reality. CD technology, when it first arrived at an affordable level, was capable of storing 650 MB of data when conventional desktop computers typically had drives of 20 to 60 MB capacity. Existing hard disk capacities have now well exceeded this technology. Similarly for DVD technology the same has now occurred and hard drive capacities are starting to even outstrip emergent BluRay technology. Optical media, however, is one of the best solutions currently available for long-term archival storage for digital forensics.

One of the common problems with this form of technology is the ability to accurately estimate the longevity of the media. The layers that are used for the recording of the data on optical media are subject to the perils of oxidization in the same way as magnetic tapes.

A current industry norm is that it takes five years for CD or DVD media to start to deteriorate, delaminate, rot, or give trouble. This figure has reemerged at various times since the discovery of the issues related to the deterioration of the recording layers. This issue is a serious one and there are now published standards for estimating the longevity of CD media (ISO18921 and 18927). It should be noted, however, that these are simply models for estimating the longevity of the media. If you lose one bit of data in a digital recording of a song the impacts are relatively minor, but for digital forensics a one-data-bit change can invalidate the hashing checksums and make the remnant evidence possibly invalid.

Consistent in the literature relating to this issue of optical media longevity is that the quality of the physical media production is one of the major determining factors. It is therefore important when purchasing media for use in optical drives for archiving that the best quality media be sought for use in the process. The other critical factor is adequate environmental control to reduce temperature change, eliminate humidity, and reduce exposure to UV light. The optimal temperatures and humidity levels are the same as for conventional IT equipment. The reduction in the levels of UV light can be achieved by simply making sure that the optical media is stored away from sources of direct UV light and preferably stored in a wrapping or receptacle that eliminates light. The current wisdom is that the CD or DVD of good quality can be relied upon for 20 to 50 years if stored properly.

Large Disk Drive Clusters (RAID, NAS)

RAID, NAS, and SAN are basically large assemblies or clusters of commodity hard drive mechanisms. These technologies typically are set up to provide some redundancy, however hard disk drives also have a finite lifetime. They also have significant power and space implications for a digital forensics laboratory. They typically are used for high availability applications and are not the most suitable for deployment as an archival solution mainly due to the large setup costs and the ongoing maintenance required for the equipment. This may change as solid-state memory capacities start to increase and become cheaper.

Management and Maintenance of the Archival Storage

Having decided on the type of media on which to store your archival material, the next phase is to determine a management plan and support systems for the archive. The management plan should include what material is to be archived, how is to be stored and maintained, and then, ultimately, expired from the archive. The overall management system for electronic evidence should actually take into account the archival needs. A management system would ideally have a facility to progress cases from active to archive while still keeping the records intact, accessible, and maintaining the strict authority and authentication required to maintain continuity for evidentiary purposes.

One of the problems that is unique to law enforcement is the long-term storage of archival material. Some jurisdictions mandate as long as 75 years after the sentence has been handed down for the material to be kept, when even storage for periods of five or seven years still presents a significant problem for organizations.

The first major issue to overcome is how the archives are to be managed. The management of archives is a specialist skill and for large organizations the hiring of a specialist archivist/librarian may be warranted. Large organizations will produce considerable volumes of archival material that has to be catalogued correctly, stored, and preserved. This is not within the normal skill set of a digital forensic practitioner. This archival material may actually include the physical devices in addition to the electronic record. The impetus behind the archiving of the case record(s) is so that they can be retrieved at a later date, for example to reexamine the specific case as a result of appeal proceedings. Archival material may also be used in the investigation of other crimes or incidents that, at the time of the original incident, were not related but now are. The material may also be subject to analysis and study for the purposes of improving outcomes for law enforcement or the profession in general.

Maintenance of archive is a key issue and, as previously mentioned, optical media may last for 50 years at the maximum. If any data is to be preserved accurately then maintenance is a necessary phase in the preservation of the record. This may involve the periodic testing of archival samples for deterioration to ensure that the records are still in an accessible form. In some cases it may eventually require the moving of the archival material onto a new media format, as was highlighted previously as an issue when using tapes for archival purposes.

In the case of those jurisdictions that mandate long periods of retention this will involve significant costs to maintain and preserve the archive. It should be noted that these costs are in addition to the existing base costs that should already have been factored in for the storage of the material within a safe, secure, and environmentally controlled facility. Remember that not only must the electronic record be preserved but also the equipment on which it was produced. This equipment must also be maintained in good working order and tested on a regular basis.

One key phase of archive management is the deletion and destruction of redundant records. As mentioned previously, the record should have been catalogued and should be readily retrievable and accessible. At some stage the record itself will become redundant and will need to be completely removed from the system and the archive as it is no longer required. The record may require subsequent destruction or further archiving in a long-term archival facility. This can be simply managed by completing a redundancy cycle every quarter from which all expired records are extracted from the archive. Should a record require destruction then this would have to be carried out in accordance with any legislative requirements.

Conclusions

The management of evidence at any time is an involved task that is fraught with complexities and pitfalls. Continuity of evidence is paramount and any piece of potential evidence must be accounted for and be able to be tracked at any time up until its eventual disposal.

Digital evidence has its own endemic issues such as volatility, transportability, and long-term retention on potentially problematic media. It does however also have some benefits in that there is a relatively easy method of verification and validation of its integrity via hashing. The evidence is easily replicated and copied for examination and relatively easy to transport in a reliable form.

As with physical evidence, the creation and utilization of sound and robust systems to manage the storage of evidence is not to be underestimated. The adoption of stringent audit and compliance procedures is also essential. However, unlike conventional evidence, digital evidence also requires strict logical IT controls that restrict, track, and monitor access to electronic evidence. A stable, high-speed IT infrastructure and careful ongoing maintenance and planning of the same can bring significant advantage in terms of speed and the resolution of cases.

Finally, the archiving of electronic evidence presents some unique problems due to the relative immaturity of the technologies involved, as well as creating the appropriate environment for containment and security. When you consider that paper has been around since the Egyptian era and we still are getting the management and handling of that wrong, we can assume that there is still a significant amount to be learned in the handling and management of digital media. The best that we can do, as with all evidence storage, is the prudent application of the best available science at the time to protect and preserve it.

Chapter 13

Quality Assurance

Introduction

This chapter will address the vitally important issue of Quality Assurance (QA) and will describe when it should be carried out, who should do it, and to what standards.

Quality assurance is a vital task in any modern digital forensics laboratory. QA, as it is sometimes colloquially referred to, is a planned, systematic set of actions to provide an assurance that a product or service will satisfy the requirements for quality. Forensic science is the application of scientific method to determine facts for presentation in court as evidence. Considering that some of these courts will impose long custodial sentences or the death sentence there is no greater argument for stringent quality assurance. All parts of the digital forensic process should be subject to rigorous and continuous quality assurance processes to ensure that all processes are carried out to the highest quality and standard possible. QA is also an integral part of the process improvement, which in the long term should save the organization time, effort, and money.

Forensics is embedded in a scientific tradition of proof by scientific methods and techniques to create evidence via stringent peer review. This is not in with QA, but rather they compliment each other. QA should occur across all three phases of digital forensics activity, namely acquisition, analysis, and presentation. The three components that need to be subject to quality assurance in any digital forensic process are the software, the hardware, and the personnel/processes.

What Is Assurance?

Assurance is the process of validating, testing, or verifying that a particular process functions as specified or completes in the way that was intended. This is normally achieved by the application of testing procedures to a given context or set of variables. The tests are applied to assure that the process or functions perform as specified within the given operational or acceptable limits.

What Is Quality?

Digital forensics has its own intrinsic metric of quality that is the analysis of the case, which produces evidence that is able to be admitted into court and withstand cross examination. Quality is a measure of the output of an organization that is produced as a result of the implementation of its procedures and policies, processes, and people in the course of their work. Quality does not really occur naturally but is constructed as a result of planning, preparation, and performance. In an organization this works only when there are efficient management systems in place to maintain a focus on producing a quality outcome that addresses the three aspects of planning, preparation, and performance.

One of the applicable quality-related standards or models is ISO 17025 *General requirements for the competence of testing and calibration laboratories*, which specifies the requirements for the competence to carry out tests and calibrations, which is largely what a digital forensics laboratory does. There are 15 management requirements and 10 technical requirements that are specified in the standard for compliance. The requirements outline what a laboratory must do to become accredited and some digital forensic laboratories in fact are trying to achieve ISO 17025 accreditation. The standard refers to and revolves around a management system—an organization's structure for managing its processes or activities that turn inputs into a product or service that meets the organization's objectives. In this case, it means the production of evidence that must be suitable for presentation in court. There are others that would fall into the scope of the intent of the standards such as satisfying the customer's quality requirements, and complying with laws and regulations.

Another suitable model that can be used in a quality paradigm is the Capability Maturity Model (CMM) and its newer incarnation, the Capability Maturity Model Integration (CMMI). These models are based around continual improvement of quality outcomes with a focus on improving organizational capability while allowing a progression in maturity. The landscape is littered with other quality programs such as TQM and ISO 9001, the goal of which is ultimately the enforcement or development of a management structure to plan, prepare, and produce a quality outcome.

Fundamentally, these systems and standards can be summarized as the Shewart Cycle, made popular by Deming, which is PDCA (Plan, Do, Check, Act) or its various other incantations:

- Plan—Establish the objectives and processes necessary to deliver outcomes.

- Do—Implement the processes.

- Check—Monitor and evaluate the processes and results.

- Act—Apply actions to the outcome for necessary improvement, reviewing all steps (Plan, Do, Check, Act), and modifying the process to improve it before its next implementation.

The Shewart Cycle in reality looks a lot like the cycle Francis Bacon started using around 1620 and is now known as the scientific method. The only fundamental difference between the scientific method and many of these quality processes systems and standards is that they have a substantive management architecture to support the PDCA approach.

Regardless of which system becomes your chosen organizational mantra, the first step in producing quality outcomes is the understanding of what a quality outcome is for your organizational context. This understanding is achieved only through the use of cogent policy statements that describe what the quality aims are. These strategic aims then turn into practical procedural documentation and actions to achieve that quality. The ISO 17025 standard in Section 4.2.2 further defines the minimum requirements for a quality policy statement indicating that it should have top level management endorsement and be contained within a document of its own standing. The minimum requirements are:

1. The laboratory management's commitment to good professional practice and to the quality of its testing and calibration in servicing its customers.

2. The management's statement of the laboratory's standard of service.

3. The purpose of the management system related to quality.

4. A requirement that all personnel concerned with testing and calibration activities within the laboratory familiarize themselves with the quality documentation and implement the policies and procedures in their work.

5. The laboratory management's commitment to comply with this International Standard and to continually improve the effectiveness of the management system.

Underpinning a policy statement such as this is the production of suitable procedural documentation that aligns to the quality policy. This procedural documentation should be aligned with the tasks that are undertaken within the organization that should have the PDCA cycle or similar cycle enforced upon them. In the case of a digital forensics laboratory this procedure is within the areas of acquisition of evidence, analysis of evidence, and presentation of evidence.

Separate and apart from the actual production processes, the underlying supporting infrastructure that is used in the production processes itself needs quality assurance processes undertaken upon it. This infrastructure includes all hardware and software used within the facility. This hardware and software should also be subject to various quality assurance tests to ensure the software and hardware is operating as specified. The other often forgotten part of a system is "wetware" or the human elements that also need quality assurance performed on them.

Finally on top of all of the processes, software, hardware, and wetware, should be a comprehensive set of supporting documentation. The documentation of processes and procedures is vital, as is documentation of the processes of review and structuring of tests that will be applied to assure quality.

QA in Digital Forensic Acquisition

Acquisition is one of the most critical steps in the digital forensic process. If acquisition is not carried out correctly, there is often little that can be done to recover the situation. The acquisition process is based on a very simple principle, which is to obtain a forensic copy of the original evidence without changing the state of the original evidence or using the principle of least intrusion or destruction. This typically means applying a standard procedure, using verified tools to produce a verified forensic copy. The processes and tools each need quality assurance processes applied rigorously to them. Likewise the personnel need testing in proficiency of use for these tools.

- Acquisition should be conducted only through the use of documented procedures, using verified tools operated by proficient personnel, that are peer reviewed and tested.

- External validation of these processes is also a very good idea and for some laboratories may be a requirement.

- The processes themselves should use standardized documentation for the production of reports.

- The processes and documentation should be subject to regular review.

The QA involved in the acquisition phase should be a relatively simple process. The procedure for acquiring an image of a hard disk, for example, should rarely change. The main focus here will be on assuring that procedure has been followed rigorously and that this can be readily substantiated using valid science. In addition, the software and hardware tools and the personnel should be subjected to relevant standards of verification and proficiency.

QA of the Analysis Phase

Documented processes should also be applied to the analysis phase using verified tools and methods to extract evidence from forensic copies of the material. This phase is the largest and the most problematic for quality assurance within the digital forensics paradigm. This problem relates back to the entropy within the IT industry. Software developers are constantly changing the parameters by which programs operate. As hardware operating platforms are released so too are operating system platforms and then application platforms that take advantage of the "new" features. This means that proven and validated methods that were once effective quickly become redundant or in need of serious revision or in some cases will simply fail to work on the new hardware.

There are some basics that thankfully remain reasonably static; these are file system formats onto which data is stored. Processes and procedures for file system related tasks should likewise be less entropic. However, they should still be subject to review as a result of patching or other changes to the operating system that may affect its file system formats or how it writes the file system to the storage media.

Most of the effort in this stage is quality assurance that verifies the results obtained from various software tools used in the analysis of digital evidence, and will be dealt with later in the chapter. Critical once again in the analysis phase is the use of standardized forms and documentation to record any actions underpinned by sound scientific processes.

QA for the Evidence Presentation

The final phase is the presentation of evidence either to the customer or in a court of law. Quality assurance is achieved in this phase first by rigorous peer review of reports and analysis conducted during the analysis phase. Second, feedback from customers and court processes is also important as there is little point in producing reports or analysis that do not meet the customers requirements or fail to be entered as evidence in court processes.

QA for Software

Software tools are the mainstay of the digital forensic process, replete with all the associated benefits and drawbacks. Software used on a typical computer system can be divided into two main areas. These are application systems (EnCase, FTK, Autopsy, Paraben Device Seizure, etc.) and operating systems (Windows XP, Windows Vista, Linux, MacOS X).

Operating systems are the underlying systems onto which everything else is built and are relied upon to be stable. Operating systems should be tightly controlled via a standard operating environment methodology that creates a stable version of a particular operating system to use within the laboratory environment. The resultant standard operating environment (SOE) can be verified using a range of tools and methods to ensure that the operating environment is stable and uses certified drivers. Most operating system manufacturers have programs that certify drivers and equipment for use with their operating systems. The exception to this rule is open source software such as some Linux-based distributions that typically do not have these programs. At all times certified drivers should be the only ones deployed on an SOE for use. It is also important that this is a fully documented installation and that all levels of patches applied and service packs are recorded and documented. An SOE in software takes considerable time to develop and should be revised every six to 12 months at the most.

To be effective, the use of an SOE for software also really mandates the use of standard operating environments for computing hardware. Preferably all computers of a particular generation within an organization should be built in exactly the same way. This is where the main boards, processors, network cards, video cards, RAM, and hard disk controllers are all certified to work with one another and are the same for each computer. In some organizations this will not be practical for all their systems and when this occurs they can be dealt with in several batches. This will require the creation and maintenance of multiple copies of documentation for each particular identified operating platform.

This standardization of platform helps a quality agenda in several ways. The maintenance and revision can be planned and is not ad-hoc in nature (i.e., each machine becoming an exception to the rule due to disparate hardware or software). The use of SOE also performs a vital assurance function for this.

A proper standard operating environment should contain not only the underlying operating system but also all the required application software to be built to a known patch level. This may go down to the level of the desktop on each computer looking exactly the same. This means that staff then are focused on the outcome and procedure in front of them rather than trying to decipher someone else's computer desktop to perform a task.

The applications or the level of patching for either the operating system or the applications should not change until they have been tested and validated to work. For each piece of software that is being deployed there should be standardized tests to ensure that the software functions as prescribed. This will require the production of known goods or metrics to be used for testing of the software function; some organizations already provide tested samples for this purpose. These types of sample are used to test proper copying, validation, and extraction of evidence using digital forensic tools.

It is important that the tests actually check for the correct functioning of the software under standard work or operating conditions. It is also important that the tests relate specifically to the functions that the software is required to perform, in the particular roles within the organization. There would be little value in rigorously testing the hyphenation qualities of a word processing program when that feature is actually turned off in the preferences and never used.

One of the problems of validation and verification is that, if a complete software suite was to be fully tested, it would cost significant amounts of time, money, and effort to test, and potentially would cost millions of dollars for a piece of complex forensic software such as EnCase, FTK, or Autopsy. Forensic software is complex and has many functions that may not be used within a particular role or function, or laboratory for that matter. Also computer systems and software are a reasonably fast-moving problem when compared to other traditional forensic laboratory equipment such as a test tube or burette. The underlying foundation software that is the operating system may change as a result of necessary patches to secure the machines or remedy critical errors. Similarly the application software may itself have patches that need to be applied to correct problems with the software. There is a double-edged sword within application software that may see changes being mandatory as a result of changes to the patch level of the underlying operating system. These issues are often complex and resolving it can result in significant testing and verification of the various systems.

Although ISO 17025 and other verification, validation, or testing frameworks almost all typically mandate the complete testing of components, it is simply not currently achievable within IT and related areas due to significant ongoing developmental change within the area and the complexity of systems. This problem, however, does not remove the need to assure key processes that are undertaken within the digital forensics laboratory environment with software. There are key processes that utilize software that are fundamental to maintaining continuity and the extraction of evidence. It is critical that these processes are subject to rigorous quality assurance. These include:

- Any software that requires a forensic copy of a device or artifact

- Any software that produces a checksum, timestamp, or similar device that is used to verify or validate an artifact

- Any software that extracts data from an abstract structure; for example a chat log

To test and verify software such as this, an approach called blackbox testing can be undertaken. This type of testing involves the production of a known sample that contains known artifacts that this tested software should be able to extract or process without error. For tests where the software is producing checksums or timestamps these can be performed and then verified by matching the results against other known good sources. The range of testing should test across the scope of uses and activities the software would undertake in the course of conducting investigations within the digital forensics laboratory. It is also productive with this type of testing to use known goods from other reliable sources such as other digital forensics laboratory and certifying institutions. Support organizations such as the National institute for Standards and Technology (NIST) has the Computer Forensic Tool Testing (CFTT) project to establish a usable methodology for testing computer forensic software tools by development of general tool specifications, test procedures, test criteria, test sets, and test hardware. They have developed extensive guides for testing of disk imaging, write blockers (software and hardware), deleted file recovery (carving), searching, and indexing. These types of guides should be used in developing testing procedures for quality assurance of software.

QA of Hardware

Operational hardware such as write blockers, hard disk caddies, hard disk drives, and combined systems such as desktop computers need regular and complete testing. Unlike specialist software, digital forensic specialist hardware typically has been verified and certified to work to a particular level or standard. This does not however remove the need for it to be tested for faults. In most instances, testing and verification is a less arduous task as you are dealing with devices embedded in silicon.

For hard drives:

- Hard disk drives used for analysis should be tested for faults on a regular basis with vendor certified diagnostic tools.

- Any hard disk that is used for the storage of forensic images should be zeroed and this should have confirmation tests performed on the drive before any new images are written to it.

For write blockers and disk imagers:

- This type of equipment should be tested on a regular basis to verify correct operation. This should ideally be performed before attachment to any original evidence.

- This type of hardware should be able to copy and image known goods without failure or error. They should be periodically bench tested.

For computers and workstations:

- Periodically diagnostics should run on the hardware in the computers. This includes the main board, the RAM, and the hard disk. Most quality vendors supply diagnostic utilities with their components.

Regular testing of these mechanisms should be embedded into any QA management system used in the digital forensic laboratory, again leveraging guides from security organizations like NIST or CERT to help formulate context relevant tests.

Process QA

This is quality assurance of process whereby each of the individual processes are examined, reviewed, and hopefully improved. Review of process should ideally be undertaken independently of any hardware or software issues. This involves critique of processes that are undertaken in the laboratory to produce an outcome by suitably qualified experts.

QA of the Documentation

Documentation is the method by which we as humans transfer information, knowledge, and experience to one another. The documentation process is a fundamental undertaking that is often poorly executed by most organizations. Within a digital forensics laboratory there must be stringent quality checking of any documentation that is produced and management systems should strictly enforce the use of documentation, its review, and its reuse.

QA of Process Documentation

This form of documentation is concerned with the processes and procedures that are undertaken within a given task context. This documentation should include generic procedures for tasks such as the acquisition of a hard drive, the acquisition of a mobile device, how to extract information from a USB mechanism. This generic documentation will rarely need to change if it is set up properly.

Then there would be documentation based on these processes that would note specific exclusions, oddities exemptions to the generic steps that you would take to perform a particular task. These can be incorporated in to the main documentation, but it is far more expedient, efficient and productive to produce them as appendices to the main core documentation. By using a system of appendices it allows appendices to be retired or revised as required without disrupting the core process documentation.

The aim here is to produce comprehensive documentation that will allow a quality outcome with a minimum of disruption to workflow and which can produce the correct output to the required standard or burden of proof. Documentation is a living process and it should at all times be subject to scrutiny and revision to produce better and higher quality outcomes.

This process documentation is separate to the case based documentation. It should be tightly revision controlled and periodically revised by internal and external entities for completeness, accuracy and efficiency.

Case-based Documentation

This is the documentation that revolves around a particular case that is being processed by the laboratory. This documentation should use standardized forms that have low revision cycles. These should be monitored and recorded, and training should be given to laboratory personnel on how to fill out the form in the correct and accurate manner for that particular organization.

Review Documentation

This is documentation about the processes of operational reviews that are undertaken within the organization. This includes the processes necessary to conduct a review and how to achieve the standards necessary to achieve compliance with the review. A review process should take account of:

- The suitability of policies, procedures, and processes

- The standard of reports or analysis produced

- The outcomes of any previous reviews or audits and subsequent corrective and preventive actions from same

- Changes in work patterns, loads, or type

- Errors or failures and subsequent avenues for improvement

- A review of training or improvement possibilities

- A review of resources and staffing

A high-level review of the complete laboratory should be undertaken on a regular basis. This is, of course, dependent on the case load, the size of laboratory, and a number of other factors, but should be at least every six months.

Specific area, task, or team reviews should occur on a monthly basis. The reviews do not have to be onerous but should be sufficiently rich in detail to indicate any problems that may be arising within the lab that may impact on quality outcomes being produced.

Conclusions

QA is a cyclic process that is vital in demonstrating proficiency and expertise in the tools, processes, procedures, and work produced. QA is about seeking continual improvement in process that brings about a resultant change in quality. It is really the pursuit of excellence using a management rather than academic imperative.

QA is ideally suited to the philosophical underpinnings of forensic science, its practice and its execution. It is especially applicable to an emergent discipline such as digital forensics as a validating and verification mechanism and also one that provides a comprehensive management framework.

Chapter 14

High Technology Crimes: Case Summaries

Introduction

Throughout the previous chapters of this book, basic concepts, definitions, and methodologies for digital forensic investigations and the management of incidents and the laboratory have been discussed.

This chapter gives a range of cases that illustrate the types of incidents that may be encountered under the general grouping of high technology crimes. There are examples of cases that have been successfully investigated and other examples that highlight occasions when a lack of good processes and procedures have led to investigations that have failed, resulting in considerable embarrassment.

High Technology Crime Cases

In the following paragraphs, a number of cases that highlight a range of management issues have been detailed. As you read through the cases of crimes that involve digital devices[1] that are detailed below, we hope that an understanding of a range of actual high technology crimes or incidents will provide some awareness as to what you may be facing with regard to the investigation and management of this type of incident. We hope that it will also give you some insight into the issues involved in the management of an investigation—the steps that need to be taken and the order in which they will need to be taken to manage the investigation of an incident. An emphasis has been placed on selecting cases that were either large, complex, or both, or that, at some point, have attracted adverse comment. This is in no way intended as a criticism of those investigations, but they do provide the opportunity to highlight the issues that, in many of the cases, became apparent only at a later date. Comments have been made with regard to each of the cases to highlight the management issues and problems that need to be considered.

Operation Buccaneer

This was the name that was used in the United States to an operation that was mounted to close down the Drink-Or-Die Group in 2001. This was a massive multinational copyright infringement and software piracy case—the Drink-Or-Die group was an underground warez (software cracking and trading) network that was known to be in operation from 1993. The group was finally put out of business by a coordinated operation that ended in a major series of raids in 2001. According to FBI and other reports, the Drink-Or-Die group started operating in 1993 and was led by a Russian[2] with the handle "deviator" and another individual using the handle "CyberAngel." By 1995, two years after it started its operations, the group had spread around the world. This group, which consisted mostly of individuals that were employed as network or system administrators (trusted positions), used their positions to gain access to software that was then pirated. Among the group's exploits was the release of the Microsoft Windows 95 operating system two weeks before the official Microsoft release. Other software that the group obtained included business software and multimedia files including a number of films. One of the authors witnessed the scale of the operation when he visited the UK National High Technology Crime Unit after raids carried out in the United Kingdom. The quantity of media, mainly CDs, that was confiscated as a result of the raids in the United Kingdom covered the whole of the floor of one of the operations rooms. The activity of the group gradually declined and by the year 2000, they were no longer considered to be a major player in the warez scene. When it was finally shut down in December 2001 as a result of the raids, the group was reputed to have two leaders, one based in the United States and another in Australia.

The Australian-based leader of the group, Hew Raymond Griffiths, known as Bandido, subsequently was extradited to the United States and charged with one count of conspiracy to commit criminal copyright infringement and one count of criminal copyright infringement. He pled guilty and was sentenced to 51 months in prison in June 2007. As a result of a plea agreement and Griffiths agreeing to become an informant on other pirates, the second charge was dropped and the three years that he had served in custody in Australia was taken into account.

The Operation Buccaneer raids were part of a coordinated international operation by law enforcement agencies in six countries that targeted a total of 62 people. A total of 56 search warrants were required, and the raids resulted in 130 computers being seized. Raids were also carried out in Australia, Finland, Norway, Sweden, and Britain.

For further information, see these web sites:

- http://www.defacto2.net/news.cfm?mode=comments&id=185

- http://www.ibls.com/internet_law_news_portal_view.aspx?s=latestnews&id=1778

- http://news.bbc.co.uk/1/hi/technology/4518771.stm

- http://www.usdoj.gov/criminal/cybercrime/ob/OBMain.htm

- http://pw1.netcom.com/~jstorres/infosec/OperationBuccaneer.pdf

NOTE

This was a huge investigation that took place over a period of a number of years. The coordination for the raids that took place on December 11, 2001, was an immense undertaking that involved the coordination of a number of agencies, in the United States and in a number of other countries, to try and ensure that the raids took place simultaneously and that none of the suspects received warning from a raid taking place elsewhere.

The evidence that was collected in a raid in one location had to be recovered in the knowledge that it may be used against a person who was being investigated in another jurisdiction. Consideration also had to be given to the level of effort that was required to ensure that sufficient evidence was secured from the immense amount of data that was recovered so that convictions could be achieved.

Although this was an exceptional case, it helps to illustrate the complexity that such cases can take on and are likely to take on in the future.

The huge volumes of data that were recovered in a number of countries and seized under a range of national legislations had to be collected and stored (in some cases for years) in a manner that was evidentially sound. In the case that took place in the Old Bailey courts in the United Kingdom, some of the evidence that was used and accepted in the U.K. judicial system had been recovered from servers located in the United States by U.S. federal agents. This evidence was used to prove that one of the individuals had carried out the actions for which he was charged.

Although this operation was one of the largest and most complex that has been undertaken and is at the top end of anything that you may ever encounter, it shows what it is possible to achieve if the right processes, procedures, and resources are used and the operation is managed properly.

From a computer forensic management point of view you can begin to see that without well-established and practiced procedures that conform to accepted standards, it is probable that the huge amount of effort that went into this investigation would have been wasted.

The Trojan Defense

In two cases in the United Kingdom that were reported in 2003, the Trojan Defense was used successfully. In the first case, Aaron Caffrey, aged 19, of Shaftesbury in Dorset, U.K., was acquitted of an attack on the Port of Houston's vulnerable NT-based computer systems. The prosecution and defense in the case both agreed that the attack that slowed the massive American sea port's Web systems to a crawl was launched from Caffrey's home PC. Caffrey claimed that the evidence was planted on his machine by attackers who used an unspecified Trojan to gain control of his PC and launch the assault. Forensic examination of Caffrey's PC found attack tools but no trace of Trojan infection. The prosecution alleged that the attack was the result of a misdirected attack by Caffrey against a fellow chat-room user.

Caffrey was cleared after a jury of six women and five men unanimously decided he was not guilty of causing the unauthorized computer modifications in the attack in September 2001. The case was seen as a major setback for police that would have profound implications to the future of criminal prosecutions for computer crime in the United Kingdom. Caffrey's case is the first ever in the United Kingdom decided by a jury under the Computer Misuse Act, and the case hinged on whether the jury accepted the defense argument that a Trojan could erase itself or expert testimony, or the argument from the prosecution that no such technology existed. The Trojan defense already had been used successfully before in a British court and this case again raised the question as to whether complex computer crime cases should be tried before a panel of experts, rather than a jury.

The following sites provide more information:

■ http://www.theregister.co.uk/2003/10/17/caffrey_acquittal_a_setback/

■ http://www.compseconline.com/digitalinvestigation/trojancase.pdf

NOTE

This was a significant case in the U.K. legal system. It was the first case of its type to be tried by a jury and was unique in that Caffrey was allowed to act as his own expert witness, despite having no qualifications to do so or having any experience. The case demonstrated that a jury could be persuaded that there was sufficient doubt in the case presented for it to be unsafe to find the defendant guilty. This was based on the unproven assertion that a Trojan could carry out a set of actions that caused the evidence to be present on the computer and then delete itself and leave no trace of its presence. Such a Trojan has never been identified. This poses a significant issue for the management of a digital forensic investigation, as it places an increased burden on the investigator to foresee this type of 'curve ball' of an argument.

In the second case, Julian Green, aged 45, of Torquay, England, was cleared of child pornography charges after experts found 11 Trojan horse programs on his computer. According to press reports, the U.K. Courts accepted that the malicious programs probably downloaded the 172 images for which he had been charged. The basis for this was the apparent acceptance by the court that once installed, a Trojan horse can carry out malicious acts such as in this case, downloading illegal material from the Internet or destroying data.

For more information, see the following web sites:

- http://www.theregister.co.uk/2004/01/20/the_giant_wooden_horse_did/

- http://www.out-law.com/page-3783

NOTE

The Trojan Defense came to attention in 2003. These two cases are from the United Kingdom, and highlight two separate issues. In the first case, we are at a loss of the advice that could be offered to a digital investigation manager when a court can find it credible that a Trojan not only could be responsible for a hacking attack but also could be self-deleting and remove all trace of itself, even when such a Trojan has never been seen. In the second case, if the investigators had examined the Trojans that were identified on the system and determined what their purpose and capabilities were, it may have been possible to show that the Trojans were not capable of downloading the images. The problem here, for the investigation manager, is how much time can be invested into each case, even when sufficient material has been collected, to ensure that any arguments that are raised by the defense with regard to Trojans and viruses can be addressed.

Insufficient Evidence

In a case from the United States in 2007, a federal judge has denied the Recording Industry Association of America's (RIAA) motion for a default judgment in the case of Atlantic v. Dangler. Judge David G. Larimer decided against awarding the RIAA's motion for a default judgment of $6,000 plus court costs, citing significant issues of fact with regard to the RIAA linking of the KaZaA username to Dangler and the lack of details provided with regard to the date and time the alleged infringement took place.

This was the second time in a two-month period that the RIAA has failed to obtain a default judgment against a defendant. In the case of Interscope v. Rodriguez, the judge cited the lack of specific details with regard to the alleged infringement in refusing the label's attempt to obtain a default judgment. In this case, Judge Brewster commented that "the complaint is simply a boilerplate listing of the elements of copyright infringement without any facts pertaining specifically to the instant Defendant." The RIAA was to be allowed to present the results of a MediaSurvey investigation at a future date.

In another case involving MediaSentry, the Dutch District Court in Utrecht decided that the MediaSentry investigation into p2p file sharing was not only flawed, but was also "unlawful." The Utrecht court ruled that Dutch ISPs did not have to provide customer information to the counterpart of the Recording Industry Association in the Netherlands. Two expert witnesses from the Delft University of Technology stated that "the technical information provided by MediaSentry is limited and their measurement procedure is simplistic." The experts then went on to highlight a number of areas in which they considered that the evidence provided was inadequate.

For details, see the following web sites:

- http://www.p2pnet.net/story/6977

- http://arstechnica.com/news.ars/post/20071028-riaa-denied-default-judgement-as-judge-cites-doubt-over-positive-id.html

- http://www.pp-international.net/node/369

> **NOTE**
>
> The failure to provide the required level of detail in the submission to the court is one that should not be underestimated. Good management and clear policies and procedures that are adopted for all cases should help to ensure that when case work is reviewed, all the essential questions have been answered to a level that is forensically sound. Remember, you need to address the who, what, when, where, how, and why.

Discrediting of Expert Witnesses

This case was from the United Kingdom, and involved a person who had been involved in more than 100 child pornography cases and whose company had developed one of the early forensic tools, DIBS (Disk Image Backup System). The credibility of Mr. Jim Bates was called into question when he claimed to hold an academic qualification that in fact he did not possess. In court papers dated September 1998, which were seen by the BBC News, Mr. Bates stated, "I hold a Bachelor of Science degree in Electronic Engineering," but in 2004 it emerged that he did not hold the qualification and had never been to university; subsequently he admitted that he had erred in claiming he had a Bachelor of Science in Electronic Engineering in court documents. Prior to this, Mr. Bates had served as an advisor to the Scotland Yard's computer crime unit and had lectured at the police training school at Bramshill in the United Kingdom. At the time that this came to light, Mr. Bates was the President of the Institution of Analysts and Programmers (IAP) and had been involved in a number of high-profile cases as an expert witness both for the prosecution and defense.

As a result of this it was reported that a CPS statement had been issued that stated, "Prosecutors would have to disclose to the defense that allegations have been made against Mr. Bates if we were using him as a prosecution expert," and that "if he was appearing as a defense witness it may be appropriate to challenge his credibility."

Information about this case can be found at:

- http://news.bbc.co.uk/1/hi/england/london/6124616.stm

- http://www.people.co.uk/news/tm_headline=soham-sex-cop-expert-facing-court&method=full&objectid=19722008&siteid=93463-name_page.html

NOTE

As a result of this type of incident, where the integrity of the expert witness is called into question as a result of false qualification claims, it is not surprising that the courts will have difficulty in believing any evidence that they have presented. The management problem here is that this could lead to a review of all the cases in which the expert has been involved. This reinforces the need to ensure that members are properly qualified and that they accurately reflect this, and that the qualifications of any external expert that is engaged are validated.

Police Accused of Negligence in Porn Case

The Chief of the Halifax Regional Police in Nova Scotia, Frank Beazley, and two detectives were accused of negligence in the investigation of a Mark Wayne Smith, who was convicted of possessing child pornography. A computer expert who was hired by Smith to analyze his computer hard drive after he had been found guilty, established that the child pornography located in the "unallocated space" had been downloaded by previous users. As a result of this evidence, Smith subsequently was acquitted.

In a statement of a claim for damages, Smith accused Casella, one of the two detectives, of failing to properly analyze the computer, and accused the other of giving incorrect and misleading evidence at the trial. The statement also claimed that Beazley was negligent for not ensuring that Casella was properly trained in computer forensic analysis.

For more information, see

- http://www.hfxnews.ca/index.cfm?sid=80791&sc=89

- http://www.forensicfocus.com/index.php?name=News&file=print&sid=799

- http://multimediaforensics.com/index.php?topic=284.0

NOTE

This appears to be one of those occasions where the evidence found was sufficient to gain a conviction, but where the provenance of the ownership of the computer throughout its lifetime was not verified. Once again, this is the management issue of, when you have gathered sufficient evidence to satisfy the investigators' question, how much more effort should be invested in addressing issues that might be raised at a later date?

Operation Avalanche

This was the name given to a two-year nationwide U.S. investigation involving the Dallas police and the U.S. Postal Inspection Service (USPIS) that resulted in the arrest of 100 people who had been subscribing to the largest commercial child pornography ring ever discovered in the United States.

The Landslide web site was first detected by the U.S. Postal Inspectors, who were able to trace many of the customers through the credit card details used for Internet transactions to gain access to pornographic images and films of children being sexually abused. The Landslide Web site had an estimated 250,000 visitors, who were paying $30 per month in subscriptions to the service. One expert commented that the organization was unusual for a pedophile ring because pedophiles usually operate as a club; membership is not usually sold for profit.

For more information, see the following:

- http://news.bbc.co.uk/2/hi/uk_news/2445065.stm
- http://www.usps.com/postalinspectors/avalanch.htm
- http://www.usdoj.gov/opa/pr/2001/August/385ag.htm

Operation Ore

In the United Kingdom, a police operation named Operation Ore was mounted to investigate the 7200 U.K.-based people whose credit cards were recovered from the Landslide Site. As a result of the investigations and subsequent arrests in the United Kingdom, there have been more than 33 suicides, including that of Commodore David White, the Commander of British Forces in Gibraltar. Jim Bates, one of the computer experts who was discussed earlier in this chapter and who had acted as an expert witness in more than 100 of the cases, later commented that many of the Operation Ore cases were likely to collapse or be overturned in the Court of Appeal as the result of the U.S. police testimony being discredited and the forensic methods that had been used being called into question. Mr. Bates is reported to have stated that he believed records of credit card transactions on the Landslide web site were unreliable and therefore the names of alleged subscribers could not be used as evidence.

Refer to the following web sites for more information:

- http://news.bbc.co.uk/1/hi/uk/2652465.stm
- http://www.theregister.co.uk/2005/04/22/uk_police_internet/

NOTE

This operation in the United Kingdom took place as a result of the information that was obtained by Operation Avalanche. If the comments made by Mr. Bates with regard to the information used from the United States are substantiated, then a number of the U.K. convictions could be unsound. Bear in mind that many of the accused in Operation Ore pled guilty and in many of the cases, this evidence from the United States was not used, as sufficient other evidence was obtained when the computers of the accused individuals were examined. From the perspective of the management of computer forensic investigations, it highlights the importance of ensuring that evidence collected is evidentially sound as it may have an effect far beyond the initial case.

Operation Cathedral

This operation, which was initiated in California and subsequently led by the British police, took place in 1998. The investigation was sparked by a 1996 U.S. police investigation in a Californian farming community that started as an investigation into a routine child abuse allegation. This resulted in the arrest of two men and the seizure of computer files containing pornography and also digital equipment capable of broadcasting live pictures of abuse on the Internet. It was subsequently discovered that the two men were part of an international pedophile ring known as the Orchid Club. During this investigation, three U.K. residents were identified as being involved in the club and when computer equipment that was seized as a result of raids on their premises was analyzed, it became apparent that a far bigger and more sophisticated pedophile ring, known as the Wonderland Club, existed.

The subsequent investigation into the Wonderland Club spanned 12 countries and led to the arrest of 107 people in countries including the United Kingdom, Australia, Austria, Belgium, Finland, France, Germany, Italy, Norway, Portugal, Sweden, and the United States. In the United Kingdom, nine men were arrested and charged with conspiring to distribute indecent images of children. One of the men subsequently committed suicide. This was the largest international investigation that had been led by U.K. officers and resulted in the seizure of computer equipment, 750,000 computer images of children, and 1,800 computerized videos.

This was a more typical type of pedophile group, where a group of people used the Internet to swap images of children among themselves. New members were recruited only if they were identified as being able to bring at least 10,000 indecent pictures of children to the club and remain separate from other pedophile groups. Membership was strictly by invitation, with individuals that were nominated having to be approved by senior figures in the club.

For more information, see:

- http://www.theregister.co.uk/2001/01/10/child_porn_ring_smashed/
- http://news.bbc.co.uk/1/hi/uk/250800.stm
- http://edition.cnn.com/2001/WORLD/europe/UK/02/13/paedophile.police/

NOTE

This investigation was both large and complex. The individuals involved in the Wonderland Club went to extraordinary lengths to protect their identities and the security of their activity. The membership of the club was organized into a number of levels with new members being given access to the lowest level and earning promotion to higher levels. The group had a security officer and was given advice on how to maintain security. In addition, several of the members used encryption on their computers to hide their activity. In addition to the number of jurisdictions that were involved in this investigation and the huge number of images that had to be handled, the investigation of this was further complicated by the use of encryption and the need to associate the names that the individuals used on the Internet—their "handle" or screen names—with the Internet Service provider that they had used in order to identify their real names.

Operation Site-Key

This operation, which was named Site-Key after a California company called Site-Key, provided credit card services for a number of illegal child pornography sites. It was a large and sophisticated Internet pedophile investigation that involved more than 23,000 individuals that were believed to have used their credit cards to subscribe to child pornography web sites. The operation started in 2002 and ended in April 2004 and resulted in the arrest of more than 700 individuals. Unfortunately, in Texas, it was subsequently found that detectives had obtained at least nine of the search warrants that were used based on information that was more than a year old, far longer than what constitutional protections from unreasonable searches allow. The delay had been caused by the need to refer the names on the lists that had been obtained to prosecutors and other law enforcement agencies in order to verify that the names did not belong to people who had been the victims of identity theft. Once this had been completed, search warrants had to be obtained to search the homes and computers of the suspects. The delay occurred as a result of having to deal with the massive number of cases.

For more information, see the following web sites:

- http://www.securityfocus.com/archive/1/412398

- http://www.cybertipline.com/missingkids/servlet/NewsEventServlet?LanguageCountry= en_US&PageId=1582

- http://seclists.org/fulldisclosure/2005/Aug/0242.html

> **NOTE**
>
> The problem here for the digital forensic investigation manager is that of resources. When such large numbers of individuals need to be checked, it will be necessary to obtain a large number of resources, but suitable numbers of these with the correct qualifications and training may not exist. At this point decisions have to be made as to which of the suspects should be pursued.

Israeli Industrial Espionage

Police in Israel uncovered a large industrial espionage ring in May of 2005, which used a Trojan horse piece of malicious software to hack into rivals' systems. In all, 20 people were arrested, with 18 of them arrested in Israel and another two by British police. More than 15 Israeli firms were implicated in the espionage plot, including three private investigation agencies, a Volvo importer, two cell phone providers, Cellcom and Pelephone, and Israel's largest satellite television company, YES, and a number of media companies. The investigation spanned Britain, Germany, the United States, and Israel. It was estimated that in excess of 60 Israeli and international companies were either involved or affected. One of the Israelis arrested in London, Michael Haefrati, is suspected of writing the software and then charging $2,000 a month to supply and maintain custom designed Trojan horse spy software. The software was distributed both on CD and as e-mail attachments.

The Trojan horse is thought to have been used to gain information from the Rani Rahav PR agency (whose clients include Israel's second largest mobile phone operator, Partner Communications), the HOT cable television group, Champion Motors, the importer of vehicles made by Audi and Volkswagen, Strauss-Elite, Mei Eden mineral water, Ace DIY, and Zoglobek sausages.

More information can be found on these sites:

- http://www.bbc.co.uk/

- http://www.computerweekly.com/Articles/2006/02/01/213977/israeli-trojan-espionage-writers-extradited-for-trial.htm

- http://www.msnbc.msn.com/id/8145520/

- http://www.techweb.com/wire/security/163702797

- http://www.sophos.com/pressoffice/news/articles/2006/01/israeliesp.html

NOTE

The problem with this investigation relates to the fact that the investigation spanned a number of countries and that there were so many large organizations involved as both perpetrators and victims. This was not really one case, but a collection of separate cases that resulted from the common source of the tool of the crimes. For the manager of the digital forensic investigation, the issues that would have to be considered would include liaison with the investigations in a number of countries and the scale of the investigation into a large number of separate private companies.

The Paul Grout Case

Paul Grout, a 46 year old U.K. medical consultant at the Hull Royal Infirmary, was cleared of four pedophilia charges after a judge criticized the prosecution and ruled that no reasonable jury could have found him guilty. This was one of the cases investigated under the Operation Ore inquiry. His credit card details were among those found on the Landslide computer and the prosecution claimed that Dr. Grout had paid to view two sites that contained pedophile images of children as young as three; however, the examination of the computers he used at work and at home found no evidence that they had been used to view any indecent images.

Dr. Grout maintained throughout that he had never registered with Landslide and that someone must have hacked into his computer and stolen his credit card details. He was able to show that he had alibis for a number of the relevant times when he was supposed to have carried out the activities of which he is accused and that on one of the occasions he was actually conducting a police custody officer training course.

The judge at his trial instructed the jury to find Dr. Grout not guilty on two charges of attempting to incite the distribution of indecent photographs of children and two of incitement to distribute indecent images of children and conclude that "no reasonable jury, properly directed, could exclude on this evidence the possibility that the applications were made not by Dr. Grout but by someone who had obtained his details by hacking into his machine."

For more information, see:

- http://www.bbc.co.uk/insideout/yorkslincs/series6/computer_doctor.shtml

- http://www.timesonline.co.uk/article/0,,8122-1083739,00.html

- http://www.id-protect.co.uk/news.php?news_id=5

NOTE

The problem that became apparent with this investigation was that the case was based on uncorroborated information that had been provided by another agency. It is difficult to understand why the alibi information was not checked before the trial and, in the United Kingdom, it is unusual for a case to be brought in the absence of evidence from the accused person's computer(s). The issue for the digital forensic manager in this case was absence of any evidence to corroborate the external evidence.

Not So Anonymous

A company web site was under a sustained and heavy attack that resulted in extended periods where the denial of service was complete. The site in question had excellent logging capabilities and accurate time-stamps on the log files that were created by the servers. The suspected attacker initially was interviewed as he was a recently retrenched IT specialist and the parting from the company had been acrimonious. The suspect was helpful when initially interviewed and surrendered his IP address and connection details, and it was found that there was no evidence to be found of the attacks coming from his IP address or ISP.

Upon further investigation, it was found that the origin of the attacks was several anonymous proxy services on the Internet. The suspect was again interviewed as he was reported to have been bragging about having brought down the systems. The attacker was found to have been using an Apple Macintosh laptop computer. He was also found to be using a web cleansing tool that removed the Internet cache and its files, or so he thought. The web cleansing tool that he was using was found not to completely remove all the evidence of his activities and it left behind the cookies from his web sessions. In this case, the anonymizing proxy servers that he had used employed a cookie to record the initiation of the network sessions.

The suspect, being an IT expert, had also fastidiously kept the time on all his devices synchronized, and this was eventually part of his downfall. This allowed the investigator to match the creation time of a number of cookies from the anonymizing server that were found on the laptop to the time of initiation of attacks on the web site.

NOTE

The issues that the digital forensic investigation manager has to address are those of complexity and jurisdictions. There are a number of sites that have to be considered in this case, including the victims' site and those of the anonymizing proxy servers, the collection of evidence from each of which must be addressed.

Pornography Access

This case involved the accessing of pornography in the workplace; the offender in this case previously had been warned about visiting web sites that contained inappropriate material during work hours. This was the third time that such an incident had been noted and was a potentially sackable transgression. The offender claimed that this was a conspiracy to have him sacked and claimed that he had not accessed the images in question and that someone else used his computer account to access to web sites in question.

An initial investigation by internal resources found that the computer account had been used on a number of machines within the same office space, giving some credence into the claims of the suspect. There were significant differences in the time shown on the clocks on each of the computers in question and, in addition, the proxy Web server that had been accessed also had accurate timekeeping and was not synchronized with the mainstream servers of the organization. There were no cameras in place at the organization to confirm or deny the claims of the offender.

It was noted however that a large proportion of the illicit activity had occurred around conventional breaks where people would vacate the office space. This was mainly during the morning, lunchtime, and afternoon breaks. As part of the investigation the examiner needed to visit the organization to collect further evidence in the form of proxy logs. During the visit the examiner noticed that the access to all the areas within this organization was through a swipe card access system. The proxy logs once again proved inconclusive, with multiple machines being used to access the pornographic material over the relevant periods. The examiner had some knowledge of how the swipe card systems worked and where the logs of the swipe card access system were stored.

The investigator discovered that it was possible to isolate the times at which the suspect had had access to the facilities and that the swipe card system was accurately time synchronized with the main server core. On investigation of the timeline for the access by the suspect and other staff to the relevant area it was possible to match the times when the offender had swiped into the room and was alone and his logging on and accessing the web proxy. Further investigation revealed that any of the computers that had been used to access the illicit material on the Internet had a clear and open view of the door that gave access to the area. It was then found by the human resources staff that the use of those particular workstations matched the records of sick days for the regular users to those workstations.

> **NOTE**
>
> The digital forensic investigation manager's main problem here is that of the number of systems that were relevant to the investigation that were not synchronized, and also the need to ensure that the investigator had the relevant skills to examine the systems for the card swipe system.

Unique Identification

An investigator was required to seize and image 32 computers that were thought to have been involved in a large corporate fraud. The computers were client computers that were connected to a local server, which connected to a number of external parties. The first member of the investigation team arrived and dutifully photographed the scene and each desktop computer before they departed. A team of junior investigators then created an image of the hard drive for each of the machines and placed it on a uniquely numbered hard disk. The computers were then bagged and placed in a secured van for transportation and further processing back at the laboratory.

Upon arrival at the laboratory the machines were laid out in a room ready for final tagging, reconciliation, and then storage as evidence. Ongoing through the procedural documentation, one of the experienced officers noted that no disk serial numbers had been recorded, nor were any of the cases marked with an exhibit number or tag.

The senior officer then checked the photographs that had been taken at the scene and found to his horror that none of the photographs contained an exhibit number or distinguishing feature. Fortunately, each of the drives had been imaged prior to their removal from site and appropriate hashes had been taken of the hard disks. It took the junior investigators three days to reconcile the hard drives with the exhibits and to ensure that this time the exhibits had identifiable tags and exhibit numbers.

If the hard drives had not been imaged on site and using standard procedures this could have been a complete and catastrophic failure. There remained, however, the issue of resolving of placement of the particular computers within the crime scene. In this case there had either been a severe breakdown in the observance of the procedures or a complete lack of a procedure for the seizure of the computers.

NOTE

The first issue here for the digital forensic investigation manager was that, having had an obvious failure in the initial processing of the computers, how could the situation be recovered and the impact minimized? The second issue was, what had caused the issue and what action needed to be taken to ensure that it was not repeated? In reality, there will always be problems that result from noncompliance with procedures or inadequate procedures to meet new situations. It is important that the manager maintains the balance of perspective to support the staff and ensure that the right procedures are in place and also ensure that the impact of any failure is minimized.

Crunchy the Courier

The use of certified and appropriate couriers to transport evidence is highlighted in this case. An organization wanted 10 hard disks analyzed for a potential intellectual property breach by a member of staff. The organization was located some 500 miles from the digital forensic laboratory.

The organization was given strict instructions on how to remove the hard disks from the computers and to photograph the items and document them. The documentation was undertaken to a high standard and was sent to the digital forensic laboratory via e-mail and also in printed form several days later by registered mail. The hard drives were entrusted to a courier company for transportation to the laboratory. The hard disks arrived at the laboratory and were received into the laboratory and readied for analysis. The investigator in charge of receiving the hard disks noted that the box in which the drives had been packed was somewhat misshapen. Subsequently, of the 10 disks that were sent to the laboratory, only three were able to be imaged. The other disks had what could be described only as severe mechanical failures and made distinctive noises when powered up.

The organization was immediately called and they confirmed that all drives were functional at the time that they were dispatched. The courier company was then contacted to ascertain whether any of the packages were involved in a motor vehicle accident; the courier company confirmed that no accident had occurred and that there were full tracking details of the package available. One transfer of the package had occurred at the main depot of the courier and this all had been recorded on video. The courier company subsequently checked the video of the exchange and found that there was no indication of the package being dropped or damaged.

The digital forensic laboratory also had footage of the goods receivable area and this video showed a different story. The courier responsible for the delivery was observed throwing the package out of the van, with the box in question landing from a drop of six to eight feet onto a hard concrete surface. Suffice to say this was the cause of the failure of the hard drives.

NOTE

The issues here for the digital forensic investigation manager are twofold. The first is that of ensuring that suppliers and service providers are trusted and can be relied upon to provide the requisite level of service. The second is again that of looking at all the available sources of information to determine what has happened. In this case, the video cameras that were covering the receiving area of the laboratory were the source of the relevant information.

The Disappearing Evidence

This again was a case where a suspect had been accessing inappropriate material from a computer within the organization. The security manager had noticed the accessing of inappropriate material in the form of graphic hardcore pornography by a particular staff member. The issue was raised with the Human Resources (HR) department of the organization and a plan of action was put into place.

The images that had been viewed appeared to have an underage orientation such as lolita1.jpg, which was of significant concern. Of further concern was that many of the web sites had since been taken down or removed. Upon return to work the next day, the suspect was met by a member of the HR team and a member of the investigation team. The staff member in question was escorted from his office where he left his laptop. The suspect was then interviewed with regard to his accessing the inappropriate web sites. During interview the suspect said little in response to any questions; after the interview was concluded by the HR and security staff it was decided that the matter would be referred to police for further investigation.

The HR officer left the interview room with the offender as it was near the morning break. The investigator assumed that the offender was being escorted at all times. To the investigator's horror he found the HR officer sitting alone in the staff room some 30 minutes later, after they ventured into the room for their morning tea break. When the HR officer was asked where the offender was he replied that he had released the offender to go back to his office and tidy up his desk and collect his keys and personal possessions because he was being placed on suspension until the matter had been resolved. The investigator and the HR officer then hurried to the offender's office only to find the offender had disappeared along with the laptop computer that contained the evidence. When the laptop was subsequently recovered, the hard drive had been completely erased.

When the investigator looked for other potential sources of evidence, they discovered that the organization's proxy caching server was overloaded and was caching material for only approximately seven days. Unfortunately, the last access to a site containing inappropriate material had been some 14 days earlier—this meant that no images could be retrieved from the cache server.

NOTE

The main issue here for the manager is that of ensuring that when collaborating with other organizations and departments, that the respective responsibilities are clearly understood and that the action plan is thought out in advance. It is also essential that the other parties are briefed with regard to the requirements of the investigator to ensure that the potential evidence is not compromised.

The second issue here is, when you are part of a larger organization, ensuring that their processes and procedures are in place to ensure that evidence will be available. If the server had been set up differently or the logs recovered on a more regular basis, there may have been evidence available that, in this case, was lost.

Summary

Crimes that involve computers and other digital devices are continuing to increase. The problem of using evidence that is gathered from these devices is exacerbated by a whole range of issues including inconsistent approaches to evidence collection, a lack of professionalism and standards, poorly framed and implemented laws, and potentially from the international nature of crimes involving digital evidence and the vagaries of the judicial systems.

Loss of personal data resulting from identity theft is one of the fastest growing areas of concern, as has been highlighted by the data losses by a number of government agencies in the United Kingdom. As the range of digital devices and their storage capacity and capabilities continue to increase, together with the ways in which they are used, it is inevitable that the digital forensic investigator will continue to encounter an ongoing set of challenges to the collection, analysis, and presentation of evidence. The increasing sophistication of high technology devices used by organized crime and reputedly national and state organizations will continue to test the ability of investigation managers to ensure that the response to these crimes is managed properly.

The cases in this chapter have been selected to highlight the problems that a manager of a digital forensic investigation may have to deal with. These cases have been selected because they represent some of the most complex investigations that have been undertaken. Although these cases are all police investigations, and you may consider that they are not relevant in a corporate environment, they have been selected because they have been reported in the public press, whereas most corporate investigations are not. They are also the most extreme examples and are best for highlighting the issues. It should be remembered that the information on these cases is only the information that was reported in the public media. It is almost certain that in the majority of these cases, the perspective of those involved in the investigations and involved in the decisions that resulted in the reported outcomes will have made the decisions that they did on the information available at the time. Twenty-twenty hindsight is a wonderful thing.

Notes

1. Although the reports of the incidents have been combined and reduced for clarity and brevity, the original sources of the reports are identified for each of the cases.

2. The cases of the Drink or Die group and the Russian Business Network that is reported later in this chapter have a number of characteristics in common that should be considered.

Overview of the Digital Forensic Investigations Profession and Unit

This section gives an overview of the management issues related to a digital forensics unit and the investigations profession. The section looks at the roles within the laboratory and why and how to develop credible plans for the laboratory at all levels. It also examines a number of methods for the measurement of the effectiveness of the unit—figures that will be vital in workload management and supporting the plans that are put forward. The section also looks at the wider issues of information sharing and sources of valuable information that can enhance the capability of the unit. In this section, the development of a career in the area is also examined.

Chapter 15. Understanding the Role of the Digital Forensic Unit Manager. The objectives of this chapter are to describe and discuss the major functions of the high technology crime investigative unit manager that need to be carried out, and describe the flow processes that can be used to establish the baseline in performing the functions.

Chapter 16. The Digital Forensics Unit Strategic, Tactical, and Annual Plans. This chapter describes how to establish the plans for the digital forensic laboratory, which provide the subsets of the Strategic, Tactical, and Annual Plans of the parent organization. These plans will set the direction for the Digital Forensic Laboratory's program while integrating these plans into those of the parent organization. This will ensure that the digital forensic laboratory plans are compliant with the aspirations and requirements of the parent organization, thus indicating that the digital forensics program is an integral part of the organization.

Chapter 17. Sources of Information, Networking, and Liaison. This chapter identifies, describes, and discusses a range of information sources of various types, such as joining and establishing networks with your peers, and liaison with outside agencies.

Chapter 18. Digital Forensics Investigation Unit Metrics Management System. The objective of this chapter is to outline and discuss the identification, development, and use of suitable metrics to assist in managing a digital forensics laboratory to ensure that the team is profitable, their efforts are directed in the correct way, that they are adhering to best practice and that the procedures are evidentially sound.

Chapter 19. Workload Management and the Outsourcing Option. Having the right level of resources to meet the demands that will be put on the unit will not always be achievable, but should be planned for. Outsourcing is a management tool that can help in balancing the workload and can also help to save money. This chapter looks at the possibilities of outsourcing this function and at a process that can be used to make that determination.

Chapter 20. Developing a Career in Digital Forensics Management. The objective of this chapter is to provide the digital forensic investigator with a career development plan outline that can be used in developing a career as a digital forensic unit manager.

Chapter 21. A Summary of Thoughts, Issues, and Problems. This chapter discusses what might happen in a dynamic organization that drastically changes the high technology crime investigations unit and the unit manager's role.

This section provides an overview of the digital forensics unit and investigations profession management issues. The section examines the roles within the laboratory, business plans and their relationship with other plans within the organization, and the measures that will need to be initiated to measure the effectiveness of the laboratory. The section also looks at the wider issues that relate to the environment and the relationship of the laboratory and the manager with other groups within the organization and other laboratories.

Finally this section looks at the development of careers within the digital forensics arena and finishes with some thoughts by the authors on changes that might affect the laboratory or the role of the manager.

Chapter 15

Understanding the Role of the Digital Forensic Laboratory Manager

Introduction

The word *manager* usually evokes feelings of panic on the part of the person that finds themselves holding this title as well as those whom he or she is managing. This is especially true in the area of digital forensics. This market is on the leading edge of technology; as such, managing people/technologies/processes in this area can be a chaotic undertaking. Nonetheless, a digital forensic laboratory manager must execute certain core functions. Even though this execution can be delegated, ultimate responsibility for the entire operation rests with the manager.

This chapter will describe the major functions of the digital forensic laboratory manager as well as the responsibilities comprising each of those functions.

The Laboratory Manager's Major Functions

The laboratory manager is typically responsible for four major functions: financial, human resources, case management, and facilities management. Each function includes certain responsibilities, as outlined in Figure 15.1. We will discuss those roles and responsibilities in the following sections.

Figure 15.1 Major Functions and Responsibilities of the Digital Forensic Laboratory Manager

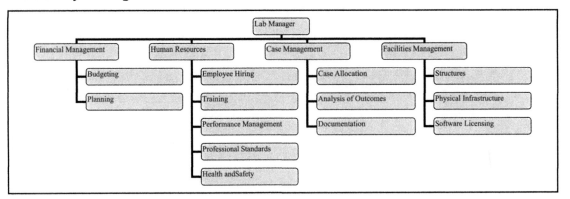

Financial Management

The financial role comprises two main responsibilities: budgeting and planning.

Budgeting

Budgeting includes tasks such as handling staff payroll, billing customers, creating job estimates and budgets, paying bills for goods and services purchased, and negotiating contracts for provision of goods and services. In this role, the manager must constantly be aware of the bottom line. These budgeting tasks may be spread across several roles within the laboratory, but the manager is the person ultimately responsible for the financial outcomes of these tasks, good or bad.

The details of payroll are typically handled by individuals who have expertise in this area and includes complex issues such as pay awards, overtime rates, and superannuation, among others. This is a function that most corporate businesses now outsource, and digital forensic laboratories should consider doing the same. Whether this responsibility is outsourced or not, however, the laboratory manager still must ensure that the staff is paid correctly and appropriately.

Job estimations are a learned skill for the individual and the organization. Establishing performance baselines will allow accurate prediction of resource input required to accomplish a given laboratory task. The process of job estimation is a crucial function of a manager in an organization. If a manager underestimates a job, the organization runs the risk of significant losses. Similarly, if a manager overestimates a job, the organization may not see any business at all. This task is not suitable for a junior staff member or for staff members who have had little exposure to the commercial realities of this area.

Like payroll, billing is also usually outsourced. This includes issuing bills to customers and any subsequent follow-up should they be slow with respect to meeting their financial obligations. In small practices, this responsibility will typically be undertaken by the principal of the organization. This part of the laboratory manager's role also includes the timely payment of bills from external providers of services or goods, and this can only really be done with some oversight of cash flow and the overall budget, as there is no point in writing checks that people cannot cash!

Negotiation of contracts is another skill that is not innate and must be learned. This is tied to job estimation but also links strongly to business viability. Just because your estimates are lower than your competitors' doesn't mean you'll win a particular contract. Modern contracts often have non-financial conditions that must be met to satisfy the purchaser. These may include such matters as the laboratory meeting certain known applicable standards such as ISO 17025, provisions on meeting gender or equity issues, or the ability to execute tasks to a known or given standard based on prior work.

Planning

Financial planning involves a strategic or long-term sustainability focus. To stay current with technology, it is important that the equipment in a digital forensic laboratory is updated regularly; outdated or obsolete equipment can bring a laboratory to its knees. Avoiding this problem takes prudent long-term planning, as mentioned in previous chapters. Not having long-term strategic plans in place to handle replacement and redundancy of laboratory equipment will place the organization behind its competition. This includes decisions that must be made regarding the laboratory's resources and the subsequent movement of capital within the business to cater for this.

For a digital forensic laboratory, the ongoing need to replace hardware as it becomes obsolete is a significant issue. As such, often laboratory managers will question whether it's more advantageous to lease or to purchase equipment. Leasing allows you to replace outdated equipment, but it requires a significant ongoing cost. Purchasing costs money in the beginning, but it typically has the advantage of much lower ongoing costs. Because there are advantages and disadvantages of both approaches, a laboratory manager should decide which approach to take based on the organization's financial characteristics such as cash flow, funding cycles and asset disposals.

Long-term ignorance or avoidance of the issue of equipment obsolescence can impact a laboratory's ability to process its workload in a timely fashion. In turn this will make a business unprofitable or noncompetitive. Even law enforcement officials who may not be competing on price against other providers must still compete with the known adversary: criminals. A manager who is not up to speed with this can rapidly ruin a facility, either financially or in terms of its reputation.

Human Resources

This part of a laboratory manager's job comprises ensuring that those working for the organization are adequately trained and compensated and that they are working in a safe environment.

Employee Hiring

One of the key criteria in this role is to ensure that staff members are qualified to perform their jobs such that any analysis produced can be presented without issues or concerns regarding competency issues in a court of law. A manager must possess several key skills to ensure the best possible outcome for the organization in this regard. Before an interview takes place, the manager must have a thorough understanding of salary rates and work conditions to attract suitable candidates. Also, before an interview, the manager must verify the candidate's qualifications. This takes time, expertise, and knowledge of suitable qualifications. Although the vetting of qualifications may not clearly fall into the domain of the laboratory manager, he or she is in the best position to aid in the process as he or she should have unique knowledge with regard to qualifications required of future employees.

Recruitment processes can go only so far in assessing the expertise and competence of an individual seeking employment. There is often more to the recruitment process than employing a candidate with the correct expertise. One of the critical factors is to achieve the right organizational fit. Teamwork is seen as an essential component within a digital forensic environment and careful selection of staff members who fit into the team is crucial. The employment of a brilliant loner may actually be more destructive than you think.

Training

We discussed training earlier in the book, but it's worth mentioning here that the overall responsibility for training rests with the laboratory manager. As outlined previously, ongoing training is an important aspect of a laboratory's sustainability and viability and should be undertaken to maintain baseline competency.

Technology is changing at a rapid pace. In addition to scheduling regular competency-based training on base applications and operating systems investigators use within the laboratory, the laboratory manager must also be aware of changes in technology that the criminals are using. Take the iPod, for instance. iPods are now considered potential sources of evidence, requiring laboratory managers to ensure that investigators understand how to capture and analyze them during an investigation.

Here again the manager must find the perfect balance between too much training and not enough training. Excessive training is an expensive undertaking and may result in staff being unavailable for tasks for protracted periods or to staff members leaving because they do not have the required skills or because they are very well qualified and an attractive recruit for other laboratories Conversely, if investigators have too little training or education their competency can be questioned or the laboratory may become unable to process artifacts for potential evidence. The operational and strategic planning decisions for training are clearly within the laboratory manager's responsibility.

Performance Management

Regular reviews of employees' work output, as well as its quality, timeliness, and volume, are mandatory when it comes to maintaining a laboratory in good standing and ensuring that it is running efficiently. Managing the performance of employees is critical to business success, efficiency, and ultimately, the long-term sustainability of the laboratory.

Employee performance reviews will uncover skill gaps, competency issues, changes in personal circumstances, or issues that are significantly impacting a staff member's ability to work efficiently and appropriately. Skill gaps and competency issues are usually addressed through mentoring or training and subsequent testing. In most cases, this closes the gap. However, in some cases competency issues may not be resolved and retrenchment processes will have to be undertaken, in which case a working knowledge of appropriate dismissal procedures and human resources legislation and procedures is crucial.

Where there are personal issues the provision of counseling services may be appropriate. As mentioned in previous chapters, some digital forensic practitioners are regularly exposed to material of a highly graphic, disturbing nature, and prolonged exposure to this material may precipitate issues requiring counseling. The manager has an obligation under occupational health and safety laws to ensure that staff members are monitored for this.

Inappropriate work behaviors may result from not following procedures correctly, work shirking, or in some cases, incorrect instruction or advice from peers. A regular review of work practices measured against known norms should uncover these types of issues before they become significant problems for the laboratory.

Managing employees is often hard, and the laboratory manager is often the one who has to deliver the bad news. It is important, therefore, that in the process, the manager also takes the time to deliver good news.

Professional Standards

Professional standards are closely tied to QA outcomes, but they also cover issues such as general conduct, punctuality, and dress standards and protocols both within and outside the laboratory. Establishment of a work ethic and laboratory ethos is often intangible, but again, it is the responsibility of the laboratory manager to maintain a level of esprit de corps. The last image that a laboratory wants to project is that of a group of unprofessional time wasters.

A laboratory manager has an obligation to ensure that the practices within the laboratory are professionally accepted and completed to an externally valid professional standard. Enforcement of an internal peer-reviewed and documented, enforced QA apparatus can provide a mechanism to ensure this in part and this is also the responsibility of the laboratory manager. The external review of the laboratory as whole is important and should be conducted on a regular basis, but not so regular as to cause significant stress among employees.

External recognition of personnel in the profession is important. Staff members should be members of the relevant professional bodies. For most digital forensic practitioners, a good starting place is the relevant computer society. The laboratory manager's role in this regard is to lead by example and support the staff in making this happen.

Finally, the digital forensic laboratory manager will also need to continuously monitor the levels of expertise within the lab. This will involve engagement with external agencies and professional associations to ensure that the laboratory practice and staff expertise are consistent and closely aligned with others within the industry.

Occupational Health and Safety

Most countries have occupational health and safety legislation. These acts of legislation typically require that a workplace—in this case, a laboratory—is maintained as a clean and safe working environment. Therefore, a laboratory manager has a legal obligation to provide a safe working environment for the organization's employees. In some countries, the onus is also on the employees to proactively maintain a safe work environment, but the oversight responsibility still falls on management.

In a digital forensic laboratory, this would include regular checks for potential hazards—for example, electrical cables for leakage as a result of faulty wiring or trip hazards. Ensuring the correct ergonomic use of personal workstations and the correct movement and handling of heavy or hazardous materials are also matters that need to be considered. In fact, all aspects of the workplace where a hazard could impact the safety or health of the employee and could reasonably be foreseen and prevented must be addressed by identification and remediation.

Case Management

Case management involves oversight of all the processes, tasks, and duties that must be executed to complete a case and requires a detailed working knowledge of digital forensics. This knowledge would be the result of considerable practical experience in digital forensics, and ideally some previous management experience of personnel in this context.

Case Allocation

It is the laboratory manager's job to make sure cases are allocated appropriately, and this requires organizational maturity and significant insight into digital forensic processes as well as individual staff members' abilities. Over time, each staff member will reveal talents and expertise for a given set of tasks that he or she performs well and with minimal overhead. Staff members should be matched to tasks for which they have an aptitude, as this makes good business sense most of the time. The manager must, however, also take into account the transfer of knowledge as well as staff development and satisfaction.

One drawback with optimized use of the staff is that the development of specific niche expertise can work against the organization's capacity to perform tasks or recover from staff moving to another organization. There also has to be a balance between organizational efficiency and overall capacity through prudent management. In addition, when staff members are undergoing training there is an extra burden on a digital forensic laboratory to ensure that the competency of the work cannot be brought into question. Although it may be desirable to share the workload and increase capacity, any work conducted by novices should be undertaken with the strict supervision of a competent peer, another complexity that is in the role of the laboratory manager to organize.

Prioritization and the sequencing of cases is also a skill set that the laboratory manager must have. The correct sequencing of tasks within a case can have a major impact on the timeline and overall resolution of a case. Task prioritization within a case is a skill of laboratory management or a senior staff member and is typically learned through raw practical experience. Depending on the details of the case, certain techniques and avenues of inquiry may yield a quicker outcome—for example, the use of specific searches or the examination of particular critical files. Although standard procedures are a necessary function, they should not become an impediment to the rapid progress of a case while maintaining forensic integrity. Deciding on the appropriate time to use nonstandard procedures is the laboratory manager's professional prerogative.

Almost every day, cases will come into the laboratory and any one of them could change the priority with which other cases are to be investigated and completed. Too much change may produce unnecessary turmoil and uncertainty within the laboratory. However, any inherent inflexibility in task or case reallocation may result in significant loss of income for private practices, or the release of undesirable individuals back into the population as a result of the noncompletion of a task for a law enforcement laboratory. In situations where rescheduling of cases is necessary, this is best carried out by the laboratory manager, who should oversee all tasks being completed. In some cases, this will involve significant renegotiation of outcomes with external third parties and is a significant political skill that a laboratory manager must have.

With case allocation a significant issue concerns resources, and this should be done on a cost benefit or opportunity cost basis. After the initial job estimation, the pursuit of a particular outcome or case may not be viable. This nonviability may be due to financial restrictions, human resources restrictions, infrastructure restrictions, time constraints, or a combination of all of these. Once again, this is a management decision and typically involves informing the client and realigning expectations or outcomes for the case. It may also involve the recommendation of another, more suitable laboratory, or a new avenue of inquiry to yield the required result.

One potentially contentious issue is management of the workload and its fair allocation. Just because a staff member is efficient and professional and produces timely results, he or she should not be given larger or excessive workloads. Transparency in workload allocation can also help a manager to manage in this regard as staff members can measure their performance against their peers or realize that they have little cause for complaint.

Analysis of Outcomes

Analysis of outcomes is the application of QA and other metrics to work that has been or is being produced in the laboratory. It is simply not good enough to produce work in this type of environment and not assess its outcomes without some rigor and routine. The ultimate failure that a digital forensic laboratory can suffer is that any analysis produced is inadmissible in court as evidence, thereby allowing a criminal to walk free on a technicality. It is clearly the laboratory manager's function to ensure that this outcome does not occur.

This function involves a proactive, interventionist approach to case review and the analysis of outcomes produced by the laboratory. Quality assurance can go only so far, as this is often done post incident and may not prevent problems or adverse findings from occurring. Therefore, the laboratory manager must actively monitor case milestones and analyze the processing of evidence at the point of initial production. By actively reviewing cases, the laboratory manager can eliminate errors or reduce their likelihood before lots of resources are committed unnecessarily to the case or are required to turn the case around. In large and sometimes small laboratories, it is simply not feasible for the laboratory manager to be personally involved in all cases, but it is his or her responsibility to ensure that active reviews of cases take place.

Documentation

The production, maintenance, and security of appropriate documentation with respect to cases are some of the most important tasks that a laboratory manager will oversee. Adequate documentation is a hallmark of the scientific process, and it is one of the key ways that we transfer knowledge or give our opinion about a particular subject. For digital forensics, appropriate documentation is a requirement to prove the integrity and continuity of evidence by the provision of an auditable, witnessed trail of documentation. Documentation also provides underpinning detail for the investigative techniques used on the evidence, allowing for peer review and for review by external experts. Although QA processes should ensure that this happens, it is the laboratory manager's responsibility to set and enforce the standards and levels of documentation for evidence.

Evidentiary documentation requirements change over time, and it is the laboratory manager's responsibility to be aware of these changes. The changes in documentation requirements are normally a result of changes in case law or legislation, the implementation of new procedures, or changes in current professionally accepted practices. This issue will require environmental scanning on the part of the laboratory manager to become aware of instances where documentation has been found to be lacking, the reason for this, and how to remedy it. This scanning is not only internally focused, but should also involve review of cases and adverse rulings.

Facilities Management

In digital forensics, facilities management is the management of all aspects of the digital forensic lab. This includes management of structures—buildings, gates, and the supporting critical infrastructures they house. It also includes management of physical assets, such as special storage technologies, desks, chairs, benches, and filing cabinets, as well as soft assets such as software licenses.

As mentioned in previous chapters, some areas, such as secured evidence storage, require expert knowledge of things such as appropriate shelving as well as appropriate security measures including swipe cards and locks. In addition, this can require knowledge and management of IT archive media longevity and suitable environmental and fire controls.

Structures

This area of management is primarily concerned with the actual structures of the laboratory, i.e. buildings, gates, rooms and access ways. It should be noted that although there is significant overlap with the physical infrastructure management aspects, there are discrete requirements. Included in the management of structures is ensuring that the leases, etc. for use of the building are maintained and are appropriate for the business being conducted. Depending on the leasing or ownership arrangements, there may be on-going maintenance that may need to be addressed to ensure the safety and security of the facility.

Management of structures involves making sure that they are sound and can withstand natural hazards and malicious attacks. Natural hazards are typically and frequently in the form of storms, tempests or flooding. Depending on the site of the buildings they may also be subject to major natural hazards, such as earthquakes and fires, the impact of which can be mitigated by proper management or selection of the site, i.e. keeping it clear of debris or sources of fuel for fire, or ensuring that the building is earthquake rated.

Malicious attacks are disruptions of operations, or destruction of assets by human agents. This type of vector may seem alien to private enterprise but it should be remembered that some of the material being processed could relate to crimes perpetrated by organized criminals, terrorists or a nation state. This type of hazard could include forceful penetration of the facility by unauthorized individuals or denial of access to utilities via destruction or tampering with supply. These hazards can be managed by ensuring the structure and surrounds are sufficiently resilient or hardened against these threats. This includes active management of basics such as ensuring that entry points, both egress and ingress are secured and/or monitored with resulting appropriate response based on level of threat, which is ultimately a management decision.

Physical Infrastructure

Physical infrastructure is the actual physical assets e.g. desks, chairs, benches and computer hardware contained within the structures or buildings. The management duties involve responsibility for the purchase/lease, tracking, maintenance and eventual disposal of these physical assets. These duties are substantive, on-going tasks and must be addressed directly or suitably outsourced. Managing the physical infrastructure in good working order is also a basic requirement of sound occupational health and safety.

The laboratory manager also must oversee such tasks as the management of access to critical utility infrastructures—for instance, the power grid, for provision of adequate power supply to the laboratory both now and in the future—as well as to communication infrastructures and systems that allow for fast, accurate, and reliable access to telephone, Internet, and wide area network technology. He or she must also oversee the provision of adequate environmental controls to control the building at temperature ranges which minimize damage to or deterioration of materials and items stored or used at the facility. Additional responsibilities include the following: provision of adequate internal physical security for the facility to prevent loss or incursion; regular testing of internal support systems such as fire control mechanisms, standby power arrangements, and standby communication; and management of physical resources including physical internal and external security systems (e.g., barriers such as keys, doors, locks, swipe cards, guards, and CCTV systems).

Software and Hardware Facilities

The provision of the necessary hardware and software to enable analysis of evidence is also a facilities management issue for which the laboratory manager is responsible. This includes tasks or processes that require oversight of software evaluation and testing, software licensing and monitoring, hardware recommendation, requisitioning, and recalibration, and recertification. It also includes production and enforcement of schedules for the regular maintenance, testing, and auditing of this infrastructure. As mentioned in previous chapters, standard operating environments can help in this regard; however, it is the laboratory manager's responsibility to ensure that these are developed, enforced, and maintained in an orderly manner. It is also important that the manager maintain software licenses. Additionally, some hardware devices may need maintenance in the form of updates to achieve currency of certification or recalibration.

The maintenance of critical information systems and architectures is also a part of facilities management. This includes systems such as an evidence database or tracking systems, mass secondary storage facilities, archival tape drives, and their resultant libraries. Many of these large IT systems and their specialist administrative functions can be outsourced, but the responsibility still ultimately lies with the laboratory manager for oversight and management to ensure stable operation of the laboratory.

Summary

This chapter focused on four key roles of the laboratory manager—roles that are crucial to the ongoing successful management of a digital forensic lab. Managing a laboratory requires a wide range of skills, from financial management and human resources to case management and facilities management. It is simply not possible for one person to be omnipresent or omnipotent within a modern digital forensic laboratory, as the tasks and processes are simply too varied and complex. Therefore, the function of a laboratory manager is one of oversight and appropriate delegation of key processes and functions within the lab.

To be successful in this position, laboratory managers must strike a balance between operational and strategic imperatives. These imperatives are sometimes antagonistic to one another, presenting the manager with a chicken-and-egg scenario: On the one hand, operational matters must be attended to and are the lifeblood of the laboratory if it is to succeed; on the other hand, digital forensics is changing rapidly, and these changes must be addressed to ensure the lab's survival in the future.

The laboratory manager's job is difficult and complex, and inevitability the person holding this position will make a mistake or two along the way. Like all management positions, this position is often the loneliest place in the entire lab, requiring the manager to make tough decisions. But it can also be extremely rewarding, and in many cases, those rewards can make the job worth undertaking.

Chapter 16

The Digital Forensics Laboratory: Strategic, Tactical, and Annual Plans

Introduction

The objective of this chapter is to establish the plans for the digital forensic laboratory that will provide the subsets of the Strategic, Tactical, and Annual Plans of the parent organization. These plans will set the direction for the Digital Forensic Laboratory's (DFL's) program while integrating these plans into those of the parent organization. This will ensure that the DFL plans are compliant with the aspirations and requirements of the parent organization, thus indicating that the digital forensics program is an integral part of the organization.

This will be of greater or lesser relevance depending on the type of organization to which the laboratory belongs. The strategic plans will be of less relevance for laboratories in the government, military, and law enforcement areas, as may the tactical plans, but all organizations normally require annual plans of one type or another.

For the purposes of this chapter it has been assumed that the DFL will be subordinate to the security department, although depending on the organization, it may be subordinate to Security, Audit, Finance, IT, or even answer directly to senior management as an independent department.

Relationship of the Business Plans

Throughout this chapter there is continuous reference to the organization, department, and laboratory strategic, tactical, and annual plans. All these plans must be coherent and mutually supportive, both top-down and bottom-up. Figure 16.1 shows these relationships.

Figure 16.1 Relationship of Business Plans

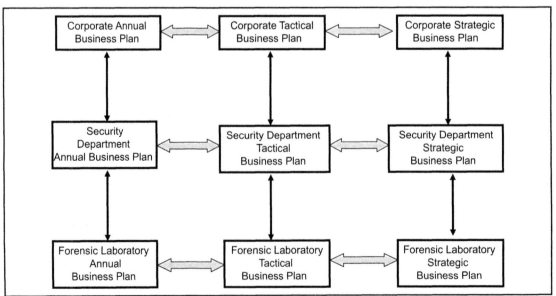

The Digital Forensic Laboratory Strategic Plan

In order to be successful, the laboratory's forensic investigators must be working to the digital forensic laboratory strategic plan. That plan should be integrated, or at least compatible, with the parent organizations' Security Department and overall organizational Strategic Business Plan (normally referred to as the Five or Seven-Year Plan). It is this plan that sets the long-term directions, goals, and objectives for the digital forensic laboratory program.

When developing the digital forensic laboratory strategic plan, the digital forensic investigator-manager must ensure that the following basic, DFL principles are included, either specifically or in principle (since it is part of the DFL strategy):

- Conduct professional, effective, and efficient investigations

- Ensure compliance with internal and external standards

- Maintain laboratory certification

- Produce reports for management on the investigations conducted, broken down by type

The Digital Forensic Laboratory Strategic Plan Objective

The objectives of the DFL Strategic Plan are to:

- Ensure compliance with organizational and external standards

- Minimize costs

- Meet contractual requirements

- Build a comprehensive digital forensic investigation environment

- Be flexible in order to respond to changing requirements

- Support a range of customers' digital forensic investigative needs

- Incorporate new digital forensic investigative techniques as soon as required

- Assist in attracting new customers, and provide new services to existing customers

- Maximize the use of available resources

Communication and Coordination of Digital Forensic Laboratory Strategic Plan

To have a successful DFL program, the strategy will need to be sensitive to and address the office politics and internal relationship aspects of the organization. It should always be borne in mind that the ultimate aim of the strategic plan is to meet the aspirations and needs of the parent organization and that the objectives of the DFL and the security department must be tailored to meet them.

In order to ensure this, coordination with all levels of the organization's management and employees and their cooperation are essential.

Many of the functional areas within an organization will have an interest in the DFL-related plans. In order to ensure buy-in from these groups, such as the auditors, security staff, human resources personnel, legal staff, and so on, the plans should be discussed and agreed with them. This will help in ensuring that the plans are optimized for the organization and integrated into the plans of the organization.

The DFL Strategic Plan should be discussed and input requested from a range of the employees of the organization. This should include groups such as union representatives and the organization's managers. This is essential as the digital forensic laboratory is part of the larger organization and will not only need to comply with the rules, processes, and procedures of the parent organization, but will also contribute to it and will inevitably have an impact on it. By discussing the plans as widely as possible, the communication and interaction will lead to a plan that is integrated and inclusive and is one that has a broad-base support.

The consultation with, and input from, the management and employees of the organization and their understanding of what the digital forensic investigation manager is trying to achieve will assist in ensuring broad-based support for the DFL plans and ultimately a successful program.

Planning Considerations for the Digital Forensic Laboratory Strategic Plan

The planning considerations for the DFL Strategic Plan must also include:

- Good business practices
- Quality management
- Innovative ideas
- Risk management philosophy and techniques
- DFL Vision Statement
- DFL Mission Statement;
- DFL Quality Statement
- Providing channels of open communications with others such as the employees, auditors, systems personnel, security personnel, users, management, etc.

All these factors must be considered when developing a DFL strategy and documenting that strategy in the parent organization's strategic plan.

The process flow of plans begins with the parent organization's strategic business plan through to the organization's tactical business and annual business plans. The goals and objectives of each of the plans must be able to support each other, both top-down and bottom-up. Once the parent organization's plans are understood, then it is possible to map the DFL Strategic Plan into the goals and objectives of the Strategic Business Plan of the relevant department within the parent organization.

Mapping the Digital Forensic Laboratory Strategic Plan to the Security Department's and Parent Organization's Strategic Business Plan

It is normal for the Strategic Business Plan or the organization to identify its projected annual revenues for a period of around seven years together with other projections such as market-share targets. In order to meet these projections, the DFL program will have to be shown to be cost-effective, and any digital forensic investigations must also reflect this goal.

When used as an internal capability as opposed to a revenue earning external service the digital forensic service is a cost to the organization and will inevitably be viewed as a "parasite" on the profits of the organization. Effort must be made to demonstrate the value-add that the maintenance and use of the service provides (the value that the service provides in support of the bottom-line). Therefore, the DFL strategy must show that the laboratory is efficient (cheap) and effective (good) and must ensure the capture of statistics that demonstrate the contribution that the forensic laboratory's services will make. If that can be accomplished, then the DFL program will be in a position to support the organization's strategy relative to earnings and market share.

Taking these points into consideration will help the digital forensic investigation manager develop a strategy prior to documenting it in the DFL Strategic Plan. Mapping the points to the departmental and organizational strategic objectives will assist the digital forensic investigation manager in focusing on the strategies that support those strategies.

Some examples of mapping include:

- An organizational strategic goal to increase employees' productivity

- The security department's supporting goal of minimizing the adverse impact of incidents by rapid and efficient investigations and the early restoration of full productivity

- A DFL goal of efficient and effective digital forensic investigations in support of the security department

Writing the Digital Forensic Laboratory Strategic Plan

You will find that writing the DFL Strategic Plan is much easier when the mapping to the organization's plans has been completed. Once that is accomplished, the digital forensic investigation manager will be able to write the DFL Strategic Plan using the organizations standard plan writing format.

Normally the format used within organizations will include the following elements:

1. Executive summary

2. Table of Contents

3. Introduction

4. Vision statement

5. Mission statement

6. Quality statement

7. Standards compliance statement

8. DFL strategic goals

9. Description of the way in which the DFL strategies support the parent organization strategies

10. Mapping charts

11. Conclusions

The Digital Forensic Laboratory Tactical Plan

The tactical plan is a mid-range plan (normally a three-year plan) that supports the DFL Strategic Plan goals and objectives. The tactical plan should:

- Identify and define, in more detail, the vision of a comprehensive DFL environment, as defined in the DFL Strategic Plan

- Identify and define the current DFL environment

- Identify the process to be used to determine the differences between the two

When these have been identified, the digital forensic investigation manger can develop the projects that will be required to progress from the current Digital Forensic Laboratory environment to where it needs to be, as detailed in the DFL Strategic Plan. The DFL Strategic Plan should also take into account the:

- Business direction

- Customers' direction

- Direction of high technology

When these factors have been taken into account, individual projects can be developed and implemented. This will normally start with the DFL Annual Plan (DFL-AP).

An example of the mapping to the annual plan is as follows:

> The organization's Tactical Business Plan goal that stated "it is expected to be able to integrate new high technology hardware, software, networks, and devices with minimum impact to schedules or costs."

> The Security Department's Tactical Business Plan is in support of this, which stated that it would provide adequate protection to the new high technology equipment and devices at least impact to the organization schedules and costs.

In the Digital Forensic Annual Plan, this could be addressed by establishing a project with the objective of arranging training a suitable number of the digital forensic investigators on the new high technologies at the earliest opportunity to ensure that the laboratory will be able to support investigations in the environment.

The digital forensic investigation manager must then also consider that in the DFL Annual Plan, a project would be created to address the upgrade, if necessary, of the digital forensic investigative tools and methodologies that would be used to conduct investigations in the new environment.

Writing the Digital Forensic Laboratory Tactical Plan

Writing the DFL Tactical Plan should be easier when experience has been gained from mapping the goals for the DFL Strategic Plan and DFL Tactical Plan, and the writing of the DFL Strategic Plan. Once that is accomplished, the digital forensic investigator manager will write the DFL Tactical Plan following the standard organizational format for plan writing.

Normally the format used within organizations will include the following elements:

1. Executive summary

2. Table of Contents

3. Introduction

4. DFL strategic goals

5. Description of the way in which the DFL tactics support the DFL-SP

6. Description of the way in which the DFL tactics support the organization tactics

7. Mapping charts

8. Conclusions

The Digital Forensic Laboratory Annual Plan

The digital forensic investigations manager will also have to develop a DFL Annual Plan to support the security departments and the overall strategic and tactical plans of the organizations. The plan will need to include suitable and realistic goals, objectives, and projects that will support the goals and objectives of the Annual Business Plans of the security department and the organization.

The Annual Plans of the security department and the organization are used to identify and implement projects to accomplish the goals and objectives as stated in the Digital Forensic Laboratory Strategic Tactical Plans. These are the "building blocks" of the DFL Program.

The DFL annual program will require the following elements:

- Identification of a project leader

- Project management techniques

- A schedule (Gantt charts)

- Identified start date for each project
- Identified end date for each project
- Objectives for each project
- Budgeting and cost tracking

Projects within the Digital Forensic Laboratory Annual Plan

When the DFL is established, the first project that will form a part of the first DFL Annual Plan might be to identify the current DFL environment within the organization. In order to achieve this, the following projects might be established:

Project 1—Title: The Digital Forensic Laboratory Organization

Project manager: Digital forensic investigation manager

Objective: Establish a DFL organization

Start Date: October 1, 2008

End Date: October 15, 2008

Project 2—Title: Digital Forensic Laboratory Team

Project Lead: Digital forensic investigator

Objective: Establish a DFL Working Group to assist in the creation and support for a DFL program

Start Date: October 1, 2008

End Date: December 31, 2009

Project 3—Title: Development of Digital Forensic Laboratory Policies and Procedures

Project manger: Digital forensic investigation manager

Objective: Identify, document, and review all DFL-related documentation, and establish a process to ensure relevance and currency

Start Date: October 16, 2008

End Date: November 30, 2008

Project 4—Title: Development of Digital Forensic Laboratory Roles and Functions

Project manger: Digital forensic investigation manager

Objective: To Identify and establish DFL roles and functions and the associated processes procedures

Start Date: December 1, 2008

End Date: December 31, 2008

Mapping the Digital Forensic Laboratory Annual Plan to the Security Department and the Overall Organization Annual Business Plan

As shown before, mapping the digital forensic laboratory Annual Plan to the security department Annual Business Plan and the organizational Annual Business Plan should be easily achievable. However, in this specific case, the organizational Annual Plan and the security department Annual Plan objectives were not mapped to the DFL Annual Plan.

Writing the Digital Forensic Laboratory Annual Plan

As indicated earlier, wherever possible, the writing of the plans should follow the format used by the rest of the organization. The DFL Annual Plan is no exception and the following format is fairly standard:

1. Executive summary
2. Table of Contents
3. Introduction
4. DFL annual goals
5. DFL projects
6. How the DFL Projects support the Annual Plan goals
7. Mapping charts
8. Conclusion

Mapping the Digital Forensic Laboratory Strategic Plan, the Tactical Plan, and Annual Plan to Projects Using a Matrix

Another approach that can be taken to mapping is the use of a matrix. This approach can be used in a number of ways, and at a number of levels, for example, the organization's Strategic Business Plan to the security department to the DFL Strategic Plan. This method should identify any holes in the plans that need to be addressed.

Summary

In summary, when it comes to DFL planning, the digital forensic investigator–manager must integrate the plans for the laboratory with those of the organization's security department and the parent organization overall. Remember that:

- The DFL Strategic, Tactical, and Annual Plans must be mapped and integrated into the Strategic, Tactical, and Annual Business Plans of the organization.

- The DFL Plans must incorporate the Vision, Mission, Quality, and Compliance Statements, and their philosophies and concepts.

- The DFL plans must identify strategies, goals, objectives, and projects that are not only coherent and support each other, but also support and integrate with the organization plans.

- By mapping the DFL plans with the goals of the plans of the organization, the required information fusion can take place.

- The process of mapping will make it easier for the digital forensic investigation manager to write the appropriate DFL plans.

- The DFL-AP will normally consist of a set of projects that form the individual elements of the DFL program and that follow the strategies and tactics of the DFL-SP and DFL-TP.

It must be reiterated that the plans at all levels and for the short, medium, and long term must be coherent and mutually supportive. Although it can be time consuming to ensure that the plans are mutually supportive, it is essential and will actually help with the justifications for staff, equipment, and training.

Chapter 17

Networking, Liaison, and Sources of Information

Introduction

The field of digital forensics is complex and rapidly changing. If the staff of the digital forensic laboratory are to maintain the high level of competence that is essential and its ability to deliver a professional quality of service, it is important that relationships with other parts of its parent organization and other organizations are developed and maintained. With the range of skills and the number of specialist areas that impact the digital forensics arena, access to up-to-date, accurate information on technical and regulatory developments and access to the latest tools and techniques is essential. Allied to this is the need to capture and store this knowledge and information in a manner that makes it accessible and searchable so that if an item of information exists, it is always accessible to the people who need it. For those issues that are encountered for which there is not a known solution, access to the network of your peers and the domain specialists is invaluable.

The objective of this chapter is to identify, describe, and discuss a range of information sources of various types, joining and establishing networks with your peers, and liaison with outside agencies.

Knowledge and Skills

In today's high-technology environment, developments have, and are continuing to take place in information and communications technologies at an ever-increasing rate. It would be incredibly expensive and difficult for one laboratory or group of people to obtain and maintain an up-to-date and leading edge level of knowledge in all the relevant areas. It is essential for the manager of the laboratory, with the help of the staff, who will have their own specific areas of knowledge and contacts, to develop a comprehensive portfolio of sources of knowledge and contacts that can be accessed when there is a specific problem to be addressed.

Networking

It is important that digital forensic laboratory managers maintain their networking efforts with their counterparts, who they have met as a result of work or at conferences, association meetings, or even as a result of a chance encounter. These contacts should be recorded in a database and categorized by their area and level of knowledge or skill (e.g., operating systems, networks, live memory forensics, PDA forensics, etc.). The digital forensic laboratory managers will also have to establish their and the laboratorys' credentials and credibility with their peer group and will have to show that they can contribute to the knowledge pool before they will gain a great deal from the relationships. This can take time and will certainly take effort, but is invaluable in gaining access to the information that will be needed for the digital forensic examiners to carry out their role effectively and to the appropriate standard.

In the high-technology environment in which digital forensics takes place, the people that the manager will need to interact with will certainly have e-mail addresses and in fact will normally do most of their communication via this means. Contacting them periodically via e-mail and making the occasional telephone call are very cost-effective ways to maintain the relationships, gather information, and keep abreast of developments in your areas of interest. Often, the information that is obtained as a result of these communications can provide the knowledge or expertise needed for a particular investigation.

For example, if a new forensic tool or technique that addresses a problem that the laboratory could not solve in the past, or that makes the task easier to carry out was discovered, then it could be passed to others who could benefit from it through the peer network. Doing this can have a number of major advantages: first, it gives others the tool that they also need to address the problem for investigations in their laboratory. Next, it shows the laboratory as a credible and knowledgeable organization (this earns it credits with its peers). It can also provide a "sanity check" for the tool or technique and allow for peer review and even an external contribution to its future development.

Liaison

The word liaison is taken from the French language and is defined[1] as "communication for establishing and maintaining mutual understanding and cooperation (as between parts of an armed force)." For the manager and staff of the digital forensic laboratory, it means just that: communicating between the laboratory and government and law enforcement agencies and other laboratories and organizations.

Liaison with other groups and individuals will always be in the best interests of the digital forensic laboratory as part of their involvement in the professional community, and the exchange of information with law enforcement agencies on digital forensic issues will be of mutual benefit to all parties.

Good examples of the types of organization that will enable the interaction needed to foster a relationship of trust and support will include membership and active support of groups such as your local High Technology Crime Investigation Association (HTCIA) branch or the FBI Infraguard program.

Networking with Contacts inside the Organization

It is important for the digital forensic laboratory manager to develop and maintain a good working relationship with a range of individuals and groups both inside and outside the organization. In developing a network of contacts within the organization, the manager will be putting in place the infrastructure that will help the investigators to gain the information, knowledge, and goodwill that will support them in carrying out their role. The range of people inside the organization with whom the manager will normally need to have at least a working relationship will include:

- The manager of the organization's legal department

- The manager of the organization's information security team

- The manager of the organization's accounting and finance department

- The organization's human resources department

- The manager of the organization's audit department

- The organization's systems management team

- The organization's physical security staff

- Depending on the type of organization in which you work, it is probable that you will need to add others to this list.

As the manager of the digital forensic laboratory, it is important that you:

- Meet and get to know the relevant people

- Get to know their departments and their individual roles and responsibilities

- Understand how they can help your team and how you can support them

Networking outside the Organization

The external contacts and sources of information can be anyone outside the organization or anyone inside it who is not a direct employee, for example a contractor or a consultant who is working at one of the organization's facilities.

Outside the organization it is also important to maintain a good working relationship with a range of organizations, which will include the local, state/province/regional, and federal/national security and law enforcement agencies in those places where the organization's facilities are located, regardless of which country they may be in.

Effort should also be made to maintain good relationships with the local community, as this can not only enhance the image of the organization, but can also result in the acquisition of useful information and assistance. All this is in addition to those other individuals and organizations that will have the information and knowledge in a whole range of digital forensic and other topics that will be of relevance.

As the digital forensic laboratory develops and the investigators become established it is a good idea to assign each of them a number of organizations with which to develop relationships. They will need to keep in contact with them when they are not actively involved in conducting investigations, inquiries, briefings, surveys, research, and the like. It will always be necessary for the digital forensic manager to personally handle some of the relationships because of the role that they carry out or the authority and position that they hold.

Maintaining the List of Contacts

The details of anyone who has provided digital forensic related information should be recorded for future reference. In the past, this type of contact information was kept on index cards (Roladex's or similar) or in collections of business cards. These days, this information is more easily maintained on the digital forensic laboratory's contacts database, where searches can easily be conducted to find contacts that have provided information on a specific topic in the past or that are recorded as having knowledge in that area.

Some of the basic information that normally would be entered onto the database for a contact is:

- Name
- Position/title
- Organization
- Address
- Telephone number

- Fax number

- E-mail address

- Time, date, and location of first contact

- Details of subsequent contacts

- Area of knowledge or skill and assessment of level of expertise

- Name of investigator providing contact details

These details can be expanded and include more details as required. However, caution must be used to ensure that the collection and storage of this information can be shown to be necessary and that it stored in an appropriate manner and in compliance with relevant legislation (e.g., the Data Protection Act in the United Kingdom). This type of information also should have a short expiration date (people do move around and get promoted fairly regularly in this area). If there hasn't been a contact with the person in a year, then they either should be contacted and the relationship renewed or the information should be deleted; however, this will be a judgment call by the digital forensic unit manager.

Collecting and Storing Information

The staff of the digital forensic laboratory will bring with them and develop or collect a wealth of knowledge that is fundamental to the ability of the laboratory being able to carry out its role in a competent and professional manner. Any good investigator, whatever their field of expertise, will know that he or she is largely only as good as his or her information resources. In the digital forensic area, where the range of information that is required and the diversity of potential sources is huge, it is important that any information that is collected is stored in a way that makes it easily accessible to the staff. The individual staff members will bring with them and then further develop knowledge and skill in their specific area of expertise, but the manager must ensure that there is a system in place that captures that knowledge, the "corporate body of knowledge," so that it can be used by all the staff when required. This is a good way of making available and transferring the knowledge from one staff member to another, and is also a way of maintaining that knowledge within the organization, even in the event of a specialist leaving.

Other Sources of Information and Knowledge

The range of sources for information that is relevant and of use to the digital forensic laboratory is huge, and a selection of those that they would expect to use will include, but is in no way limited to:

- Organizations
  - Local, state, regional, and federal or national government agencies and departments
  - Local, state, regional and federal or national law enforcement agencies
  - Other Digital Forensic Laboratories

- International Organization Of Computer Investigative Specialists (IACIS)
- High Technology Crime Investigation Association (HTCIA)
- Defense Cyber Crime Institute
- The Scientific Working Group on Digital Evidence
- Web sites, newsgroups, and listservers
  - The HTCC listserver (limited access)
  - Forensic Focus
  - geschonneck.com
  - Forensic Wiki
  - Dave Dittrick, University of Washington
  - Computer Forensics World
- Journals
  - Journal of Digital Forensics Security and Law
  - Journal of Digital Forensic Practice
  - Digital Investigation Journal
  - International Journal of Digital Evidence
  - The Small Scale Digital Device Forensic Journal
- Academia
  - Edith Cowan University
  - University of Glamorgan
  - Longwood University
  - University of Alabama at Birmingham
  - University of Western Sydney
  - Queensland University of Technology
  - University of Louisville, Kentucky
  - University of Rhode Island
- Research Organizations
  - National Institute of Standards and Technology (NIST)
  - Brian Carrier, Digital Forensic Organization
- Vendors
  - Guidance Software— Encase
  - E-Fense—Helix

- Access Data Corp—Forensic Toolkit (FTK)
- WetStone Technologies—LiveWire Investigator
- Technology Pathways—Prodiscover
- Paraben Corporation—Mobile device forensics
- Oxygen—Mobile Phone Manger
- Conferences
  - Australian Digital Forensics Conference
  - ADFSL Conference on Digital Forensics, Security, and Law
  - TechnoForensics
  - The Computer Forensic Show
  - Black Hat
  - WORLDCOMP
- Networking meetings
  - High Tech Crime Investigators Association
  - First Forensic Forum (F3)
  - FBI Infraguard Program
  - Digital Forensic Research Workshop
  - National Cyber-Forensics & Training Alliance

NOTE

A more comprehensive list of useful resources, together with relevant URLs, can be found in Appendix A.

Classifying the Reliability of Sources and the Accuracy of Their Information

There are a wide range of individuals and organizations that have specific knowledge or skills with which you may need to interact to obtain information. There are also a large number of web sites that contain information that may be of value. When gathering information from any of these potential resources, always remember that there are a range of levels of expertise out there and also a number of reasons why people are willing to share that information or knowledge. Some of the resources will be people with a high level of expertise and who are motivated to support and improve the digital forensic capability. Other sources will be less skilled but well intentioned, and others, who may be highly skilled and have valuable knowledge, may be motivated to mislead and obstruct if they have the opportunity. As a result, when you are gathering your storehouse of knowledge, it is essential that you develop a track record of the information sources and annotate each "gem" of information with the source from which it was obtained, and the value and accuracy of the information that they have provided.

This may seem tedious and a waste of time, but it is essential for a number of reasons. The first is that, over time, the track record will start to reveal the good sources, the "just OK" sources, and the downright unreliable ones. This will help you in developing the relationships that you will need and help you to avoid wasting time. It will also act as a pointer to the sources that are most likely to provide you with the right information when you need it in a hurry and have to make a phone call or send an e-mail for advice.

One way of achieving this is for the digital forensic manager to develop a system within the unit, which will provide the user of the information with an indication of the reliability of the source of the information and the probability that the information is accurate. One of the easiest ways is to use the system that has been employed in government for a considerable period of time and that undoubtedly will be familiar to a number of the readers. This is to include two fields in the record of each database entry that will assist in evaluating the source and the information provided by the source. The two fields are:

- Reliability of Source
- Reliability of Sources Information

Whenever anyone adds an item of information to the database they are required to make an assessment and to "grade the source and information" using the following grades:

- Source Reliability:
    - Grade 1: Always reliable
    - Grade 2: Usually reliable
    - Grade 3: Sometimes reliable
    - Grade 4: Questionable reliability
    - Grade 5: Has never been reliable
    - Grade 6: Reliability unknown at this time
- Information Provided by the Source Has Proven to Be:
    - Grade A: Always accurate
    - Grade B: Usually accurate
    - Grade C: Sometimes accurate
    - Grade D: Accuracy is always questionable
    - Grade E: Never accurate
    - Grade F: Accuracy of the information is unknown at this time

If the information database is kept up to date, then every digital forensic investigator within the laboratory will have a ready source of reference material that is up to date and spans the knowledge available to the laboratory. The database will give a good indication of the reliability of the information and a pointer to the source of the information that can be used if more detail or information is required. The database should be queried prior to any meeting with an individual to determine if they previously have provided information and whether their information was useful and accurate.

Summary

The digital forensic laboratory will not be able to function to its full potential without having access to a whole range of information resources and people who have specific knowledge and skills. Maintaining the relationships, networking, and actively liaising with outside groups and government agencies are all excellent ways to:

- Help develop the skills and knowledge of the staff
- Obtain the information needed to keep up to date with the latest developments and events in the profession
- Exchange information with peers and peer organizations
- Engage with the local community, which can be invaluable for the organization when the digital forensic laboratory needs support and input from the community
- Develop the relationship and support the local law enforcement agencies and others

Given the requirements for accuracy, repeatability, accountability, and a quality that make the results of an investigation acceptable in court, the peer group can have incredible value in communicating best practice and in establishing the validity of new tools and techniques.

The second issue is that, having expended time and effort in gaining the knowledge and information from a wide range of sources, it is important that it is stored in a manner that allows it to be validated, graded, cross referenced, and searched to ensure that the maximum value is gained from it.

Note

1. In the Merriam Webster online dictionary, http://www.merriam-webster.com/dictionary/liaison

Chapter 18

Computer Forensics Investigation Unit Metrics Management System

Introduction

Tracking the life of any assignment from receipt in the laboratory to return to the customer is of crucial importance. Within this process must be embedded the requirement for continuity of the evidence or chain of custody records so that the courts may be satisfied as to the veracity of the process. Also, there must be a record of the hours spent so that the profitability is not sacrificed to the inherent curiosity of an examiner or his or her desire to examine every last artifact.

The tracking and the hours spent on imaging and analysis need to be carefully accounted for so that each assignment provides a profit, and although there may be a view that the collection of what seems to be minutiae is for the "bean counters," the resultant information will be of use in a number of ways.

This chapter will look at the variety of metrics that may be used by the laboratory manager to ensure that the team is profitable, directing their efforts in the correct way and adhering to best practice, and that their procedures are evidentially sound.

The Metrics

The following sections give a breakdown of the areas where metrics need to be obtained, and the specific topics on which they should be collected.

Management Issues

In order to understand the cost of the operation of the laboratory, you will need to have an understanding of a range of elements, and be able to support it with evidence, including:

- Cost of laboratory space and running costs
- Cost of salaries
- Cost of media to image to and back-up
- Storage costs of submitted digital media
- Storage costs of backup copies of imaged media
- Cost of training for analysts
- Cost of continued training (professional development training)
- Cost of specialist training
- Cost of membership to professional organizations
- Cost of security vetting
- Cost of running disaster recover or business continuity site
- Throughput of investigations
- Balanced workload for analysts
- Cost of psychiatric well-being interviews

- Cost of equipment
- Cost and timetable of refreshing equipment
- Allocation of hours per investigation
- Time taken in supervision by laboratory manager
- Time taken managing appearances of staff within the criminal and civil court system.
- Time taken managing the asset register
- Time taken to upkeep weeding and disposal of digital media
- Time taken managing the quality assurance / ISO 9001 process

The Quotation Process

In order to create a quotation for a piece of work by the laboratory, you will need to take into consideration a range of issues that will have an impact on the cost of the work.

- Number of submitted tower/desktop computers
- Number of submitted laptop computers
- Number of submitted loose hard disk drives
- Number and capacity of submitted hard disk drives
- Number of submitted floppy diskettes
- Number of submitted CD-ROMs
- Number of submitted DVDs
- Number and capacity of other digital media that will be submitted
- Cost of collection/return of items submitted
- The required turnaround time
- The imaging time for the submitted media
- The type of investigation required
- The complexity of the investigation
- Time needed to run key word searches
- Time needed for the analytical process
- Time needed for the reporting process
- Time needed for the quality assurance process
- Cost of independent quality assurance review

The Imaging Process

In order to understand the cost of the operation of the laboratory and to enable you to determine the most effective way to carry out the individual processes that are undertaken in the imaging process, you will need to have an understanding on the metrics of a range of elements including:

- Time taken in opening and recording details in case file

- Time taken in examining, photographing, and recording physical details of submitted digital media

- Time taken copying photos to case file and WORM (Write Once Read Many) media

- Time taken in removing hard disk drives from target machine and for checking for inserted CD-ROMs/DVDs or floppy diskettes

- Time taken to connect media to write blocking media and software

- Time taken to image target digital media

- Time taken to record contemporaneous notes of process

- Time taken to conduct and record BIOS time and date

- Time taken to reseal imaged digital media and record details thereof

- Time taken to write report/statement of actions taken and results obtained

The Analytical Process

Again, in order to understand the cost of the operation of the laboratory and to enable you to determine the most effective way to carry out the individual processes that make up the analytical process, you will need to have an understanding on the metrics of a range of elements including:

- Time taken to open analyst's case file

- Time taken to read case file/notes submitted by the case officer

- Time taken to create a contemporaneous note file to record actions/decisions

- Time taken to contact and discuss with the case officer the objectives of the examination

- Time taken to create key search words/expressions/grep expressions

- Time taken to run searches for keywords/files/pictures/movies, etc.

- Time taken in manual recovery of files from unallocated or slack space

- Time taken to complete dual-tool verification of primary artifacts

- Time taken to review finding with case officer

- Time taken to deal with defense requests

- Time taken to deal with encrypted items

- Time taken in cross-reading reports

- Time taken in peer review of reports

- Time taken in report writing

- Time taken in statement production

- Time taken for independent quality assurance review

When quoting for unseen computers, laptops, and other digital media it is important to gain as much information on the type and size of media to be submitted.

- Is there media that may necessitate the purchase of software not currently owned within the laboratory?

- What is the total size of the submitted media and how much time will it take to image?

- If there are quantities of CD-ROMs, DVDs, or floppy diskettes, does the client require all to be imaged or only those that show particular attributes such as photographs or Excel spreadsheets?

- How detailed is the investigation going to be? Is this a hunt for traces left by a hacker, or looking for live/deleted Word, Excel, Sage documents and spreadsheets together with recovered e-mail for a suspected fraud?

- If the case is one being undertaken under contract to law enforcement, then are there hundreds or possibly tens of thousands of indecent pictures that will need to be viewed and graded?

- What is the turnaround time for the client and can it be balanced against current workload, or does the manager, indeed can they, subcontract?

- What media will be used to return the images to the client and at what cost?

The final quotation needs to take account of all the metrics contained within this chapter. Although it may seem obvious, the first factor to consider is the method of transmission of the submitted media from the client to the laboratory. If the case is likely at any stage to become part of the criminal justice system whether civil or criminal, there must be enforced the continuity of evidence or chain of custody so that the submitted media may be tracked from origin to receipt at the laboratory, through all processes with the laboratory until return to the client. A break in this process gives rise to the possibility that the evidence obtained, however compelling, will not be put before the tribunal or court. The fallout for the laboratory will inevitably be a loss of client confidence.

The cost of this and the logistics of collection and return must be factored into the costs of the examination.

Many of the issues expressed in the management issues metrics are self-explanatory, however there are some that do not immediately spring to mind when thinking about how the metrics will drive a successful and useable pricing policy.

The training needs for forensic analysts must be carefully balanced so as to provide the right mixture of skills in the laboratory. Although every analyst will need training to a high level on the forensic software(s) of choice, not every analyst needs to be trained in every tool in the kit box. The costs of software licences and refresh of computers should also be factored into the cost. The speed of the analytical process is dependent to a great extent on the processing power and memory available. Storage media for the analysts is crucial to allow them to work on one investigation while running searches on another.

Allocation of hours to each investigation, if the metrics just described are taken into account, should ensure that the laboratory is run on a profitable basis while enabling the analyst to complete a thorough investigation. It is important that supervision is maintained to ensure that the hours are not either underused or exceeded without management knowledge and authority.

The throughput of investigations is the most obvious metric on which to judge the performance of the laboratory as a whole and the individual members of staff; however, the complexity of the investigation and requirements of the client must be factored in.

If the laboratory is contracted to law enforcement and deals with pedophilic material on a regular basis, then health and safety concerns dictate that all staff that come into contact with this type of material have the ability to talk, in confidence, to independent suitably trained practitioners. Many laboratories have chosen to have contracts with psychiatric practitioners, and as part of their contract of employment, staff are required to attend interviews on a regular basis. The cost that this imposes must be factored into the cost.

Training is a continuing requirement and continued professional development training should be factored into the cost of the laboratory. Academic qualifications are to be encouraged, and a number of universities now have degree programs in forensic computing, or have forensic computing as a module of the course, particularly at the Masters level. It is of importance that analysts are kept current with trends in investigation and new developments both in hardware and software.

If the laboratory has, or is required to keep, a back-up archive of imaged data then that cost together with the cost of maintaining the archive in useable format must be factored in. There will also be the cost of managing the security of the premises and the retained data.

The metrics suggested for the imaging and analytical processes may be used in a number of ways. The most obvious is that of judging the efficiency of the individual imaging technician or forensic analyst in terms of throughput of cases. This is useful to review at times of annual appraisal and salary reviews.

The data collected will also, if recorded over time, give the laboratory management information with regard to the efficiency of process, software tools, computer equipment, and whether there needs to be improvement in any areas. Evaluation of software that is used to search for artifacts can be set against known data sets to test whether or not efficiency is improved, and therefore there is a cogent spend-to-save rationale for purchase.

A prerequisite of a successful laboratory is a well-founded quality assurance process; the ISO 9001 charter mark is one example of such a process that fits neatly with the workings of a digital forensics laboratory.

The QA process needs to capture the entire flow of activity in the forensics laboratory from initial receipt of an enquiry, to quotation, arrangements for collection/receipt of the digital media, imaging and analysis, report writing, quality assurance regime, return of exhibits, and finally the invoicing process and something that all laboratories seek to avoid but nevertheless becomes necessary at times, a disputes resolution procedure.

The metrics devised and collected in the processes described will aid enormously the process mapping of policy and procedure for the company and employees, which will ensure that all adhere to the quality assurance processes and maintain the standards.

A successfully run quality assurance regime ensures that employees understand and promulgate the standards set, and ensures that the customer sees a product that is useful, understandable, well presented, answers the questions posed, meets evidential stands, and most importantly represents value for money. The client satisfaction with the process, their knowledge that there is a simple, understandable dispute resolution procedure with escalation points built in will lead to repeat business, the object of every successful forensic laboratory and something that every business wants.

Summary

This chapter has looked at the metrics that will need to be collected during all phases of the operation of the laboratory in order for the manager to understand the cost base of the digital forensics process, to be able to make objective decisions on changes to the processes and equipment and software, that the laboratory is adhering to best practice, and that their procedures are evidentially sound. The range of metrics that are required may seem excessive, but it is only when you have this level of detail available that you can understand the effect that changes may have.

Summary

Chapter 19

Workload Management and the Outsourcing Option

Introduction[1]

This chapter will discuss whether to outsource or keep in-house either whole digital forensic investigations or individual tasks within the investigation. Having the right level of resources to meet the demands that will be made of the Digital Forensic Laboratory will not always be achievable, but should be planned for. There are a number of ways in which the workload of the laboratory can be managed and two of these will be detailed here. The alternative option of outsourcing is a management tool that can help in balancing the workload and can also help to save money.

This chapter will look at the possibilities of outsourcing either specific tasks or whole investigations, and a process that can be used to make that determination.

In-house Workload Management

Inevitably, the flow of work that comes into the laboratory will have peaks and troughs, both in the flow of work and the type of specialist knowledge required. The reality is that in most laboratories it is normally a case of peaks and higher peaks, with an ever-increasing workload and ever greater demands made on the staff. In order to address this ever-present problem, it is essential that the digital forensic manager puts in place measures that can help to ensure a balance between the requirements of the customers and the capacity and capabilities of the staff.

The traditional way of dealing with the workload is for the manager of the laboratory to take in more work than can be dealt with immediately, and accept that there will be a backlog that will be dealt with on a first-come, first-served basis. With experience this can work with some degree of success, as the manager should be able to predict when there will be periods that are quieter than others, when the laboratory can catch up and deal with the backlog.

There are a number of potential problems and shortcomings with this approach. The first is that there is no prioritization of tasks so that those with a higher priority are dealt with first. The second is the time lag that can occur between the acceptance of a task and the production of the report of the findings. This may turn out to be a significant period of time and may have an impact on the actions that can be taken as a result of the investigation. Another issue is that this approach relies on there being periods of lower activity that will allow the staff to catch up with the backlog, but if this does not happen, the backlog remains and will probably continue to increase.

There are steps that can be taken to support this type of approach. The first is to procure new software and hardware that will allow for a faster throughput of jobs. This can address either a particular bottleneck in the processing or all aspects of the investigation. The second approach could be to automate steps within the digital forensic process to reduce the manpower required to achieve the same level of productivity. A third option is to recruit or train additional staff to meet the extra workload, but this should be considered only when the level of work in the laboratory is consistently higher than can be addressed by the existing staff.

Using Triage Techniques

Another approach that can be adopted is that of using a process called *triage*. In this process the jobs coming into the laboratory are ranked according to their importance or priority. This approach has been used for a long time, particularly in the area of medical emergencies and disaster management situations, where either the resources available are limited or the probability of a successful outcome varies.

The concept of triage, in the medical/disaster context, separates casualties into a number of categories depending on the severity of the injuries.

- The first group is the deceased, who are left in situ and those casualties that will not survive, even if they are evacuated to a hospital.

- The second group are those for immediate evacuation, who have a chance of survival if they receive medical care as soon as possible. These people will be in a critical condition and would probably die without rapid assistance.

- The third group consists of those who are less seriously injured and are in a stable condition but will still require medical assistance. The evacuation of this group can be delayed until all those in the second group have been evacuated.

If the concept of triaging is adapted for tasks in the digital forensic laboratory, it can be successful only if it is undertaken on a basis of good knowledge. In order to manage this, it is essential that enough information is obtained to make a decision regarding the material that is presented for investigation.

The issues that will need to be addressed will include the seriousness of the suspected incident. It is sensible that incidents that are considered to be the most serious will receive a higher priority and be dealt with first. However, incidents that have a high potential value or impact or that are likely to be part of a larger investigation must also be allocated an appropriate priority. Other ways in which the work can be prioritized include ensuring that there is an understanding of how much evidence is enough (how much evidence is required to satisfy the investigation). Account should also be taken of what skills will be required to address the task and how much resource in that area is available, whether the task can be automated, and the level of detail of reporting that is required.

In-house or Outsource?

For a digital forensic laboratory that is part of a large organization, always remember that the laboratory will normally be considered to be an overhead. As a result, the laboratory manager must always be conscious of the expense of running the laboratory and the value for money that it provides. They need to keep under constant review the practices and procedures that are in use to try and find ways in which they can be accomplished more effectively and efficiently. One way in which this objective might be achieved is to examine the option of outsourcing either parts of or all of the digital forensic investigation function in some of the cases.

Within an organization, it is probable that the digital forensic laboratory will be asked to carry out a range of tasks that will vary in importance and also in the skills that are required. Some of these will be jobs that clearly fall within the remit of the laboratory, but it is inevitable that some of them will be outside the scope of the original remit. Although this will help the triage process, when the laboratory has spare capacity (well we are hypothesizing, aren't we?), these tasking requests should not be discounted, as they can be interesting, allow the team to gain additional skills and experience, and potentially earn a wealth of goodwill and credibility within an organization.

The types of assistance that may be requested have been discussed in earlier chapters but the tasks may well range from recovering important data from a failed system, to data discovery for the audit or legal departments, to digital forensic support to a security or criminal investigation or live digital forensics on a network.

Like any manager, the digital forensic laboratory manger will have a limited set of resources available to provide this range of services to the organization. The laboratory manager must be able to provide the best possible range and quality of services at the lowest cost. To do this, the laboratory manager must evaluate the cost effectiveness of outsourcing some forensic investigation functions. In order to carry out this process there are a number of actions that the laboratory manager must take and items of information that will be needed in order to carry out a comprehensive analysis. This analysis is normally undertaken in two parts:

- The first part of the process is an initial assessment. This must be carried out to determine whether outsourcing elements of the digital forensic investigative function is a viable option.

- Second, a detailed analysis must be made to determine whether outsourcing is the most cost effective option.

A Definition of Outsourcing

Outsourcing is defined as contracting for outside services that are a necessary part of doing business, but are either not core competencies or allow the laboratory to deal with a workload in excess of its resources. A core competency may be a service, activity, or process that is fundamental to the role of the laboratory and will not normally be candidates for outsourcing unless the process of outsourcing is used to enhance the capability of the laboratory (provide additional resource). There are a number of tasks that should not be considered for outsourcing and these include tasks where intellectual value will be generated, those that are of a sensitive nature or are for classified material, those that rely on either the management's or the laboratory's trust relationships, and those that do not easily lend themselves to outsourcing.

The Advantages and Disadvantages of Carrying Out Tasks In-house

The decision to develop and maintain a team and the laboratory in order to be able to carry out investigations using in-house facilities will have been made as a result of a reasoned and costed evaluation of the need for the capability. There are always reasons why a task should or should not be carried out in-house. Depending upon conditions and circumstances there will always be advantages and disadvantages, and depending on which is the stronger, it will affect the decision as to whether the task is conducted in-house or not. Detailed next are a number of the more significant pros and cons of an in-house digital forensic capability.

Pros

The following are a number of the main reasons for conducting the digital forensic investigations in-house:

- **Corporate Knowledge:** Since in-house staff work within the organization, they have knowledge of the organization that an external supplier (outsourced) will have difficulty in developing. This will be invaluable in easing the conduct of an investigation.

- **Development and Maintenance of Expertise:** An in-house team of investigators develop the relevant skills and experience that best meet the needs of the organization. As the team develops skills to meet the needs of the organization they will be available for use within the organization in a variety of ways. The maintenance of an in-house team will allow the manager to keep that functional expertise within the company and under control of the laboratory.

- **Continuity:** The turnover of digital investigative staff within an in-house laboratory is generally less frequent than that of staff with an outsourced provider. Since in-house digital investigative staff are generally better paid and have appropriate training and employee benefits within the organization, they tend to move less frequently. There will also tend to be a degree of belonging and loyalty to the organization from in-house staff.

- **Management control:** An in-house laboratory facility provides for direct management control over tasks and the performance and career opportunities of the staff. This means that the processing of tasks is fully under the control of the organization.

Cons

The following are reasons for not maintaining an in-house digital forensic capability or for outsourcing tasks or functions:

- **Costs:** Maintaining an in-house capability will always have a set of underlying and ongoing costs. These costs exist whether there is work coming into the laboratory or not. Part of the process of making the decision to have an in-house capability will be based on the needs of the organization. This could outweigh the fact that it may be possible to get the same level of service from an outsourced supplier for the same cost or less. In addition, there are hidden costs associated with an in-house capability that are not associated with outsourced employees. These hidden costs may include things such as occasional perks provided to members of staff, and training and capital costs that are not easily identified and often are overlooked when making a comparison or assessment.

- **Availability and flexibility:** With an in-house capability, the laboratory manager will have access to a limited number of staff resources. When the level of work that is required of the laboratory exceeds the capability of those resources, there is no spare capacity available to satisfy the requirement. As a result, it might be necessary to hire temporary additional full time or part time personnel, or start or increase the use of overtime. All these options are likely to be expensive.

The Advantages and Disadvantages of Outsourcing Work from the Digital Forensic Laboratory

Outsourcing has the potential to provide either additional resource for the existing capability or to augment the existing services. If a suitable outsource service provider or providers are used, the relationship has the potential to become more of a partnership than a customer/supplier relationship. The decision to use outsourcing may be driven by cost, the available staff, and laboratory resources or flexibility. It may appear that the option of outsourcing is one to which we can turn when there is a resource issue within the laboratory, but to believe this is a serious error. In order to successfully use an external provider, the laboratory manager will have to have developed a relationship with, potentially, a number of providers. This is essential in order to understand and have tested the capabilities and range of resources that each of the suppliers can provide, and their charging structure.

As with any other situation, the time to start sorting out the arrangements for outsourcing tasks is not at the point when you need them—by then it is far too late. Once the relationships with the external suppliers have been developed, they have to be managed and there will need to be regular management oversight and a very clear, delivery-focused approach will need to be implemented. The outsourcing relationship must give value to both the organization and the external supplier. It this is not sustained then the relationship will not work. Ideally the relationship with any supplier of outsourced capability should be approached as a long-term relationship. In doing this, the required effort will be invested in establishing and managing the relationship and the maximum benefit will be derived. A number of the issues related to outsourcing are addressed below.

Pros

Detailed here are a number of the reasons why the organization might outsource tasks from the digital forensic laboratory:

- **Cost:** The option of outsourcing may be the most cost effective way of completing a task within a given timeframe. It can be used as an alternative or in conjunction with overtime payments for staff or the employment of additional full or part time staff.

- **Flexibility:** The use of outsourcing can provide greater flexibility for investigative staffing than relying solely on in-house resources. It is much easier to move, replace, or terminate the use of a resource from an outsource provider than it is to move or replace one that is an employee of the organization. The resources of an outsource provider are contracted for a specific task and are not on the payroll of the organization.

- **Surge capability:** Unforeseen events can place a heavy burden on the resources of the laboratory. With the use of in-house resources, a short-term option might be to use the option of paying staff for overtime. However, this may not always be enough to meet the requirement or may not be sustainable. If the requirement is for resource over a longer period, then additional options available to the manager will include hiring additional full time or part time staff to support the need. The use of an outsourced capability may be a better solution for a number of reasons. The first is that, by using a number of outsourcing providers, there will be access to a larger group of personnel to draw from, with specific skills, which should make it easier to meet your requirements. The second is that adopting an outsourcing option will mean that the cost of addressing the additional requirement can be accurately calculated.

■ **Resource Management:** When a task is outsourced, one of the advantages is that the day-to-day management of the relevant staff is also outsourced. This means that the day-to-day management of staff issues for the outsourced tasks is the responsibility of the outsource provider and they also have some degree of responsibility for ensuring the quality of the work that is carried out (it is in their interests to ensure that the work that is carried out by their staff is of a suitable quality). In the event of the allocated staff becoming unavailable for reasons such as ill health, the outsourcing provider will be responsible for finding an alternative resource.

Cons

Detailed here are a number of the reasons why it might not be advantageous for the organization to outsource tasks from the digital forensic laboratory:

■ **Loyalty:** The in-house staff will be perceived to have a greater degree of loyalty to the parent organization. Staff from an outsourced supplier will always be viewed as having their first loyalty to their employer. Although this should not affect their performance on the task that they are working on, it may affect the knowledge and organizational information to which they are exposed. However, if the relationship between the digital forensics laboratory and the outsource provider is a long-term partnership and has proven to be a well-defined and mutually beneficial relationship, loyalty should not be an issue, as the out sourcing organization itself will develop a loyalty to the laboratory.

■ **Quality of resource:** Although the cost of obtaining resource from an outsource provider is one of the reasons that this option may be considered, you should remember the old adage that you get what you pay for. Even with an established relationship with an out-source provider, the skilled staff that you are perhaps used to or expect may not be available when you require them. Getting quality external digital forensic resource to carry out tasks is as much about having produced a well-defined statement of work as it is about offering a competitive rate for the task. A clear and well-defined statement of work will define what skills are required to fulfill the task. An understanding of the market will enable you to determine what represents competitive rates. A failure to determine the competitive rates and not having a well-defined statement of work will lead to either disappointment or paying over the odds for the task.

■ **Organizational understanding:** In-house staff will have a good and current understanding of the organization and will have relationships with people in other departments within the organization. A person from an outsourced provider will not have this organizational knowledge or the in-house relationships. This may not be important, depending on what task they have been brought in to undertake and also whether the person from the out-sourced provider is supplementing an in-house resource that can provide the organizational knowledge and contacts. If an outsourced provider is used on a regular basis, it is likely that they will develop the organizational knowledge and relationships with the relevant staff within the organization.

Analysis or Outsourcing Options

Before the decision is made to outsource a task or function, an analysis should be carried out to include the reason for outsourcing, cost considerations, scope of the outsourcing, and quality of services required.

Initial Analysis

Outsourcing is undertaken for any number of reasons. In the case of the digital forensic laboratory, it may be to obtain access to specific skills or to gain access to additional resources during a specific time period. Once it has been determined that a task of a function requires outsourcing, it is essential that an assessment is conducted to determine whether there are any proprietary issues involved. The following questions first must be answered:

1.   Is the function a proprietary function?

2.   Is the information that will be involved of a proprietary nature?

3.   Is the task a strategic or competitive activity?

If the answer to any of these questions is yes, then consideration must be given to not going forward with the outsourcing. If the decision is that the outsourcing should proceed, then steps must be put in place to adequately protect any sensitive information through confidentiality agreements, access control, or other proprietary processes. However, if the answer to all the questions is no, a more detailed analysis should be carried out. One of the issues that should be considered is the effect that outsourcing a task or a function may have on the staff of the laboratory. This may include the staff feeling that they are not considered capable of meeting the requirement, the loss of overtime pay, or not developing new skills or maintaining current skills. If the laboratory is staffed with union personnel, another issue may be whether union agreement is necessary before the task is outsourced. There may be clauses in the union contract that prohibit outsourcing or make it problematic. In addition, outsourcing may lead to or create resistance from union staff in other areas of the organization or a lack of cooperation from them.

To ensure that outsource providers that are being considered for the provision of service can meet the expectations of the organization, it is essential that there is a relationship (partnership) between the supplier and the organization and that both parties have a clear understanding of the work that needs to be accomplished, the time frame in which it must be achieved, and at what cost. When looking for potential outsource provision partners, one way to start might be to talk with other digital forensic laboratories with whom the laboratory has contact and find out who they recommend. After all, they may well have tried and tested these providers and be able to give you an assessment of their strengths and weaknesses and also potentially the rates that they charge (although this may be confidential and not available). In developing a relationship with potential providers, the laboratory manager will gain an understanding of the type of work that they have undertaken in the past and the level of experience that they have in the different areas.

Some of the questions to which the digital forensic laboratory manager should seek to get answers from their counterparts in other laboratories with regard to the potential outsource provider include:

- What other outsource providers were considered when a provider was being selected and which were not considered and why?

- Was the expected level of service achieved?

- Were any other benefits derived from outsourcing (transfer of knowledge, flexibility)?

- Were any problems encountered?

Other sources of information that the laboratory manager may consider using on potential outsourcing service providers could include any of the major professional forensic associations such as the High Tech Crime Investigators Association (HTCIA) or the International Association of Computer Investigative Specialists (IACIS).

The information that the laboratory manager gains as a result of undertaking this process will allow them to learn from the experience, success, and failures of others who have undertaken the process in the past. This can give a considerable saving in time, effort, and money.

At this point the digital forensic laboratory manager should be able to determine the types of tasks that it will be possible and advantageous to outsource, and the relative costs of doing so. It is worth pointing out at this point that if the digital forensic laboratory is part of a larger organization, there will undoubtedly be a process in place for the procurement of goods and services, and this process should be adopted wherever possible.

In an ideal situation, a competitive bid process should be initiated. This usually would mean finding between three and five potential providers depending upon availability. However, in the digital forensic environment, this may not be achievable or desirable, if specific skill sets are required. Where it is achievable, the process of competitive tendering is normally the best way to get the most cost-effective solution, although the process requires significant effort on behalf of the laboratory manager. The bid assessment process should include:

- Skill sets of the potential suppliers

- Experience of the potential suppliers

- References provided by each of the potential suppliers

- Response to Statement of Work

- Cost and affordability

- Availability for service (time and location limitations if any)

- Available resources to perform the task

- Responsiveness and flexibility

- Quality and measurement program

As a part of the competitive tender process, each of the potential outsource service providers should be provided with the relevant statements of work.

Detailed Analysis

The next part of the analysis process is to carry out a detailed analysis of the respective costs, quality, and experience available in order to make a final assessment with regard to the potential benefit and the value of outsourcing. Always bear in mind that if the cost of outsourcing a task is too high or is liable to result in degradation in the quality of service, then outsourcing should not be considered. When you are comparing the completion of a task using in-house resources with using an outsource provider, you need to consider cost, quality, available skill sets, and experience.

Cost

When considering the relative cost and value of outsourcing tasks, the digital forensic manager must know the underlying costs and benefits of maintaining the laboratory and the cost of carrying out a task in-house. As a part of the competitive tender process, the suppliers will provide the laboratory manager with cost information. The rates charged to the laboratory will be based on the outsource provider's costs, which will include their own laboratory overhead and fixed costs, staff wages, the cost of employee benefits and other associated costs, and their profit margin.

As part of the comparison of costs, the digital forensic laboratory manger will need to use a range of information with regard to tasks carried out in-house, but these should already be available as they will have been captured as a part of the metrics and measurements process. The types of information that will be required, in order to make effective comparisons with the outsourced providers bids, will include:

1. Staff Employment Costs

   - For the digital forensic laboratory (salary bill, benefits, superannuation)

   - Total bonus costs

   - Cost of management overhead

   - Calculate the cost per employee (current and future)

   - Calculate additional costs for vacant posts.

2. Travel Expenses

   - Cost of all business travel and associated expenses

> **NOTE**
>
> Understanding the cost of travel for all of the different reasons (work, networking, training, conferences, etc.) will allow the manager to better understand what level of cost of travel is incurred for different types of tasks undertaken by the laboratory.

3. Training/Development

   - Cost for seminars/courses/conferences

   - Cost for networking and internal meetings

   - Cost for other activities

4. Facility Costs

■ Cost of office space occupied by the digital forensic laboratory

■ Cost of digital forensic laboratory equipment and software

■ Cost of common use equipment and resources

5. Other

■ Insurance

■ Legal protection (factor in claims of various types)

■ Administrative support

From this information it will be possible to calculate the cost of carrying out a task within the laboratory, taking into account the total cost rather than the direct costs. This will give the manager a baseline for comparison of the tenders provided by the outsource providers.

Quality

Although it is possible to accurately measure the cost of completing a digital forensic task, determining the quality is a much more subjective problem. There are a number of ways in which quality can be assessed, which include measurements such as the number of successful investigations, by type or the number of complaints, or by audit failures/observations. Perhaps the easiest way to assess quality is through the use of customer surveys. Once completed, the measurement of quality that is achieved internally can be used as a baseline for quality that can be used to measure the performance of an outsource service provider.

Experience

Once again, determining the relative level of experience of an outsource provider is probably best achieved by using the level of experience of the in-house staff as a baseline. The reason for assessing the level of experience of an outsource provider is to determine the probability of them successfully completing the task to an acceptable level of quality. It is reasonable to assume that the greater the level of experience available from the outsourced provider, the higher the likelihood of the task being carried out to an acceptable standard. Again, it should always be remembered that the most experienced of staff at the outsource provider will always be in high demand and may not be available when they are required by the digital forensic laboratory.

Likelihood of Successful Outcome

When determining the level of experience and the likelihood of a successful outcome, the following three major factors should be included in the analysis:

■ The experience of the staff

■ The complexity of the task

■ The sensitivity of the information related to the task

■ Any task related dependency factors

Although each of these factors will be assessed individually, they will each contribute to the assessment.

- **Experience of Staff:** The more experience that the staff has, the higher the likelihood of a successful outcome. If the outsource provider has carried out the type of task that the laboratory wishes to contract out a large number of times in the past and has a good track record for successful outcomes, then the probability is that they will perform well and deliver the required outcome. If the outsourced provider has carried out similar, but not exactly the same type of tasks in the past with success then the probability of success is reasonable. If the outsource provider has never carried out the type of task in the past, then there is a high risk in outsourcing it and the probability of a successful outcome is lower.

- **Complexity:** The issue of the complexity of the digital forensic task that is to be outsourced must be considered. A simple and straightforward task that is outsourced will have a greater likelihood of success. As the complexity of the task increases, so the likelihood of a successful outcome will, inevitably, decrease.

- **Sensitivity of Information:** A range of information will potentially be accessed during the course of the investigation and whether it is government, corporate, or personal information, consideration must be given to the risk involved with outsourcing the task. The risk may be acceptable if there is a long-term relationship with the outsource provider and there are adequate confidentiality agreements in place.

- **Dependencies:** In some investigation tasks it will be clear from the outset that there will be dependencies on other activities and tasks that are occurring. Other tasks may appear to be discrete and have no apparent relationship to other activity when started, but dependencies will become apparent as the investigation develops. If the task is to be outsourced, the less dependencies it has, the higher the probability of success. As a task has more dependencies with other tasks, the higher the probability that something will go wrong or be missed, resulting in potential failure.

Consequence of Failure

In the event that the outsourcing of a task was to result in failure, consideration must be given to the effect that this would have and also how the failure will be measured. A task can fail in a number of ways, each of which could have a consequence, but not all these consequences will have an equal effect. The areas that can be measured are:

- **Performance:** The issue that can be measured here is that of how the performance of the outsource provider compares to that of the in-house staff. A decision will have been made prior to the outsourcing of the task as to the level to which the outsourced provider must match the productivity of the in-house resource. It can then be determined how well the performance of the outsource provider matches expectations. If the timeliness of the completion of the task is a critical factor, then a failure to deliver on time may have an increasingly adverse impact as the period that the delivery is overdue increases. A complete failure to deliver would have the most significant impact.

- **Delivery on Budget:** In outsourcing, the budget for the task will have been allocated. This will have been based on one of a number of factors, which include the cost, as compared to in-house resources, the need for specific skills (which might have a premium value), or the availability of resource. When the budget is agreed with the outsource provider, there will normally be flexibility to take into account unexpected events. Within the allocated budget for the task, it is possible to measure the performance of the outsource provider. If the outsource provider completes the task within the budget, there is no adverse impact, and as the cost of completion of the task escalates beyond the budget, so the adverse impact will increase.

Final Decision on Outsourcing

Once the analysis is completed, an informed decision on whether it is reasonable to outsource can be taken. If the results of the analysis show that the risk of using one of the selected out-source providers is acceptable, then the decision can be make to proceed and a contract can be written. If the results of the analysis indicate that the risk of outsourcing (to any of the selected providers) is too high a risk, then the outsourcing either should not proceed or a new set of providers should be investigated and the analysis process repeated until one is found that can carry out the task at an acceptable risk. Alternatively, the level of risk that is acceptable will need to be reevaluated. Failing to carry out a thorough analysis before proceeding is the option that carries the greatest risk of all.

Monitoring and Review

When a decision to outsource has been made and a provider has been selected, there are a number of factors that should be identified to ensure the best chance of success and to provide metrics against which the performance of the provider can be measured.

- **Define requirement:** The work requirement should be clearly explained, including the scope and boundaries of the task. A clear understanding of the task will assist the provider in delivering what is required.

- **Define critical success factors:** Clearly identify the most important features by which the success of the contract will be measured. These are the factors that must be fully achieved for the contract to be considered a success. For example, if delivery of a report within a predetermined timeframe is considered to be essential then this should be identi-fied as a critical success factor.

- **Periodic reviews:** As the outsourcing arrangement develops into a long-term relationship, it will become increasingly important to carry out periodic reviews. This will help to ensure that any issues that have developed over time can be resolved and also help in maintaining the relationship in an ever-changing environment. This will be of benefit to both the organization and the outsource provider.

Summary

In this chapter, the management of the workload for the digital forensic laboratory has been reviewed and a number of options on ways to manage that workload have been explored. Options for the in-house management of the workload include the use of overtime working and the use of the triage technique to prioritize tasks. An alternative approach of outsourcing tasks to an external resource provider has also been explored in some detail and the main considerations that must be addressed have been examined. When managing the workload for the laboratory, prior planning is always essential—having excess work coming into the laboratory and not having considered the options to address the problem is the worst of all possible scenarios.

Note

1. This information is modeled on and some information taken from, with permissions, the book, *Security Metrics Management: How to Measure the Costs and Benefits of Security*; December 2005; ISBN 10: 0-7506-7899-2; Dr. Gerald L. Kovacich and Edward P. Halibozek; Butterworth-Heinemann.

Chapter 20

Developing a Career in Digital Forensic Management

Introduction

It is probably worth starting this chapter by saying that not all digital forensic investigators will want to be, or will have the skills and qualities to be digital forensic laboratory managers, and that not all digital forensic laboratory managers are necessarily the best investigators. It is almost inevitable that any investigator who takes on the role of manager will, over time, lose the currency of knowledge and level of skill that come from constant practice. We all know there are exceptions to this rule, where the laboratory manager leads by example and remains at the highest level of skill, but in reality this sort of person is a rarity and can normally achieve this level of status only in a small or specialized lab.

The roles of the digital forensic investigator and digital forensic laboratory manager are still relatively new. If you compare the development of digital forensics to that of information security, you can draw a number of parallels from which you can obtain insight and perhaps some guidance. As the different aspects of the information security-related professions matured, certification programs were established to provide a framework for the profession against which the skills and competencies of individuals could be assessed. In information security and digital forensics, the same technology and the associated rapid developments and change are present, and both disciplines deal with many of the same problems.

Because of the technical and volatile nature of digital forensics, investigators must constantly learn new skills. For those who aspire to manage a digital forensic lab, the problem is even more challenging. Not only must this person have a working knowledge of the job, but he or she must also make hiring decisions, as well as decide which staff members should be trained in which disciplines and to what level.

The digital forensic arena is developing rapidly, and as it does, the knowledge and skills required are becoming increasingly diverse. In the past, investigation was focused on the PC, magnetic and optical storage media (floppy disks, CDs, and tapes), and network devices. Today investigations concern PCs, handheld devices (cell phones and PDAs), magnetic and optical storage media (micro drives, floppy disks, USB sticks, CDs, DVDs, and tapes), networks, wireless devices, the capture of live memory and state information from systems, and the increasing range of devices that are not naturally thought of as computer or storage devices, such as digital cameras and MP3/4 players.

In this chapter, we will provide digital forensic investigators with a career development plan they can use to move to a managerial position. Please note that the advice we give in this chapter is based on our experience and that of our colleagues. Because the digital forensic arena is so new and the work involved is constantly changing, there is little in the way of historical precedent on which to base our advice.

What Does a Manager Do?

Before you decide that you want to be a digital forensic laboratory manager, you should understand what a person in this position does. There are four basic stages of management:

- **Planning** All management processes start with planning, and good management starts with good planning. You must recognize the difference between good planning and good luck. You can rely on the first but not on the second, and if you are going to produce good, consistent results, you need to be professional. Planning is about being clear regarding what you need to achieve and then finding the most effective way to achieve it. You will need to take into account the staff and equipment available, as well as their strengths and limitations. You also need to understand the relative costs of staffing and resources and determine the best combination to meet your requirements. To determine the best way to fulfill this task, you may need to consider a range of scenarios and plan for them, from the worst to the best. Don't forget to use all of the tools you have at your disposal, and remember that one of the best tools is the input you receive from the investigators who will be doing the job.

- **Organizing** Once you have developed your plan, you need to implement it. That is, you need to ensure that all of the preliminary activity has taken place to allow the plan to be put into action. Part of this task involves ensuring that any downstream activity that relies on the output of the plan will receive the material it needs.

- **Directing** At this stage, you need to tell the relevant people what they need to do. People need to know what is expected of them and when, who they are working with, where they need to go, what tools they have available, and what output is expected. When staff members know this, they can get on with the job and be confident that they are working as part of a well-organized and managed team.

- **Monitoring** Once everything is progressing, it is essential that you monitor the plan, and if things aren't going well you must adjust and readjust the plan as necessary. Always remember the old military adage that a plan will last only until the first contact with the enemy. That means things will inevitably go wrong, but by monitoring the situation, you will be able to adjust the activity or come up with a contingency plan to address it. Remember that monitoring is an end-to-end activity and is an integral part of the management role. When you detect the need for a change as a result of monitoring, you will devise a new plan and then implement that new plan, direct the staff on the changes, and then monitor the new plan to ensure that it is effective.

Characteristics of a Manager

A manager must have or develop a range of skills, including the following:

- **Intrapersonal skills** This means good self-awareness, confidence, and knowledge of his or her skills and limitations.

- **Interpersonal skills** This includes the ability to motivate a team, to resolve problems, and to manage conflict.

- **People skills** This refers to the ability to empower individuals and to delegate (remember that you can delegate authority, but not responsibility).

- **Communication skills** This includes the ability to conduct interviews, give briefings, write reports and briefings, and manage meetings.

Assuming you have the skills, you should ask yourself why you want to become the manager of a digital forensic laboratory. There are many positive rewards to being a manager, the most obvious of which is that managers are generally paid more than others in the laboratory. They normally also appear to have more power, prestige and status.

Once you move up to a managerial level within an organization, you must be aware that you will probably become increasingly removed from the type of work you were used to, but also that you have opened up a whole new set of opportunities for the future. The normal benefits you can expect from moving into laboratory management will include:

- **Higher pay** As the manager you would expect to be paid more than most of the team members, as you have taken on more responsibility. However, increasingly these days, many organizations, particularly in the high-tech arena, will pay staff members based on their value to the company, not on their title or position. That means people with key skills may be of more valuable to the organization than someone in a managerial position who does not have those key skills.

- **More power** It is generally considered that the manager will have more power than the people on his or her team. For instance, the manager will usually have authority for certain issues the organization has delegated to him or her. However, remember that you gain your power from the willingness of the people on your team to allow you to have it, and from the continued and increasing success of the team. You should never confuse authority with power.

- **Greater status** People aspire to achieve higher status, and the manager of a team normally is considered to carry higher status than a team member. With increased status will come increased opportunities, because people will regard and treat you differently now that you are a manager.

- **A sense of personal achievement** Although for many people in the digital forensic arena the concept of becoming a manager may not be at the top of their list of priorities, few would deny the sense of personal achievement that goes with a promotion to this level.

Positioning Yourself for the Job

Investigators who want to move up the ladder to the position of digital forensic laboratory manager must ensure that they have what it takes to be considered for the job. You can take a number of steps toward this end:

- **Perform your current job well** Although anecdotally people are promoted to their own level of incompetence, this is not something you should hope for or aspire to in your organization. It is better to develop your career based on your merit and professionalism. In most organizations, nobody is going to give you additional responsibilities if you are not good at your current job. If you have demonstrated that you are good at your current job, however, you will inspire others to be confident in you and inspire management to trust that you are capable of taking on more responsibility. Remember—the skills and knowledge you acquired for your current job will help you with your credibility and in your decision making when you become a manager.

- **Demonstrate your worth** People who come to work each day and do their job, even if they do it well, are not likely to be selected for a management position for that reason alone. You can improve your chances of attaining this position by gaining some managerial experience through helping your manager or the manager of another department. This is not considered sucking up; it you were sitting next to another digital forensic specialist to improve your skill set, you would think of this as *improving your knowledge*. Support and learn from your manager by helping him or her to prepare plans and budgets, and even by volunteering to stand in for him or her when he or she is away from the office. But remember: In the meantime, do not neglect the job for which you are being paid.

- **Develop your interpersonal skills** It may seem obvious, but the most important skill a manager needs is the ability to manage people. To do this effectively, you must understand how people think, how they are likely to react, and how well they will function when faced with problems. You do not need to be a manager to develop these skills, but they will be important to you when you get the job and they will demonstrate that you have the required attributes. If you cannot manage people, you are doomed to failure.

- **Ask questions and watch what is happening** As with anything else, you learn by asking questions. Don't presume to know what your boss does; you will find out for certain what your boss does and how if you ask him or her for the details.

- **Make sure management knows you want the job** This may also seem obvious, but unless you have told management that you want to be considered for the job, they will not know. You need to make sure they know you are interested, and you can do this by telling your manager at one of your staff review meetings or by telling someone in the human resources department.

Once You Have the Job

Once you get the job of digital forensic laboratory manager, you can do several things to ensure that you do it well. If you previously were an investigator, now you need to make sure investigations are carried out in a professional, safe, and cost-effective manner and that they meet approved standards. You will also need to ensure that you have competent support staff and equipment available, at the right time, to enable your team of investigators to do their job.

Here are some of the things you can work on to ensure that you put your best foot forward:

- **Pick the best staff** You can be only as good as the people on your team. Make sure you select people with the right work ethic, skills, and experience.

- **Create the right environment** There are always limitations on the amount of money you can spend on office space, but creating the right environment is much more about motivating and rewarding the team. People will accept working in less-than-perfect conditions if they enjoy the work and the people they work with and if they feel they are valued and reasonably rewarded. Remember that reward does not always have to be in the form of money and that recognition in the form of increased status or prestige is also valued. Part of developing the right environment will come from picking the right team. You may pick someone for the team who is not as highly skilled as another potential candidate, but you may feel he or she will be a much better team member and a more positive influence.

- **Communicate well** This takes constant thought and effort, but it is one of the major factors in good management. If you fail here, you cannot expect your team to know what you are trying to achieve or to care. Also remember that communication is a two-way process and that your team members have skills, knowledge, and opinions you need to be aware of. After all, how can you motivate your team if they do not understand what you want from them?

- **Better manage your resources** All organizations have to work within finite budgets and, in one way or another, show a return on investment. As a manager, you need to constantly look at how you can do things better, faster, and cheaper. This may mean you can get greater throughput from the investigators in the lab, or it may mean you can accomplish your goals with fewer resources, but if you are not constantly looking for ways to improve, you will become set in the way that you do things, and as a result your costs will increase. Resource management covers a number of areas—from making sure you have the most suitable (not the cheapest) equipment to do the job, to ensuring that you manage your time as well as that of your staff. It takes only a few wasted minutes here and there by each staff member to cause a significant drain over a period of time. One of the biggest drains on staff time is badly planned and managed meetings. A one-hour meeting with 10 staff members, plus preparation time, means you have used one and a half person days' of effort.

- **Ensure that you and the team work in an ethical manner** This will be crucial to the lab's reputation, but will also have a significant impact on the environment within the laboratory and the loyalty of the staff and how they feel about themselves.

Training

Throughout this book, we have addressed the skills a manager requires. When an investigator wants to advance his or her career by becoming a manager, he or she must develop a range of new skills and knowledge. For some people, the responsibility of a management role does not come easily or naturally, whereas for others it is as though they were born for it.

Many people have management responsibilities thrust upon them as a result of the needs of the organization, but others aspire to it as a route to personal development. To develop the skills and knowledge required to manage effectively, most people will require a range of training and education that is outside their normal area of operation. A well-respected digital forensic expert may find it hard to accept having to start from the beginning in a range of new subject areas, but that is essential if you are to gain the knowledge and skills that will make you a good manager.

Some of the new areas in which you will have to gain knowledge may include employment law, health and safety (from a manager's point of view), accountancy, corporate policy, quality assurance and business planning. Meanwhile, the skills you will need as a manager will depend, in part, on the size of the organization you are working in and the internal structure and support that the organization provides. Large organizations tend to have formal and structured teams that can provide advice and support in areas such as human resources, but you will always need to have a working knowledge of such topics as well.

Once you have achieved the manager role, you will need to identify any courses you will need to take to further your education. There are courses available on all aspects of the management process and the ones that you need to consider may include interviewing skills, health and safety for managers, accountancy, business planning, presentation skills, negotiating skills, etc. Only you and the organization that you belong to will know the gaps in your capability. For the person that is fully committed to the new role, for instance, at the top end of management training is the much sought after Master of Business Administration (MBA) degree.

Leadership or Management?

People often confuse management with leadership, and it is worth a short paragraph here to identify the characteristics of each of these roles. The two are not the same, but a person who is both a leader and a manager will achieve the best results. The following adage highlights the difference: Leadership is doing the right thing; management is doing things right. In general, leaders will seize opportunities and amplify the team's strengths, whereas managers will try to avoid, reduce, or mitigate any weaknesses and potential threats. Any investigator or technician who seeks to develop his or her career as a manager should aspire to have both sets of characteristics. To manage it is not essential that you are a leader, but it is extremely helpful.

Summary

One of the main questions you must ask yourself before you launch into a new career as a manager is whether it is worth it. Management is primarily about people. But like any other skill, management is something you can learn and improve on with study and experience. If you do it well, it can be hugely rewarding, but if you do not enjoy it, do not take the job because a manager who does not enjoy his or her job will create an unhappy and unmotivated staff, and that will lead to failure.

Chapter 21

A Summary of Thoughts, Issues, and Problems

Introduction

The profession of digital forensic investigator is still in its infancy. As with many other forms of forensic science, the area of digital forensics is a convergence of science, investigative experience, and the law. Where digital forensics differs from most other forensic disciplines is that the science on which it is based has a short history and is made more complex by the fact that computer technology continues to develop at an increasing pace.

Another significant difference is that although most areas of forensic science have little application outside of law enforcement, digital forensic techniques and tools have a range of applications in the commercial sector—in the areas of information security, information systems management, auditing, staff management, and litigation.

For a digital forensic investigator, the challenges are many and varied, and in several cases they include identifying what he or she already knows as well as what he or she has yet to learn. The digital forensic laboratory manager must also face these challenges, as well as understand a range of other issues, including:

- Staff management

- Relevant laws, regulations, and standards

- Digital devices (e.g., computers, PDAs, telecommunications equipment)

- Investigative tools and techniques

- Project planning

- Report writing

- Evidence seizure, collection, and analysis methods

- Forensic laboratory procedures

- Quality control procedures

- Health and safety procedures

- Laboratory and staff certification

- How to maintain security for the staff, the laboratory, the evidence, and the information systems

- How the parent organization operates

- How to handle sources of information, both people and documents

In reality, nobody can be perfect in all of these areas, and in truth you are deluded and will fail if you believe that such perfection is necessary to succeed as a digital forensic laboratory manager. However, you do have to understand these subjects in enough depth to be able to handle them on a daily basis, and know where to turn—whether to an expert person or to a highly regarded document—when you need advice. As with the digital forensic investigator, the digital forensic laboratory manager must realize the limitations of his or her knowledge and know when and where to ask for help.

This chapter addresses some of our thoughts on this subject and discusses issues and problems the manager of a digital forensic laboratory may encounter and must be able to handle.

What Makes a Digital Forensic Laboratory Successful?

A successful digital forensic laboratory is the sum of many, often disparate influences. The profile of a *successful* and *professional* digital forensic laboratory is one that, among other things:

- Is staffed by individuals who are enthusiastic and enjoy learning about a range of digital devices, software, and games

- Is respected and has a good reputation within the digital forensic and investigative communities

- Adopts, maintains and promotes professional standards

- Approaches each investigation as a challenge

- Has as its major driving force the relentless pursuit of knowledge

- Keeps current with developing technologies and understands the implications of their use, the role of digital forensics in all types of crimes, relevant laws and regulations, and their implication in conducting an investigation

- Ensures that the staff remains up to date with the latest investigative tools, techniques, and sources of information

- Is an active member of the digital forensic community and associations

- Is constantly networking with peer organizations to keep abreast of current events, and supports and works with these organizations to develop accepted techniques and methods

- Is customer-support-oriented and driven to meet all expectations

- Develops, accepts, and uses new investigative tools and methods

Although it may seem ambitious, a well-managed laboratory should aim to satisfy all of these aspirations. A laboratory that does not will be adversely affected and will be inhibited in its ability to get the job done and to retain a staff that is both happy and fulfilled.

The degree to which these aspirations are met will vary over time, but effort must be made to satisfy all of them as completely as possible all of the time. It takes a long time to establish a good reputation among your customers and peers, but it takes only one incident to lose that reputation. This is why it is so important for you as the digital forensic laboratory manager to invest the effort needed to achieve the highest possible standards.

Are You Up for the Job of Digital Forensic Laboratory Manager?

It takes a special kind of personality to be a digital forensic investigator, and even more so to be a manager of a digital forensic laboratory. Throughout this book, we have described the issues to address and consider in all aspects of managing a facility, a staff, and investigations in order to create and maintain a successful and efficient digital forensic laboratory.

Creating an environment that is both challenging and satisfying for the staff—when the work the staff performs and the rate at which the work arrives in the laboratory are not in the staff's, or to some degree the managers, control—will keep the laboratory manager occupied. Regardless of the level of effort required, that effort is a good investment because a happy staff will tend to stay with the lab. The loss of continuity and the cost of replacing and retraining staff members in an area where a skilled staff is in high demand and the services it provides are at a premium mean that retaining your staff is worth the effort.

Most of you may already be digital forensic investigators with a desire to move the next rung up the career ladder. Don't make the mistake of thinking that taking on the laboratory manager role is a way to be paid more for doing the same job! A successful laboratory manager will probably not have the time to keep up to date with the latest technology developments and will not be able to maintain his or her technical or investigative skills.

Also, although you would hope to be able to have a good and friendly relationship with your staff, in reality you can no longer be friends with your staff once you have taken on the role of laboratory manager. Some people find it difficult to make this transition, but all staff members must be treated equally, and they must believe that this is happening and this cannot happen if you are friends with some of them but not all of them.

As the laboratory manager, the credit for the lab's achievements will hopefully be attributed to your stellar skills, but it's important to realize that you'll also be held responsible for any of the lab's shortcomings and failings. Unfortunately, people tend to notice the latter more often than the former. Therefore, you will constantly be challenged by the changing requirements of your customers, of the technology, tools, and techniques available, and of the sophistication of the cybercriminals you're helping to catch.

It's also important to note that your main role as laboratory manager is to enable your staff—the investigators—to carry out their tasks to the best of their ability. This will include ensuring that you act as an interface between them and the customer/parent organization, and that they have the tools, knowledge, and leadership they need to succeed. The manager must strive to empower the staff, have confidence in them and allow them to get on with their jobs. Good management is as much about understanding and maximizing the qualities and skills of the staff as it is about control.

What the Future Holds

As technology advances and is increasingly adopted into all aspects of our personal and professional lives, the importance of digital forensics will continue to increase. The growing integration and sophistication of technology will mean that those involved in digital forensic investigations will need to constantly develop their skills and knowledge. The number of people who can do this over a protracted period is limited, so the laboratory manager will need to do his or her best to retain those who have the ability and enthusiasm to achieve this goal.

As we become more dependent on technology, criminals and people with malicious intent will find more inventive ways to use technology to their advantage. Always remember that the bad guys will lead the way and the good guys will play catch-up when it comes to detecting abuse of digital technology. Also remember that however well an investigation has been carried out, the findings will be open to question by the representatives of the other party. Therefore, the best defense the laboratory has is to follow best practices and procedures and to ensure that the highest standards are maintained.

"Management works in the system; leadership works on the system."
—Stephen R. Covey

As the manager of a digital forensic laboratory, you will, over time, gain some insight into the thinking of Donald Rumsfeld when he stated the following much-quoted nonsense:

"There are known knowns; there are things we know we know. We also know there are known unknowns; that is to say we know there are some things we do not know. But there are also unknown unknowns—the ones we don't know we don't know."

That pretty much sums up the life of a digital forensic laboratory manager, and in many ways it is why people enjoy and relish the job. You never know what is coming next.

We wish you well in your endeavors. Always remember that you are among the pioneers in this young discipline which is still finding its place in the digital environment. However, one thing is certain: You will never be bored.

Section IV

Future Digital Forensic Investigation Challenges

This section looks at the challenges in computer forensic investigations and their management, which are expected to affect the people involved in the future. It looks at the changing importance of computer forensics in the criminal justice system and the technological developments that are likely to affect our ability to support investigations. The section finishes with some final thoughts by the authors.

> **Chapter 22. The Future of Digital Forensics and Its Role in Crime Investigations.** This chapter looks at the effect that changes in the technologies and the ways in which they are used will affect digital forensics, and the role that this plays in an increasing range of criminal investigations. As computing devices become more ubiquitous, the range of crimes that will potentially involve computers will increase. This chapter looks at the implications of these changes and gives advice on the issues that will need to be considered.

> **Chapter 23. The Future of Digital Forensics in the Criminal Justice Systems.** This chapter takes a look at the role of digital forensics in the criminal justice system and the issues that will arise as technologies and crime change and legislation is modified to keep pace.

> **Chapter 24. Conclusions and Final Thoughts.** This chapter will summarize the book and provide a few final thoughts and pieces of advice from the authors.

This small final section looks at the future and the challenges that can be expected in digital forensic investigations and their management. It looks at the way in which the role of digital forensics is changing in the criminal justice system and also looks at some of the developments that are likely to affect investigations.

Chapter 22

The Future of Digital Forensics and Its Role in Criminal Investigations

Introduction

In the 1980s, when computer forensics was a new discipline, mainframe computers were the tools of the trade. With time, mainframes were replaced with PCs. Although by today's standards the processing power, data storage capabilities, and communication paths of those early PCs were extremely limited, moving from mainframes to PCs was a major breakthrough, not only for most forms of business, but also for digital forensics.

Since that time, we have seen explosive growth in the area of digital processing and data storage technologies. The devices most people carry around with them everyday (laptops, cell phones, PDAs, GPS devices, etc.) boast processing power and storage capabilities that are orders of magnitude greater and more robust than those early PCs. What's more, digital processors are now ubiquitous in such everyday items as automobiles, washing machines, and electronic devices such as MP3 players and game consoles.

At the same time, the costs of these new technologies have dropped, allowing the disciplines of computing and telecommunications to convergence. As a result, today digital devices can connect to networks in diverse ways, to enrich our lives or allow us to do things that we previously were unable to do.

For instance, in the past, to connect a computer to the Internet you had to either use a dial-up connection via a landline or connect directly into a Network. Today, we don't need a PC or a wired connection to access the Internet. Instead, we can use a hand-held device such as a PDA, cell phone, or BlackBerry and connect using a technology such as GSM, WiFi, Bluetooth, or IR.

The good news is that all of these developments have made these technologies more useful in our everyday lives. The bad news is that from a digital forensic point of view, any form of investigation has become significantly more complex, and it is now necessary to consider many more factors than were necessary in the past.

For example, consider the basic scenario of a single computer in a person's home. The conventional wisdom that is reflected in the ACPO guidelines is that you identify the system components and take the appropriate action to secure them to prevent any changes from being made to potential evidence. With the advent of wireless connectivity, however, this is now difficult to do, because not only must we consider that other devices hidden in other parts of the home might be connected to the computer of interest, but we also must consider that the computer may be connected to the Internet or to other networks via a wireless hub. This wireless hub, perhaps along with additional wireless storage devices, might be located in another home altogether, or may themselves be ineffectively secured or purposely made available for other users to connect to. As such, how can the investigator in this case identify all the elements he or she is interested in? Does the investigator have the appropriate authority to seize and secure all the elements associated with the computer of interest? How does the investigator secure these devices in a manner that ensures that any evidence is not changed? And while we're at it, what can be considered a *computer*? When identifying computers to seize and secure, should the investigator consider the TiVo DVR in the suspect's family room, since it can be used to store data and to send and receive e-mail? Should the investigator seize the game consoles as well?

And what about cryptography? The availability of tools for creating and managing encrypted files and volumes can make any digital forensic investigation and subsequent analysis significantly difficult. Although most criminals find it a challenge to install and use cryptography software to encrypt their files in an attempt to prevent investigators from accessing them, some are computer-literate enough to make this an increasingly important issue for digital forensic investigators to consider.

In this chapter, we will look at how changes in technology and the way it is used will affect computer forensics and the role it plays in criminal investigations. As computing devices become increasingly ubiquitous, the range of crimes in which they can be involved will continue to increase. This chapter will discuss the implications of these changes and give advice on the issues that will need to be considered.

The Implication of Changes in Criminal Investigations

As technology has improved, so has the way it is used in government, commerce, academia, and our personal lives. The potential value of high-tech devices has been recognized and their uses have been adopted by both criminals and investigators. There has been a constant requirement for tools, techniques, and methods that can be used for digital forensic investigations to address the increasing range of devices that contain either digital processors or digital storage media, as well as to address the complex environments in which they are found. This is part of the ongoing "arms race" between criminals and the people who investigate their crimes or try to prevent them from occurring. For every measure that is developed to prevent or detect a crime, something will be developed that either exploits a vulnerability or uses tools and techniques to create a new version of the crime so that the criminal can carry on with his or her trade.

This is both a curse and a blessing for the digital forensic investigator. On the negative side, the investigator must always keep up to speed with the latest way in which criminals have been abusing technology, or learn how he or she can use a new technology to detect criminal activity. This puts a heavy training burden on investigators and means they must constantly upgrade their skills and knowledge in order to work effectively. It also can mean a significant financial burden for the laboratory which must purchase and test these new devices.

On the positive side, digital forensics is a growing industry, and laboratories will never be short of work. Labs are increasingly investigating devices that are used in all aspects of our personal and professional lives that in the past would never have been able to provide information that might be relevant to an investigation. One example of this is an automobile engine management system that records how far a car has traveled during a particular period. Another example is a satellite navigation system that keeps a record of the routes the car has taken. As a result, investigators must examine not only the computers that are being used to commit crimes, that contain evidence of crimes, or that belong to the victims of crimes, but also devices that contain information which may indicate the movements and activities of the suspects.

Managers of digital forensic laboratories must carefully balance investments in training and equipment with the returns these investments will generate. They also must consider whether their laboratory should focus on well-established areas of digital forensics, or whether they should be on the leading edge of the field and focus on solving new problems that crop up. We would all like to think we will run a laboratory that falls into the latter category, but this will depend, in part, on the rationale for creating the laboratory and the type of organization you belong to.

The Changing Face of Crime

One of the reasons digital forensics has a growing future in the investigation of all types of crime is that technology continues to become increasingly integrated into all aspects of our lives. Investigators know that criminals will go where the money is, and because we now live in an online world, crime is increasingly moving online. Some examples of these types of crime include blackmail of online businesses, phishing attacks, identity theft, and fraud—indeed, almost any financially motivated crime you can think of.

As in the physical world, as law enforcement finds ways to counter crime, criminals find new ways to perpetrate crime. Thanks to the proliferation of technology, many old crimes have migrated to the online world, and new types of crime have formed. In addition, evidence of crimes such as assault, murder, and drug dealing are increasingly found in digital devices that either the perpetrator or the victim used. As a result of this potential evidence which did not exist in the past, investigators of conventional crimes increasingly need to consider any digital evidence that may be available.

One example of the new type of information that can be used to develop evidence is the forensic examination of a satellite navigation system on a drug smuggling craft[1]. Such an examination can not only prove the exact location of the vessel when it was captured (in case of disputes about territorial waters), but also provide important information regarding the routes the vessel took, possible meeting points, and even where the vessel started its voyage or perhaps even where the vessel had stopped and the drugs were loaded.

Another example is from a 2006 case in which a gang was found guilty of smuggling Turkish immigrants into the United Kingdom when the satellite navigation system used on their aircraft enabled the prosecution to show where the gang had flown from and to, despite the fact that they had not submitted flight plans for the trips[2]. The gang had used a light aircraft to bring Turkish nationals from airfields in Belgium and France to isolated airfields in the southeastern part of England from May to July 2004.

The Changing Role of Digital Forensics

You should have noticed by now that the authors of this book prefer to use the term *digital forensics* rather than *computer forensics*. In the early days of digital forensics, interest and effort were focused on addressing stand-alone and networked PCs. As technology has developed, focus has extended to include the recovery of evidence from any device that has a digital processor or digital storage capability.

As a result, the role of digital forensics has moved from the investigation of computer-based crimes such as hacking, to the investigation of all types of crime. Increasingly, with the information that can be recovered from car engine management systems, satellite navigation systems, and cell phones, the type of evidence that can be obtained has grown from recovery of documents, images, and network activity records to indications of an individual's movements and activities.

Investigators of conventional crimes such as murder, robbery, blackmail, and drug dealing increasingly look to the digital environment for evidence and indications of suspects' activities. In the recent past, investigators of conventional crimes did not understand the potential value of digital evidence, and as a result they would often ignore it. This is already changing, but there is still a long way to go before investigators of conventional crimes understand the potential value of digital evidence, and suitable levels of resources are available to address it.

Summary

Digital forensic investigations will continue to take on increasing importance in the investigation of all types of illicit activity. As such, the digital forensic laboratory will have to become conversant and competent with the recovery and discovery of information from an increasing range of devices.

In this chapter, we examined the effects of changes and developments in technology and the increasing integration of technology into all aspects of people's lives. We also discussed the implications of these changes and how they will affect how investigators will be trained and the tools they will use. There is no doubt that digital forensics is a growth market and that the demand for skilled investigators will continue to increase. Already we are seeing massive expansion in the area of data discovery for civil litigation cases which have resulted from increased use of computers to communicate and store information that previously was paper-based.

The decisions that the manager of the digital forensics laboratory makes on the training that the staff are given and the equipment and software that are purchased will affect the range of work that the laboratory is able to undertake. They may decide to concentrate the skill set and tools on conventional 'computer forensics' and excel in that area or they may choose to expand the scope of the types of work that the laboratory can address in order to increase the potential customer base or be able to offer a 'one stop shop' for the organization and customers that they support. These decisions will be made on the basis of the potential market, the business plan and the requirements of the organization.

Notes

1. www.satnavforensics.com/marine-sat-nav.php
2. www.cps.gov.uk/news/pressreleases/archive/2006/174_06.html

Summary

Notes

Chapter 23

The Future of Digital Forensics in the Criminal Justice System

Introduction

The term *digital forensics* is only now starting to come into common use. Up until now, we have typically used the term *computer forensics*. However, *digital forensics* is more appropriate today, for two reasons. First, forensic investigation is no longer done only on what we would generally consider to be a *computer*. We have never considered washing machines, refrigerators, televisions, or cars to be computers, but today they all contain processors and memory and can store information that may be of evidentiary value. Second, when investigators of conventional crimes such as robbery and murder hear the term *computer forensics*, they tend to feel that if no obvious computer was involved in the crime, chances are no digital evidence will be available.

The role of digital forensics within the criminal justice system has been changing for a number of years now, as the use of technology has become more widespread and the discipline of digital forensics has matured. The increasing processing power and digital storage capacity of cell phones and PDAs have done much to increase the awareness of those who are not digital forensic specialists of the potential evidentiary value of a whole range of devices.

As the technology and the way we use it have developed, the digital audit trail of an individual's activity has increased. Apart from the obvious example of e-mail replacing the letter, we now routinely conduct our banking and shopping online, and give information about ourselves through online social networks. In addition, in the past, if murderers researched their chosen method they did so through books or word of mouth. Today, they tend to conduct their research online, resulting in evidence of their Web searches remaining on their computers.

To date there have been significant problems with digital evidence and the criminal justice system. Primary among these has been the fact that most judges and lawyers are not computer-literate and do not understand how even their own computers work, let alone the subtleties of a complex network. This becomes an even greater problem when a jury is involved, as it is highly unlikely that the people sitting on a jury will understand many of the concepts and arguments being presented in a case. As a result, many computer crimes do not reach the courts, and if they do, the rate of successful prosecutions is relatively low.

Another significant issue has been the creation and implementation of adequate laws that can address the current environment. Laws, of necessity, take a long time to bring into being, as they must be carefully considered and well thought out. Unfortunately, in the area of computers and digital devices, technology is moving at a pace that far outstrips the ability of lawmakers to institute suitable and relevant laws. Not too long ago hackers and phreakers were being prosecuted under laws for the theft of the electricity they used!

The fact that many of the crimes involving digital devices are often inter- or transnational in nature also created a challenge for national legal systems. There are international agreements and protocols for the detention of suspects and capture of potential evidence in one jurisdiction for use in a case in another jurisdiction, but there are ongoing problems with the acceptability of evidence that was captured in one country for use as evidence in another country.

Digital forensics is different from most traditional forensic disciplines. The digital material that is examined and the tools and techniques that are available to the examiner are fairly new and generally have not developed from a scientific discipline that has been exposed and tested over a long period of time. In addition, most of the tools that are used were designed and developed in the private sector, and like all computer-based hardware and software, they are regularly updated with new versions.

In this scenario, it is difficult to prove their soundness for the function that they have been designed to meet, and this is an ongoing issue. To add another dimension to the problem, unlike in most conventional forensic disciplines, digital evidence collection and investigation may be required in a wide variety of locations. As a result, some of the activity will take place outside the well-controlled laboratory environment. There is also the issue of the capture of evidence from systems that cannot be replicated, along with the issue of trust being placed in the practitioner and in the processes he or she undertook to obtain the material.

Efforts to develop internationally acceptable standards for the capture and examination of digital evidence are ongoing. These efforts date back to 1991 and resulted in the formation of the International Organization on Computer Evidence, the Scientific Working Group on Digital Evidence (in the United States), the Forensic Computing Group (in the United Kingdom), and the European Network of Forensic Science Institutes (in Europe). In addition to these, a number of other bodies have been formed around the world to attempt to resolve problems in this arena. It is perhaps unfortunate that the very diversity of groups which have been created to solve the problem of standardization is likely to be self-defeating.

This chapter takes a look at the role of digital forensics in the criminal justice system and the issues that will arise as technologies and crime change and legislation is modified to keep pace.

What Is Changing

Technology continues to change at a rapid pace. This means the digital forensic investigator has access to tools that allow him or her to investigate data that was previously inaccessible or unusable, and to perform tasks faster or better. At the same time, the criminal is forever finding new ways to subvert the technology or use it to carry out new crimes, or to carry out old crimes in new ways. Unfortunately, as the technology becomes more advanced and more integrated into our everyday lives, it is being made to operate in an increasingly transparent manner. In the early days of computing, the user had to be able to operate at the command-line level and needed at least some knowledge of what the system was doing and how it was doing it. Now this is purposely hidden from the user. Users do not need to worry about how his or her PC or other device connects to the network, or the type of application that is running to achieve his or her goal. As a result, the average user is becoming less and less conversant with the underlying systems.

As the digital forensics discipline has matured and become better established, so has the level of support, training, and education. And as the number of cases that involve digital evidence has increased, their exposure in courts at all levels has increased—and with that has come a better level of knowledge on the subject within the legal system. Judges now hear cases that involve digital evidence; in many cases, these judges are highly computer-literate and increasingly use their knowledge to ensure that juries are presented with information in a form they can understand.

Another factor that is significantly affecting digital forensic investigations is the continuing increase in the volume of digital storage that is available. The near exponential growth in the capacity of hard disks has meant that the time it may take to create images of the disks and to identify and isolate relevant information is increasing, despite the development of improved tools and techniques. This issue is likely to continue to cause problems for the foreseeable future.

On final thought on changes taking place: Because digital forensics has no obvious physical context and the relevant devices may not even have been present at the scene of the crime, investigators of conventional crimes have not always considered digital forensics as a potential source of evidence. These investigators may themselves be computer users, and for many of them the workings of the computer will be as mysterious as it is to most laypeople. Educating these investigators to realize the potential evidence that digital devices may contain is a lengthy but rewarding process.

What the Future Holds

There is no doubt that developments in technology will continue at a rapid pace, and that the range and complexity of technologies digital forensic investigators must understand and work with will continue to increase. In the future, we will see the digital forensic discipline becoming more established and gaining credibility while we also see its use increasing in all types of investigations.

As a part of the increasing maturity of the discipline, we should also see improved acceptance of digital evidence in courts and tribunals. This will, in part, result from the courts' greater exposure to this type of evidence, but it will also be a result of developments such as a professional framework for digital forensic investigators and improved and agreed upon methods for presenting evidence.

The problems facing the digital forensic investigator will continue to challenge organizations, however. These problems are the result of increasing workloads due to the increased number of devices that may be of relevance and their increased storage capacity.

In addition, the issue of one's right to privacy will continue to challenge digital forensic investigators as well. When this consideration is added to the problems facing investigators regarding understanding and putting into context the increasingly vast volumes of information they face on a standard computer, those challenges are likely to continue.

It is unfortunate (or in some cases, very fortunate) that computer users rarely delete data. You can't see or touch data in the normal sense, and as long as a system does not run out of storage capacity, its user will normally retain his or her data, because to remove it takes time and effort. This means that unlike in the convention forensic environment, in this environment a huge amount of historical information may be of use in an investigation, but must be processed beforehand. Another information–related issue that may be relevant to an investigation is that in many cases, a criminal's data may be stored on a third party's computer. For example, e-mails may be stored on an ISP's server, along with information regarding a large number of other, innocent and unrelated users. Increasingly, care has to be taken to ensure that the information seized from such a system is only that which is relevant and for which there is a warrant to seize.

All told, the future will see increased levels of regulation of digital forensic labs and the investigators who work in them. In part, this is required to ensure that suitable standards are imposed and maintained by laboratories, as well as to ensure that staff members have suitable backgrounds to operate in the discipline and are adequately trained and skilled and understand the standards to which they must work. The relationship between digital forensic investigators and criminal justice agencies will continue to develop so that the understanding between the two groups can continue to improve. As this happens, the criminal justice community will become more knowledgeable regarding evidentiary requirements, which means digital forensic investigators will be better briefed on the evidence that is required, ultimately reducing the amount of data that has to be analyzed.

Summary

In the future, digital forensics will play an increasingly significant role in the criminal justice system as we continue to incorporate a range of technologies into our everyday lives. As the digital forensic discipline continues to mature, those in the criminal justice system will more readily understand and accept the contribution it can make to the discovery and production of evidence.

Chapter 24

Conclusions and Final Thoughts

Introduction

Throughout this book, we have addressed a wide range of issues relating to the management of a digital forensic laboratory. Along the way, we have discussed how to determine the function the laboratory will undertake and how to develop a business plan and identify staffing requirements and the criteria for their selection. We also have addressed training and workload management, among numerous other subjects. In this chapter, we will summarize what we've covered and provide a few final thoughts and bits of advice.

Management Challenges

Digital forensics is still in its infancy, and therefore, it is in a rapidly changing environment. As such, the digital forensic lab manager will face many challenges. Not only must he or she possess a range of skills and knowledge spanning the areas of high technology, investigations, and management, but also he or she must know how to stay abreast of the required skills and knowledge as well as this constantly changing environment. If the digital forensic lab manager can accomplish these goals, however, the manager and his or her team have the potential to reap huge rewards and a great deal of satisfaction.

Skills and Knowledge Areas

The successful manager of a digital forensic lab must have the following skills and areas of knowledge:

- **Ability to deal with and manage people** A good manager must be able to manage a group of skilled individuals in a range of environments, taking into account the demands of the job, training, and the requirements of the organization.

- **Patience** The manager will be managing highly skilled people in a complex and challenging working environment, while representing the lab to the larger organization. To maintain a balance between the two (which can sometimes be opposing forces), the manager will need the patience of a saint.

- **Diplomacy** Not only will the manager be managing the staff and operating as a part of the larger organization management structure, but he or she will also have to ensure that the laboratory is properly represented and develop relationships with its peers and customers.

- **Ability to deal with office politics** If the manager is to ensure that the laboratory gets fair representation and achieves the best possible support, he or she will need to become adept at office politics.

- **Knowledge of relevant health/safety and employment laws** To ensure that the environment is safe to work in, the laboratory manager will have to have an up-to-date working knowledge of the health/safety and employment laws that apply in his or her region.

- **Knowledge of high-technology devices and how they work** If the laboratory manager is to perform the job effectively, he or she must have a good working knowledge of the types of devices the laboratory is likely to have to process. He or she will also have to understand the types of problems the processing of these devices may create to be credible with the staff and to make informed decisions.

- **Knowledge of relevant evidentiary laws of digital forensics** The laboratory manager must have a working knowledge of relevant laws to ensure that the processes and procedures developed for the laboratory are compliant and that any evidence is forensically sound and to the appropriate standards.

- **Knowledge of digital forensic standards, procedures, tools, and techniques** The laboratory manager must know the standards, procedures, tools, and techniques that are relevant to the digital forensic arena to ensure that the laboratory is established and runs efficiently and effectively.

- **Knowledge of investigative techniques** The laboratory manager needs to understand the prevailing investigative techniques that are in use in both the physical and electronic environments to ensure that the laboratory works in a manner that is compatible with other organizations or laboratories.

- **Good project planning skills** As a laboratory is, in effect, one large project composed of a series of smaller projects, it is essential that the manager is a skilled project manager.

- **Good report writing skills** To manage the laboratory and achieve many of the skills that are required, the manager will need to be a skilled communicator. One of the fundamental requirements for this is that the manager be able to produce (and manage the production of) high-quality reports.

- **Knowledge of court procedures** The manager must understand the procedures that apply to the courts and tribunals in which the laboratory staff will have to present evidence.

Personality Profile of a Manager

The following are some additional qualifications and qualities of a successful manager of a digital forensic laboratory:

- Understands and enjoys working with and managing people, particularly those who are technically oriented.

- Keeps current on existing technologies, related crimes, and laws, and understands the implications of new technology. Also has a basic understanding of its implications in conducting an investigation.

- Keeps current on the latest investigative tools, techniques, and related sources of information.

- Takes the successful management of the laboratory as a personal challenge.

- Is good at networking and can develop relationships with peers and the team. Also is an active member of high-technology-related associations.

- Enjoys constant change and enjoys the challenges this provides.

- Is customer-oriented and motivated to meet customers' expectations.

- Is adaptive and flexible.

- Is a team player and will go the extra mile for the team.

- Is a leader who can translate management requirements into tasks the staff can achieve.

- Is imaginative and has vision regarding development of the lab and ways to make it successful.

What the Future Holds

In many ways, the future of digital forensics will be what we choose to make it. The developing digital environment and the increasing adoption of high-tech devices into all aspects of our lives will provide almost limitless opportunities for the managers of digital forensic laboratories if they have the vision and ambition to embrace them.

The Internet and the digital devices we use to access it offer fantastic capabilities, but in the hands of the wrong people who abuse it or use it to conduct criminal activity they can have a significant negative impact on individuals and businesses and be the cause of major disruptions and chaos.

Digital forensic investigators will always have to play catch-up when it comes to knowledge of the tools and techniques criminals are using and developing. After all, if the digital world has taught us anything, it is that the bad guys can think of ways to abuse technology far more quickly than we can find ways to thwart them.

The digital forensic investigation unit will always have to be part research laboratory and part investigative laboratory if it is to deliver high-quality work while keeping up-to-date with the latest developments. However, such an environment can provide the investigative team, as well as the manager of such a team, with a great deal of job satisfaction while making them adaptive and resourceful.

Appendix A

Digital Forensic Resources

Introduction

We have mentioned a number of useful resources throughout this book. In this appendix, we have grouped these resources into specific categories. Note that all the resources, including the Web sites, were valid at the time of this writing.

Laboratory and Staff Certification Authorities

The following authorities can provide more information pertaining to lab and staff certification:

The American Society of Crime Laboratory Directors (ASCLD) Laboratory Accreditation Board (LAB)   Used by a number of law enforcement organizations, this was originally designed to certify forensic labs in scientific disciplines such as DNA and fingerprint analyses. ASCLD now also covers digital evidence and has adopted ISO 17025. The ASCLD Web site is at www.ascld-lab.org.

The National Center for Forensic Science at the University of Central Florida (UCF)   In conjunction with ASCLD/LAB, this group has developed a digital evidence external test called Digital Forensics Quality Solutions (DFQS). You can use the test for a number of purposes, including external proficiency testing, competency testing, laboratory quality assurance, internal cyclic training, and potential new hire evaluations. The test examines the core competencies of evidence handling, imaging, and verification of media, partition identification and verification, and file identification and verification. The National Center for Forensic Science website is at www.ncfs.org/digital_evd.html.

International Information Systems Security Certification Consortium (ISC²)   This is a vendor-neutral organization with an international focus that provides several tiers of computer security certifications. The Web site is at www.isc2.org/cgi-bin/index.cgi.

International Society of Forensic Computer Examiners (ISFCE) The ISFCE was established in 2002 with the goal of advancing the science of forensic computer examinations. The ISFCE aims to professionalize and further the science of computer forensics and to provide a fair, uncompromised process for certifying the competency of forensic computer examiners. The Web site is at www.isfce.com/.

ISO 17025 Forensics Laboratory Certification and Accreditation This certification program has the support of the international community, many U.S. organizations and corporations, government facilities, and law enforcement agencies. This international standard gives the general requirements for the competencies that are required to carry out tests and/or calibrations. It includes testing and calibration carried out by the laboratory using standard methods and non-standard methods or laboratory-developed methods. A laboratory complying with ISO 17025 will also meet the quality management system requirements of ISO 9001.

ISO 17025 details a range of requirements that a laboratory is required to comply with including:

- Management requirements
- Document Control
- Subcontracting tests and calibrations
- Service to the customer
- Corrective action
- Prevention actions
- Internal audits
- Measurement traceability and many others.

National Institute of Standards and Technology (NIST) Handbook (HB) 150 Laboratory Certification You can use this as a foundation for many scientific disciplines such as ASCLD. HB 150 has been used as a foundation to validate various federal government laboratories. The NIST Web site is at www.nist.gov/.

Scientific Working Group for Digital Evidence (SWGDE) SWGDE has been a major contributor to the creation of the widely accepted ISO 17025 criteria detailed earlier.

Certifications

If you're interested in learning more about the digital forensic certification process as well as the different certifications and training programs that are available, here is a list of Web sites you can visit:

AccessData: www.accessdata.com/Training/TrainAceOver.aspx

Association of Certified Fraud Examiners: www.acfe.com/Membership/become.asp

The International Society of Forensic Computer Examiners: www.isfce.com/

CERT: www.cert.org/certification/

EC–Council: www.eccouncil.org/chfi.htm

Homeland Security Federal Law Enforcement Training Center: www.fletc.gov/training/programs/computer-financial-investigations/technology-investigation/seized-computer-evidence-recovery-specialist-scers

Global Information Assurance Certification: www.giac.org/certifications/security/gcfa.php

Guidance Software: www.encase.com/training/EnCE_certification.aspx

International
Association of Computer Investigative Specialists: www.cops.org/certifications

International Information Systems Forensics Association: www.iisfa.org/certification/certification.htm

Organizations

For information on organizations in this field, visit the following Web sites:

C4I.org – Computer Security and Intelligence: www.c4i.org/

Computer Technology Investigators Network: www.ctin.org/

PivX Solutions: www.computerforensics.net/

International High Technology Crime Investigation Association: www.htcia.org/

High Tech Crime Consortium: www.hightechcrimecops.org/

High Tech Crime Network: www.htcn.org/

Institute of Computer Forensic Professionals: www.forensic-institute.org/mission.html

International Association of Computer Investigative Specialists: www.cops.org/

International Organization on Computer Evidence: www.ioce.org/

International Society of Forensic Computer Examiners: www.isfce.com/

National Center for Forensic Science: www.ncfs.ucf.edu/digital_evd.html

National Cyber-Forensics & Training Alliance: www.ncfta.net/default2.asp

Regional Computer Forensics Group: www.rcfg.org/RCFGHome.html

Digital Forensic Guidelines

To learn more about digital forensic guidelines, consult these resources:

Integrated Publishing Web page regarding the issue of chain of custody: www.tpub.com/legalman/80.htm

Online version of *Electronic Crime Scene Investigation – A Guide for First Responders*: www.ncjrs.org/pdffiles1/nij/187736.pdf

Online version of *Forensics Guide to Incident Response for Technical Staff*: www.cert.org/archive/pdf/FRGCF_v1.3.pdf

Online version of *Searching and Seizing Computers and Obtaining Electronic Evidence in Criminal Investigations*: www.cybercrime.gov/s&smanual2002.htm

Online version of *Good Practice Guide for Computer-Based Electronic Evidence*: www.acpo.police.uk/asp/policies/Data/ACPO%20Guidelines%20v18.pdf

Books

Here is a list of books you can consult to learn more about digital forensics:

A Guide to Forensic Testimony: The Art and Practice of Presenting Testimony As an Expert Technical Witness, by F.C. Smith and R.G. Bace (Addison Wesley Professional, 2003)

CD and DVD Forensics, by P. Crowley and D. Kleiman (Ed.) (Syngress, 2006)

Computer and Intrusion Forensics, by G. Mohay, A. Anderson, B. Collie, et al. (Artech House Publishers, 2003)

Computer Evidence: A Forensic Investigations Handbook, by E. Wilding and G. Binger (Ed.) (Sweet & Maxwell, 1997)

Computer Evidence: Collection and Preservation, by C.L.T. Brown (Charles River Media, 2005)

Computer Forensics and Cyber Crime, by M.T. Britz (Prentice Hall, 2003)

Computer Forensics & Privacy, by M. Caloyannides (Artech House Publishers, 2001)

Computer Forensics: Principles and Practices, 1st Edition, by V. Volonino, R. Anzaldua, and J. Godwin (Prentice Hall, 2006)

Cybercrime: Incident Response and Digital Forensics, by R. Schperberg and R.A. Stanley (Information Systems Audit and Control Association, 2005)

Cyber Crime Investigator's Field Guide, 2nd Edition, by B. Middleton (Auerbach, 2004)

Cyber Crime Investigations: Bridging the Gaps between Security Professionals, Law Enforcement, and Prosecutors, by A. Reyes, R. Brittson, K. O'Shea, et al. (Syngress, 2007)

Cyber Forensics: A Field Manual for Collecting, Examining, and Preserving Evidence of Computer Crimes, 2nd Edition, by A. Marcella and D. Menendez (Auerbach, 2007)

Digital Evidence and Computer Crime, 2nd Edition, by E. Casey (Academic Press, 2004)

Electronic Evidence: Law and Practice, by P.R. Rice (American Bar Association, 2005)

The Official EnCE: Encase Certified Examiner Study Guide, by S. Bunting and W. Wei (Sybex, 2005)

File System Forensic Analysis, by B. Carrier (Addison-Wesley Professional, 2005)

Forensic Computer Crime Investigation, by T.A. Johnson (Ed.) (CRC Press, 2005)

Guide to Computer Forensics & Investigations, 3rd Edition, by A. Phillips, B. Nelson, F. Enfinger, et al. (Course Technology, 2004)

Handbook of Computer Crime Investigation: Forensic Tools & Technology, by E. Casey (Academic Press, 2001)

Handbook of Digital Evidence: Reliable Forensic Computing, by P. Sommer (Springer Verlag, 2006)

Henry Lee's Crime Scene Handbook, by H. Lee, T. Palmbach, and M.T. Miller (Academic Press, 2001)

High Technology Crime Investigator's Handbook, 2nd Edition, by G.L. Kovacich and A. Jones (Butterworth-Heinemann, 2007)

Internet Forensics, by R. Jones (O'Reilly, 2005)

Investigating Child Exploitation and Pornography: The Internet, Law and Forensic Science, by E. Casey and M. Ferraro (Academic Press, 2004)

Investigative Data Mining for Security and Criminal Detection, by J. Mena (Butterworth-Heinemann, 2003)

Mastering Windows Network Forensics and Investigation, by S. Bunting and S.J. Anson (Wiley, 2007)

Practical Guide to Computer Forensics, by D. Benton and F. Grindstaff (BookSurge Publishing, 2006)

Privacy Protection and Computer Forensics, 2nd Edition, by M. Caloyannides (Artech House Publishers, 2004)

Techniques of Crime Scene Investigation, 7th Edition, by B.A. Fisher (CRC Press, 2003)

The New Forensics: Investigating Corporate Fraud and the Theft of Intellectual Property, by J. Anastasi (Wiley, 2003)

The Science of Crime Scene Investigation: The Forensics Case Book, by N.E. Genge (Ballantine Books, 2002)

Understanding Evidence, by P.C. Giannelli (LexisNexis, 2003)

Windows Forensics: The Field Guide for Corporate Computer Investigations, by C. Steel (Wiley, 2006)

Windows Forensics & Incident Recovery, by H. Carvey (Addison-Wesley Professional, 2004)

Wireless Crime and Forensic Investigation, by G. Kipper (CRC Press, 2007)

Journals

You can learn more about digital forensics by consulting the following journals:

Digital Investigation: The International Journal of Digital Forensics & Incident Response: www.elsevier.com/wps/find/journaldescription.cws_home/702130/description #description

Forensic Magazine: www.forensicmag.com/articles.asp?pid=91

International Journal of Digital Evidence: www.ijde.org/

Journal of Digital Forensic Practice: www.tandf.co.uk/journals/titles/15567281.asp

Small Scale Digital Device Forensics Journal: www.ssddfj.org/

The International Journal of Forensic Computer Science: www.ijofcs.org/webjournal/index.php/ijofcs

Forums and Blogs

Here's a list of forums and blogs that cover the topic:

Andrew Hay's blog: www.andrewhay.ca/

Apple Forensics mailing list: http://lists.apple.com/mailman/listinfo/appleforensics

CYB3RCRIM3: http://cyb3rcrim3.blogspot.com/

Checkmate: www.niiconsulting.com/checkmate/

Computer forensics and electronic discovery blog: www.datatriage.com/blog/

Computer Forensics and Incident Response: http://breach-inv.blogspot.com/

Computer forensics blog: www.computerforensicsblog.net/

Computer Forensics, Malware Analysis & Digital Investigations: www.forensickb.com/

Computer Forensics UK: www.computer-forensics.co.uk/computer-forensics-forums/

Computer Forensics World: www.computerforensicsworld.com/

Computer Forensics/E-Discovery Tips/Tricks and Information: http://cfed-ttf.blogspot.com/

Computer.forensikblog (English version of a German blog): http://computer.forensikblog.de/en/

Dennis Kennedy's blog: www.denniskennedy.com/archives/cat_electronic_discovery.html

Digital Discovery & e-Evidence: http://ddee.bna.com/Home.html

Electronic Discovery and Evidence: http://arkfeld.blogs.com/ede/

Forensic computing blog: www.forensicblog.org/

Forensic Focus blog: www.forensicfocus.com/computer-forensics-blog

Forensic Focus forum: www.forensicfocus.com/computer-forensics-forums

Forensics Wiki: www.forensicswiki.org/

Mary Mack's Sound Evidence blog: http://soundevidence.discoveryresources.org/

Penguin Sleuth: http://penguinsleuth.org/index.php?option=com_wrapper&Itemid=8

Ride the Lightning electronic evidence blog: http://ridethelightning.senseient.com/

Sanderson Forensics ForensicsWiki: www.forensicwiki.com/index.php?title=Main_Page

SecurityBros.com: http://fleet.typepad.com/lukeup/

Subrosasoft's MacForensicsLab bulletin board: www.macforensicslab.com/Discussion/

TechNet Magazine blog: http://blogs.technet.com/tnmag/archive/2007/12/17/a-guide-to-basic-computer-forensics.aspx

Technology Pathways support forum (Prodiscover tool): http://toorcon.techpathways.com/cs/forums/default.aspx

Volatility (blog about volatile memory forensics): http://volatility.tumblr.com/

WindowsSecurity.com: www.security-forums.com/viewforum.php?f=44

Online Resources

The following additional online resources are another good source of information:

Alexander Geschonneck's Security Site: Forensic – IDS – Incident Response: www.geschonneck.com/security/forensic.html

An Explanation of Computer Forensics, by Judd Robbins: www.computerforensics.net/forensics.htm

Center for Democracy and Technology, Impact of the McCain-Kerrey Bill on Constitutional Privacy Rights: www.cdt.org/crypto/legis_105/mccain_kerrey/const_impact.html

CERIAS – Digital Forensics Resources: www.cerias.purdue.edu/research/forensics/resources.php?output=printable

Computer Forensics Laboratory and Tools: www.scribd.com/doc/136793/COMPUTER-FORENSICS-LABORATORY-AND-TOOLs

Computer Forensics, Cybercrime and Steganography Resources: www.forensics.nl/links

Computer forensics technology articles from Mares and Company: www.dmares.com/maresware/articles.htm

CyberSecurity Institute – Windows Forensics Essentials: www.cybersecurityinstitute.biz/training/wfe.htm

Computer Forensics World: www.computerforensicsworld.com

Computer Professionals for Social Responsibility Computer Crime Directory: www.cpsr.org/prevsite/cpsr/privacy/crime/crime.html/view?searchterm=computer%20crime%20directory

Digital forensics links: http://isis.poly.edu/kulesh/forensics/list.htm

Digital Forensics Research Workshop: www.dfrws.org/

Disklabs: www.disklabs.com/computer-forensics-software.asp

The Electronic Evidence Information Center: www.e-evidence.info/

Federal Rules of Evidence (Article I): http://expertpages.com/federal/a1.htm?PHPSESSID=a2d248b5ba83a082442876135682f3af

Forensic Acquisition Utilities: www.gmgsystemsinc.com/fau/

Forensic Focus – Computer Forensics Papers and Articles: www.forensicfocus.com/computer-forensics-papers

Forensics of Internet Related Evidence (FIRE): www.digitalintelligence.com/training/fire.php

Fundamental Computer Investigation Guide for Windows Overview: www.microsoft.com/technet/security/guidance/disasterrecovery/computer_investigation/default.mspx

The Forensics Science Portal: www.forensics.ca/index.php

Global Digital Forensics, Computer Forensic Resources: www.evestigate.com/COMPUTER%20FORENSIC%20RESOURCES.htm

Internet Crime Complaint Center: www.ic3.gov/

Kessler International – Forensic Accounting, Computer Forensics, Corporate Investigation: www.investigation.com/praccap/hightech/compforen.htm

Law enforcement reference links: www.computerforensics.net/links.htm

Linux LEO: www.linuxleo.com/

Linux forensics: http://tech.groups.yahoo.com/group/linux_forensics/

Mobile Forensics Central: www.mobileforensicscentral.com/mfc/

Mobile Phone Forensics and PDA Forensics: www.forensics.nl/mobile-pda-forensics

National White Collar Crime Center: www.nw3c.org/

Self Incrimination and Cryptographic Keys, by G.S. Sergienko: http://law.richmond.edu/jolt/v2i1/sergienko.html#h1

Technical articles on data recovery: www.actionfront.com/ts_articles.aspx

The Open Computer Forensics Architecture: http://ocfa.sourceforge.net/

TUCOFS software collection: www.tucofs.com/tucofs.htm

Ultimate Guide to Mac OS Forensics: http://homepage.mac.com/macbuddy/ForensicGuide.html

Zeno's Forensic Science Site: www.forensic.to/forensic.html

Academic Resources

Finally, here is a list of academic resources:

Carnegie Mellon University – CERT: www.cert.org/

Cornell University: www.law.cornell.edu/rules/fre/overview.html

Edith Cowan University: http://scissec.scis.ecu.edu.au/wordpress/

Purdue University: http://cyberforensics.purdue.edu/

University of Central Florida digital evidence site: http://ncfs.ucf.edu/digital_evd.html

University of Glamorgan: http://security.research.glam.ac.uk/

West Virginia University: www.lcsee.cemr.wvu.edu/forensics/

Risk Assessment Template

The example Risk assessment form should be completed by a competent and authorized person for each task that will involve the deployment, to a location outside the laboratory, of a member of the staff when a task is being considered. If the risk cannot be reduced to an acceptable level, the task should not be accepted. The reasons for completing this form include documenting the details of the member(s) of the staff that will undertake the deployment, detailing the known risks and the measures that can be taken to mitigate them and recording the risk that remains. All of this is important in carrying out the risk assessment and will also support the Heath and Safety and Quality Assurance requirements.

Digital Forensic Laboratory Task Risk Assessment

This form should be completed by an authorized risk assessor for any deployment carried out by an investigator before the task is accepted. The digital forensic laboratory procedures and instructions should be referred to when carrying out the risk assessment.

Name and rank/grade of person carrying out the assessment:

Deployment being assessed:

Known or expected hazards that may be encountered during the deployment:

Risk of injury and likely severity of these hazards:

Names and ranks/grades of members of the staff to be deployed:

Risk reduction measures taken:

Qualification and experience prerequisites for the staff to be deployed:

Residual risks:

Emergency actions and points of contact for assistance:

Signature of assessor: _____

Date: _____

Index

Printed and bound by CPI Group (UK) Ltd, Croydon, CR0 4YY

08/05/2025

01864781-0002